Hip-Hop in Africa

Ohio University Research in International Studies

This series of publications on Africa, Latin America, Southeast Asia, and Global and Comparative Studies is designed to present significant research, translation, and opinion to area specialists and to a wide community of persons interested in world affairs. The series is distributed worldwide. For more information, consult the Ohio University Press website, ohioswallow.com.

Books in the Ohio University Research in International Studies series are published by Ohio University Press in association with the Center for International Studies. The views expressed in individual volumes are those of the authors and should not be considered to represent the policies or beliefs of the Center for International Studies, Ohio University Press, or Ohio University.

Executive Editor: Gillian Berchowitz

Hip-Hop in Africa

PROPHETS OF THE CITY AND DUSTYFOOT PHILOSOPHERS

Msia Kibona Clark

Foreword by Quentin Williams

Afterword by Akosua Adomako Ampofo

Ohio University Research in International Studies
Global and Comparative Studies Series No. 18
Athens, Ohio

Ohio University Press, Athens, Ohio 45701
ohioswallow.com
© 2018 by Ohio University Press
All rights reserved

To obtain permission to quote, reprint, or otherwise reproduce or distribute
material from Ohio University Press publications, please contact our rights
and permissions department at (740) 593-1154 or (740) 593-4536 (fax).

Printed in the United States of America
The books in the Ohio University Research in International Studies Series
are printed on acid-free paper ⊚ ™

28 27 26 25 24 23 22 21 20 19 18   5 4 3 2 1

Cover: Kanyi Mavi at her home in Gugulethu Township, Cape Town, in 2016.
Photo by author.

Cover design by Beth Pratt

Library of Congress Cataloging-in-Publication Data
Names: Clark, Msia Kibona, author.
Title: Hip-hop in Africa : prophets of the city and dustyfoot philosophers /
Msia Kibona Clark ; foreword by Quentin Williams ; afterword by Akosua
Adomako Ampofo.
Description: Athens, Ohio : Ohio University Press, [2018] | Series: Ohio
University research in international studies. Global and comparative
studies series ; No. 18 | Includes bibliographical references and index.
Identifiers: LCCN 2018001344| ISBN 9780896803183 (hc : alk. paper) | ISBN
9780896803190 (pb : alk. paper) | ISBN 9780896805026 (pdf)
Subjects: LCSH: Rap (Music)--Social aspects--Africa. | Rap
(Music)--Africa--History and criticism. | Hip-hop--Africa.
Classification: LCC ML3918.R37 C58 2018 | DDC 782.421649096--dc23
LC record available at https://lccn.loc.gov/2018001344

This book is dedicated to
Kekeli Kaselema Anthony Numadzi,
ninakupenda sana wanangu.

Contents

List of Illustrations
ix

Foreword
"African Hip-Hop Represent!"
xi

Acknowledgments
xix

CHAPTER 1
"Boomerang"
Hip-Hop and Pan-African Dialogues
1

CHAPTER 2
"Understand Where I'm Coming From"
*The Growth of African Hip-Hop and
Representations of African Culture*
34

CHAPTER 3
"Lettre à Mr le Président"
Social and Political Representations
71

CHAPTER 4
"Femme de Combat"
Gendered Representations
118

vii

CHAPTER 5
"Make You No Forget"
Representations of African Migrant Experiences in African Hip-Hop
148

CHAPTER 6
"Brkn Lngwjz"
Language, Identity, and Cultural Appropriation
183

Epilogue
206

By Way of an Afterword
210

APPENDIX 1
Artist Interviews
217

APPENDIX 2
Companion Website
221

Notes
223

References
229

Index
257

Illustrations

Figure 1.1.	Yugen Blakrok	23
Figure 1.2.	Reggie Rockstone	27
Figure 1.3.	Zavara Mponjika, aka MC Rhymson	31
Figure 2.1.	Shaheen Ariefdien	44
Figure 2.2.	Songa	47
Figure 2.3.	Duke Gervalius	48
Figure 2.4.	Wanaitwa Uhuru	48
Figure 2.5.	Kenyan b-boys	54
Figure 2.6.	Wachata Crew graffiti art, 2010	57
Figure 2.7.	Wachata Crew graffiti art, 2014	57
Figure 2.8.	Kibacha Singo, aka KBC	61
Figure 2.9.	Guin Thieuss	63
Figure 2.10.	Helena Nyerere	67
Figure 3.1.	Albert Mangwair, aka Mangwea	79
Figure 3.2.	President Kikwete's campaign logo	80
Figure 3.3.	Sarkodie	91
Figure 3.4.	Daara J	94
Figure 3.5.	Witnesz	97
Figure 3.6.	Edem	102
Figure 3.7.	Keur Gui	109
Figure 3.8.	Nazlee	114
Figure 5.1.	K'naan	153
Figure 5.2.	Blitz the Ambassador	162
Figure 5.3.	Wanlov the Kubolor	164
Figure 5.4.	Ruyonga (formerly Krukid)	173

Foreword

"African Hip-Hop Represent!"

Quentin Williams

There are few books written on African hip-hop that capture the form and function of the culture on the African continent. There are even fewer studies that make an authoritative statement on the linguistic and cultural diversity and practice of African hip-hop. And now and then a single study pushes the field of hip-hop studies into a critical direction so that it takes seriously the contribution of African hip-hop studies in not only expanding the field of hip-hop but better capturing the future of the culture on the African continent. Msia Clark's *Hip-Hop in Africa: Prophets of the City and Dustyfoot Philosophers* is such a study.

The question of the roots of African hip-hop starts with the use of local and European languages, representing the repressed and marginalized voices by enacting the principles of the fifth element of hip-hop, and projecting it as a culture that is inclusive, original, and diverse in genres and practices. In this excellent study by Clark, hip-hop in Africa is represented as multifarious, never as a monolith. The author challenges our perception that this culture in Africa is merely "imitating American culture." But of course that is not the case because African hip-hop artists draw on a variety of ways of being and doing African hip-hop. And where they do sample American hip-hop they do so for authenticity and to go against "locationists", who seek to typify what they do. We cannot typify African hip-hop artists, Clark argues, because doing so "robs the African emcee of the power to self-identify as an African emcee."

Clark's study is a statement for advancing the practice of knowledge of self, the fifth element of hip-hop. Her study argues that hip-hop in the African continent has always focused on politically and socially conscious music: from South Africa's Prophets of da City to Kwanza Unit in Tanzania to Das Primeiro in Angola. For decades, hip-hop culture has represented the frictions and flows of all its elements: all over Africa we hear and see the embodiment of the culture and read the narratives of celebration and discontent that critically reflect on the history of colonialism, the political structures that have arisen with apartheid, the social reengineering of Pan-African identities for groups and individuals, and the economic restructuring of previously destitute countries. Hip-hop in Africa has always accounted for the flows and the frictions that have come to make it a culture on this beautiful continent, and with an increasingly technological world structure in clouds (Google Drive, Dropbox) and new forms of music-sharing platforms, the variations of the culture in Africa has come to earn its place in the global hip-hop community.

This monograph by Clark powerfully demonstrates the strength of African hip-hop not only in how hip-hop artists represent the culture, but how it codes language to draw in its audience, how it discourses and criticizes neoliberal economic policies that African states and nations often adopt wholesale, often to the detriment of the population, and that has lead to the politicization of hip-hop. As Clark puts it, "it is important to understand and further emphasize the historical and contemporary interconnectedness of the socioeconomic environments throughout urban Africa, and how that has manifested into the emergence of hip-hop artists as potential agents of change."

The idea of hip-hop artists being agents of change has been around since the inception of the culture. And given this, there will always be friction when it comes to democracy for hip-hop artists in Africa. History has shown that African governments often treat their citizens with degrees of disdain, and hip-hop on the continent has always engaged governments, often taking losses in the process. From the banning of Prophets of da City in apartheid South Africa to the recent imprisonment of Luaty Beirão (aka Ikonoklasta) in Angola, the costs for hip-hop artists in Africa are often high and unfair. But hip-hop artists who draw on the Fifth Element acknowledge that engagement with repressive state apparatuses (à la Althusser) are done so for the sake of social and democratic change. This engagement, or the production of hip-hop music that engages with the state, Clark describes, is also accomplished through "combat literature" (à la Fanon) or protest literature. That is, the production of hip-hop lyrics and rhymes that challenges the recolonization of social life by undemocratic means, such as corruption, violence, racialization, ethnic intolerance, and the criminalization of homosexuality.

This continues to be an admirable fight, but one often thwarted by hip-hop's own hypocrisy. Consider for example that hip-hop has and will remain burdened by the gender and sexuality question, and it has yet to start an honest conversation about its gender roots and principles and about its future. It is obvious as hip-hop becomes more globalized it will need to be more inclusive about gender and sexuality, and assert its support for women and queer people marginalized by nations, governments, and states who legislate against their bodies and everyday lives. Clark's study demonstrates that female African hip-hop artists know the rules of hip-hop and often "force a space for themselves in hip-hop communities" and at the same time "challenge prevailing ideas of femininity." She argues throughout that while gender and sexual identity are represented differently in African hip-hop music, women who do hip-hop in Africa not only present their own "masculinities" but also open up a dialogue about gender and sexuality that is often only held by men. Clark describes how a female hip-hop artist may use braggadocio as a way to stake a claim to her position while at the same time doing so to highlight the struggles of women in and outside the hip-hop culture. Women active in African hip-hop focus on social problems such as violence against their body: this includes rape and sexual abuse; ideological oppression via patriarchy; issues related to the LGBTQI community, and so on. But women in African hip-hop are also critical of the politics of respectability and

Foreword: "African Hip-Hop Represent!" | xiii

particularly their place in hip-hop culture. As Clark argues, "Unlike in the United States, however, female emcees in Africa operate in cultural and historical landscapes in which images of female sexuality in the media have been minimal, and in society in which public expressions or displays are either forbidden or are rare."

However, and this is Clark's point, female hip-hop artists are still seen as objects of sexual desire, and this may compromise their agency in the practice of hip-hop culture, particularly in the face of the continued misogyny and sexism that plagues hip-hop generally. It is therefore imperative, as Clark goes on to discuss, that we emphasize that hip-hop spaces in Africa generally are contested spaces for female hip-hop artists; but those spaces are also contested by migrants, particularly hip-hop migrants.

Migration and the frictions that come with it are a pervasive theme in African hip-hop. Rap artists and graffiti artists, for example, have represented the challenges that come with leaving a home you have lived all your life in and the challenge of finding a new place, and feeling at home in that place. Clark asserts that African hip-hop artists represent, and put to lyrics and artwork, the transnational character of in- and out-migration on the continent. They "bring together Afropolitanism and Pan-Africanism, in a way that challenges the classism found in Afropolitanism." But in this bringing together, African hip-hop artists also demonstrate the pain and existential urgency that come with migration. Through their music, African hip-hop artists demonstrate that migration can be a challenge but, as Clark argues, "using hip-hop culture, with its roots in urban Black America, the artists are able to reemphasize African identities . . . [and they] often talk about where they are from, give stories of their hometown, and boast of coming from a certain city."

Migration for hip-hop artists is often also an opportunity to open up new networks to expand the flow of hip-hop on the continent and beyond. Through such an opening up, new narratives of home and away evolve and the diaspora link becomes stronger. This is important to understand, as Clark aptly describes, because experiences of migration, alienation, and identity struggles are a continued theme in African hip-hop music.

The brilliance of Clark's study is in its analysis of language use by African hip-hop artists and how such language use is linked to hip-hop identities for authenticity. To her, hip-hop language, or as she cleverly puts it, "brkn lngwjz," points to new forms always being created by hip-hop artists.

For Clark, hip-hop language represents hybrid linguistic practices in the local African hip-hop context. Let's not get it twisted with language, because, as she argues, African hip-hop artists share in hip-hop cultural codes that allow them to represent their racialized identities on the African continent and by doing so bring us back to the connection between class, race, and culture. Questions of the dominance and hegemony of English on the African continent, and certainly other languages such as French and Portuguese, have been around since colonialism, and apartheid—for decades—and much ink has been spilled in critical op-eds, books, journal articles, poetry, and literature on those two issues. With calls for decolonization of not only the mind but the material reality of the historically marginalized people of Africa in this century, language has once again taken center stage, and it is through "the coded language used by African hip-hop artists," Clark claims, that we once again see the emphasis fall on the need to develop Pan-African identities. Hip-hop artists should be seen as critical language scholars, and for every artist, irrespective of which country in Africa they may find themselves in, language is central to representing a Pan-African identity. And depending on the language or language variety used, even if through "African and African American coded language and cultural symbols," such an identity does emerge.

In considering language, Clark raises an important question: Does it mean cultural appropriation takes place when African hip-hop artists mix African and African American linguistic codes to represent their identities? The answer to this is a carefully considered critical discussion of the distinctions we need to make between the "localization of art, styles, symbols, and practices between Africa and the African diaspora" and the wholesale adoption of American hip-hop. If this does happen, she asks, should we be talking about misappropriation? This clever analysis of misappropriation, as the reader

Foreword: "African Hip-Hop Represent!" | xv

will no doubt discover, is more than just a rhetorical device Clark uses to lure the reader into her critical ambit. She argues that you cannot simply suggest that African youth deeply invested in hip-hop culture are just appropriating hip-hop culture from the United States willy-nilly. This would be a mistake at best, and at worst an ahistorical approach to the local development of hip-hop across various localities in Africa. We have to focus, as she argues, on the language choices of the artist because selecting a language is not only important for the listening audience but for the social statement the artist will make.

The reason is simple: the multilingual emcee of Africa is a "super emcee." This powerful description of the linguistic biography of the multilingual emcee, as Clark quotes Chuck D, who coined the phrase "super emcee," reminds us that when African hip-hop artists write, they draw on "more than one cultural system, using multiple languages, symbols, and cultural cues to compose songs that claim ownership of multiple cultural systems." That is the norm for a multilingual emcee on the African continent.

There is of course no such thing as a monolingual emcee in Africa. This is because emcees are able to choose to rap in European languages or African languages. As Clark clearly demonstrates, emcees on the African continent may rap in Sheng, Swahili, Twi, Ewe, Wolof, Jola, and of course English and French. And though African hip-hop artists are fluent in European languages and choose to rap in those languages, they also do so in African languages—they take into account their target audience, the marketability of their music, how best to represent their political views, and how to strengthen their cultural connections. To best represent their Pan-African identity, they often code-switch between what H. Samy Alim (2007) has termed Hip Hop Nation Language (HHNL) and an African or European language to identify with the global hip-hop community and to demonstrate their linguistic authenticity.

Not fully understanding this difference in code-switching, Clark argues, not only often leads to a misunderstanding of the multilingual situation of African hip-hop artists but also leads to the unfair and unreliable description that those artists are inauthentic because they only speak like, or rap like, African American rappers or produce music that sounds too African American or generally American. Hardly. Clark hits back hard at this assertion, arguing that "one cannot appropriate from one's own culture" and that we have to take seriously the "historical-cultural give-and-take that has gone on between the two communities." The downside to the appropriation argument is the misappropriation one, and as Clark puts it powerfully: it happens "when one culture's privilege allows it to incorrectly appropriate another culture in the creation or furtherance of harmful tropes and stereotypes. For example, when performing in blackface, White actors used their privilege to appropriate what they thought was African American culture, only to further negative tropes about the lazy, untrustworthy, and stupid African American."

This powerful notion of misappropriation introduced by Clark pushes the focus on language and hip-hop performance and practice onto the localities where hip-hop is practiced in Africa. Misappropriation opens up on the racialized perceptions held not only by Africans about African Americans but also the other way around. The notion helps us tease open an often uncomfortable subject in inter- and cross-cultural communication studies: misunderstanding and politeness, or impoliteness across cultures. Clark argues convincingly that we cannot adopt a culture wholesale without adapting to it to local conditions. This means a fair amount of reworking and ultimately the production of new forms of hip-hop.

Clark's book is a welcome contribution to the growing scholarship on hip-hop in the African continent. It should be of interest to scholarship in anthropology, sociolinguistics, cultural studies, musicology, and sociology. It opens up not only debate about hip-hop culture on the African continent, but it is also a decolonizing statement on the evolving forms, functions, and translinguality of African hip-hop in the twenty-first century.

Foreword: "African Hip-Hop Represent!" | xvii

Acknowledgments

This project has been years in the making. There has been a network of scholars, artists, and activists who supported this project. Much gratitude to Kibacha Singo (KBC) and Zavara Mponjika for being down since 1996 and helping with the connects in Tanzania, Kenya, and South Africa; and for reminding me to "keep it hip-hop." Fareed Kubanda (Fid Q) for making the necessary introductions in Dar. Magee McIlvaine and Ben Herson from Nomadic Wax, who helped secure contacts in Senegal, and for starting the Trinity International Hip-Hop Festival. My brother, Becaye Dial, for hooking me up with folks in Dakar. Mamadou Sambe and the Sambe family for welcoming me into your home. Dr. Seth Markle from Trinity College for providing a space for me to meet with artists coming to the Trinity Festival. Prof. Shani Omari from the University of Dar es Salaam for our many discussions about hip-hop in Dar es Salaam and Zanzibar. Kwame Opoku (aka Quame Jr), for introducing me to most of the artists I linked with in Ghana. Sarah Hager from Amnesty International USA for helping with me with Angola links. Burni Aman and Shaheen Ariefdien for all the links in South Africa. Mejah Mbuya for being my historian on graffiti in Tanzania. Tacitus Nana Yabani for introducing me to the Pidgin Music crew and taking me around Accra. Buddha Blaze for helping put the pieces together on hip-hop in Kenya. The comrades in the All-African People's Revolutionary Party for helping me with accommodations in Ghana. Babaluku and the Bavubuka Foundation for inviting me to Kampala and allowing me to build with

Ugandan and Congolese artists. The many artists that were gracious enough to not only allow an interview but responded to my requests for clarification or translation.

To the crew, who supported this project from day one: Dr. Adryan Wallace of the University of Hartford, one of the smartest and funniest people I know, thank you for allowing me to bounce my crazy theories off you. Dr. Mjiba Frehiwot at the Institute of African Studies at the University of Ghana, Legon, and the All-African People's Revolutionary Party: Mjiba, you are the ultimate activist-academic and you have helped me understand Kwame Nkrumah better than any book. Mamertha Kente, my sister for life, your support allowed me to do my research and not break my bank.

The JCSU family: you guys always held me down. Tamitha Lewis and Hafid McIntyre, your questions about the status of the book kept me on track more than you realized. Nicole Holmes, there's no one else I'd rather go into battle with.

The illustrious women of Alpha Kappa Alpha Sorority, Inc.: so many of my sorors in academia have been there along this journey, allowing me to lean on the shield by providing advice and support when needed.

Thank you to all the mentors who have encouraged and advised me. In the Department of African Studies at Howard University: Dr. Sulayman Nyang, Dr. Robert Edgar, Dr. Mbye Cham, and Dr. Mohamed Camara. My coaches in the 2016 Junior Faculty Writing and Creative Works Summer Academy at Howard University, especially Associate Provost Okianer Christian Dark, Dr. Den'ee Mwendwa, Dr. Marie-Claude Jipguep-Akhtar, and Dr. Kehbuma Langmia. Thank you to Prof. Imani Sanga and Prof. Abdullah Hamza at the Department of Fine and Performing Arts at the University of Dar es Salaam for graciously hosting me during my Fulbright.

Thank you to my students at California State University, Los Angeles, and Howard University, who scoured the internet to assist in compiling lists of artists, music, and articles. Thank you to the research assistants who helped on the project: Magee Bwire, Lulu Garcia, Semein Abbay, and Darbrielle Thomas.

Thank you to Gillian Berchowitz, who has believed in this project from the beginning and stuck with me through its various iterations.

Thank you to my family: Seko Kibona, Nisa Kibona, and Eluka Kibona. Seko, you have been one of my biggest supporters. Thank you! Atsu Numadzi, my husband and best friend, you have been unquestionably supportive and always willing to help with my work in Ghana. You have also been married to this project and encouraged me so much along the way. My mother, Dr. Sanza Clark, professor emerita at Cleveland State University: you moved between being a mother and an adviser. You helped me crunch the numbers, and watched my son while I was off doing my research. I could never repay you for all you have done, though I am also sure you have all the receipts. To my son, Kaselema, you always seemed to know when I needed to take a break, and insisted that I do so. You also knew when I needed to work, and allowed me more quiet afternoons than I could ever ask for. You have also traveled with me to four countries in search of data, adjusting to the new climate, cuisine, and culture with ease. I love you more than you could imagine.

Funding for this project has been provided by the Fulbright Scholar Program, California State University, Los Angeles, and the Office of Research Development at Howard University.

1

"Boomerang"

Hip-Hop and Pan-African Dialogues

HIP-HOP CULTURE IN Africa has increasingly been a subject of research that recognizes the importance of the culture's popularity and its potential for influencing change. It is a culture that has had a tremendous impact on youth in Africa. Like hip-hop in the United States, hip-hop in Africa has had transformative impacts on youth. It has become more than just a style or genre of music. It is a culture that is simultaneously connected to global hip-hop cultures and local cultural systems. Hip-hop in Africa has brought African voices to a global hip-hop community. Hip-hop in Africa is a representation of African realities and of African youth cultures. In essence, hip-hop in Africa provides its own record of historical and contemporary Africa, a record no less significant than a written text, a documentary film, or oral histories. The subtitle of the book, *Prophets of the City and Dusty-foot Philosophers,* refers to the role of emcees in local cityscapes, their roles as prophets and philosophers narrating their local urban spaces. *Prophets of the City* is also an homage to the pioneering South African hip-hop group Prophets of da City, while *Dustyfoot Philosophers* is an homage to the landmark album *The Dusty Foot Philosopher* by Somali rapper K'naan.

In understanding both historical and contemporary Africa, one can look to its music. The concept of cultural representations in cultural studies asserts that to understand any society or culture one "must understand the practices that surround the production and consumption of its music" (Ingram 2010, 106). While the focus of this research is primarily the music, music is not the only form of cultural representation. Written text, song, poetry, film, television, fine art—all are cultural representations. The concept of cultural representation is found within cultural studies and was advanced by scholars such as Stuart Hall. According to Hall (2013), there are the "reflective, the intentional and the constructionist approaches to (cultural) representation." Cultural representations may reflect what is going on in society, they may be an expression of the creator's intentions, or they may construct meaning for the audience consuming the representations. This research takes a more constructionist approach, looking at how hip-hop, as a cultural representation, constructs certain narratives for its audiences.

This research focuses on the importance of cultural representations (hip-hop) in constructing understandings of political institutions, social change, gender, migration, and identity in Africa. Most of what we know about the world is through "mediation," or representations, whether it be a newscast, a textbook, or a film. These representations can come in the form of a blog, a website, Twitter, a Facebook post, or a YouTube video. When we take in these representations by watching, listening, reading, and experiencing; reality is being shaped (Ingram 2010; Barker 2012). Cultural representations, in this case hip-hop, shape how the consumers of those representations view society and what realities they adopt.

When news directors at the BBC, CNN, or Al Jazeera reduce the day's events to thirty- or sixty-minute segments, they shape how viewers interpret the world (Barker 2012). Truth and reality are not neutral but constructed. As a form of cultural representation, hip-hop is no different. The artists themselves decide what is relevant and what realities they want to construct. Whatever is produced—be it music, a graffiti tag, a graphic design on a T-shirt, or a film—the cultural production encompasses the ideologies and backgrounds of the artist(s). Participants and observers of African hip-hop facilitate the process of creating reality by defining what information is important and interpreting it based on their own social, cultural, and ideological perspectives. The street language used in hip-hop, for example, may cause some to dismiss the music as troublesome, and disrespectful, while others may be drawn to the music because they feel connected to the words being spoken.

For the purpose of this research, African hip-hop will include hip-hop music performed by individuals born in Africa, and who identify as African, regardless of where they live. The definition will also include those who are recent African migrants as a result of migrations of African communities outside Africa, especially in the West, in the past fifty years. While there are African hip-hop artists all over the world, this research will focus primarily on hip-hop in Africa, as well as hip-hop produced by those who migrated from Africa to the United States, the birthplace of hip-hop culture.

While the concept of representation is often discussed by hip-hop artists, it is also a core concept within cultural studies. According to Hall, "To say that two people belong to the same culture is to say that they interpret the world in roughly the same ways and can express themselves . . . in ways which will be understood by each other" (2013). Hip-hop music speaks, through the use of shared languages, to individuals within certain cultures. Hip-hop is a vehicle by which artists represent locations, experiences, and identities. It is also a vehicle through which African realities are shaped and told. Representation in hip-hop serves to validate, depict, and define a place, a people, and experiences.

This research contributes to defining African hip-hop and recognizes hip-hop culture in Africa as a form of cultural representation by urban youth on the continent and in the diaspora. African hip-hop culture is tied to both African cultures and global hip-hop cultures. Hip-hop uses the power of words and wordplay while simultaneously understanding and harnessing the power of representation.

The research is based on the premise that hip-hop is a musical form with African roots, roots that predate hip-hop's contemporary origins in the South Bronx between 1970 and 1973 (Chang and DJ Kool Herc 2005; Kitwana 2002). Hip-hop is part of years of back-and-forth music flows between Africa and the African diaspora. African hip-hop has also been influenced by the continent's own musical history. Hip-hop artists all over Africa have used local, continental, and diasporic elements in their music.

"Boomerang": Hip-Hop and Pan-African Dialogues | 3

The research will examine representations within this varied and complex culture, on a continent with multiple hip-hop communities. Some hip-hop communities are larger than others. Most began in the capital cities but have spread to smaller towns and villages. There are also a growing number of African artists in the US diaspora, as a result of the large numbers of Africans who have migrated out of Africa and into the United States in the past thirty years. Hip-hop is bringing these artists together through collaborations and is creating both diverse and common narratives of African society.

This book examines the role that female artists play in constructing contemporary representations of African women. These artists are influenced by both hip-hop and local cultures, and they use their music to provide additional perspectives on, and depictions of, women in Africa. Many challenge constructions of femininity and womanhood, or the policing of women's sexualities. Others direct their commentary toward gender oppressions or gender identities. It is important to understand how the representations created by female emcees contribute to our understandings of urban African women. Media representations of African women present skewed single-story narratives of passive, poor, rural African women. Female emcees offer representations that present narratives of African women having agency, women in both urban and rural contexts, and women who recognize and grapple with privilege in its many manifestations.

The research looks at African hip-hop as a representation of African society, as a representation through which Africa is discussed, defined, and represented. The events and experiences that have influenced the content of hip-hop in Africa, and the representations of Africa it chooses to depict, are significant. These events and experiences differ across Africa, but there are some important similarities. For example, the depictions of African economic and political realities, interactions with state institutions, and access to resources bear significant similarities in hip-hop coming from various parts of Africa. Topics like migrations west, across the Sahara, and in boats, as well as via Western embassies in search of visas, are depicted in a similar way across the continent by both anglophone and francophone artists.

4 | *Hip-Hop in Africa*

As part of the global hip-hop community, African hip-hop artists have advanced the culture artistically and have created new spaces where Africans are able to tell their stories. In its examination of hip-hop in Africa, this study will also illustrate the transition artists have made from providing political commentary and protest music to actually becoming agents of social and political change. As the increase of youth mobilization globally has resulted in popular uprising, the roles played by hip-hop artists and hip-hop culture in specific countries need to be understood as having local and global significance.

The Pan-African Connection

In 2003 the Senegalese rap duo Daara J released an album entitled *Boomerang,* based on the premise that when Africans left the continent in bondage during the transatlantic slave trade, they took with them their musical traditions, which evolved into hip-hop, which returned to Africa in the 1980s. These music traditions that were taken with enslaved Africans developed and were cultivated on the plantations of the Americas and included drumming, rapping, and storytelling (Keyes 2008; Manning 2009; Appert 2016). Over time, African American culture incorporated these music traditions into new forms of African American music and self-expression.

Hip-hop's roots in African culture have been discussed in three major ways: by linking hip-hop music to African rhythms and drumbeats, by linking modern rapping to traditional African forms of rapping or poetry, and by drawing parallels between the hip-hop emcee and the West African griot.

Robert Walser (1995) looks at the "percussive sounds, polyrhythmic texture, timbral richness, and call-and-response patterns" found in hip-hop and links them to origins in Africa. Cheryl Keyes (1996) also looks at the continual repetition of particular rhythms in African music, which are similar to the hip-hop DJ's tradition of repeating and extending the playing time of parts of a song, while mixing in the next song. Keyes says this "reaffirms the power of the music" and creates a connection with the listener (1996, 236). This is

"Boomerang": Hip-Hop and Pan-African Dialogues | 5

manifest in the call-and response traditions practiced at hip-hop performances. Walser's (1995) article shows similarities in rhythms and beat patterns found in African and hip-hop music, specifically the polyrhythmic nature of both. Music is polyrhythmic when it contains two or more conflicting rhythms at the same time. Many early hip-hop drumbeat patterns have similarities with patterns found in many African drumbeats.

Lyricism with rhyme styles similar to those found in hip-hop lyricism can also be found in some African languages. Keyes says hip-hop rapping can be traced from "the African bardic traditions to the rural oral southern-based expressive forms of African Americans" (2006, 225). The language most often cited as having a form of rap is Wolof and the tradition of *tassou*. Tassou is a form of rapping that is often accompanied by drumming and is found in Senegal and the Gambia (Tang 2007; Gueye 2011; Penna-Diaw 2013; Appert 2016). In other countries, like Somalia and Tanzania, artists have reflected on associations between rap and poetry.

The role of the emcee as a griot has also been discussed by scholars, who point to American hip-hop artists as being among the first to draw the parallels. Hip-hop pioneer Afrika Bambaataa, Professor X (a member of the 1990s rap group X-Clan), Nas, and Kanye West have all referred to themselves as griots (Tang 2012; Kimble 2014). Scholars who discuss the parallels between the rapper and the West African griot point to the griot's role in their community as a storyteller and historian (Smitherman 1997; Dyson 2004; Tang 2012; Sajnani 2013; Appert 2016). While Sajnani's (2013) article reflects on the griot's position among the elite to debunk this connection, the similar functions the griot and the emcee play in their societies remain evidence for many of the connections between the two roles. The collaborative nature of African music and the traditions of call-and-response are also used to point to relationships between hip-hop and African music. A lot of African music is collaborative music, similar to the cyphers, sessions, and battles that take place in hip-hop culture.

In the twentieth century the African music traditions that were present in the African American community would merge with African-influenced Caribbean sounds as an increasing number of Caribbean immigrants arrived in the United States (Kalmijn 1996; Foner 2001). With similar patterns of music retention, the Caribbean population that would emerge in New York City was large. It would be members of that Caribbean community who would collaborate with African Americans to create a cultural revolution. The music that would develop into hip-hop has its roots in these retained musical traditions.

Hip-hop emerged in the Bronx borough of New York City in the 1970s, where African American residents exchanged creative influences with the West Indian and Puerto Rican communities (Chang and DJ Kool Herc 2005). Caribbean immigrant artists such as Jamaican-born DJ Kool Herc (Clive Campbell), Barbadian-born Grandmaster Flash (Joseph Saddler), and Antiguan-born DJ Red Alert (Frederick Crute) were among the pioneers who helped found hip-hop (Perry 2004; Chang and DJ Kool Herc 2005). The Caribbean influence on hip-hop also came with the importation of two music trends that emerged in the Caribbean, specifically in Jamaican music, in the 1960s (Hebdige 2004; Perry 2004; Chang and DJ Kool Herc 2005).

First was the introduction of dub music, which consisted of remixing and manipulating sound recordings, often removing the vocals to work with the drumbeats; second was the Jamaican style of toasting, or talking over beats (George 2005; Veal 2007). As Caribbean artists like DJ Kool Herc and Grandmaster Flash integrated into the African American community in the Bronx, they brought their Caribbean influences with them. Out of this fusion came hip-hop music and culture, and a new sound that would soon have a global reach.

Pan-African Dialogues through Music

The musical flows between Africa and the African diaspora are more than a century old. There has been a constant movement of peoples and cultures between Africa and the African diaspora, with cultural styles being adopted, transformed and renamed, and then borrowed again. Tsitsi Jaji (2014), in fact, talks about the "continuities" between African American music and various parts of Africa and the diaspora. Rather than seeing Africa as simply the source of diaspora music and culture, Jaji sees it as part of the cycles of taking, transforming, and giving between connected communities and cultures. Often when we speak of Pan-Africanism it is through the diasporic gaze, through the diaspora reflecting on African connections. We seldom consider the African gaze and African reflections on diasporic linkages. It is crucial to consider both, and in fact to look at Pan-Africanism using multiple lenses, and in consideration of the cultural linkages that encompass a global African (race as opposed to citizenship) population.

According to Edmund John Collins (1987), some of the earliest arrivals of diaspora music in Africa began in the 1880s with the arrival of former enslaved Blacks into West Africa from the United States, the Caribbean, and Latin America. In Ghana and Nigeria, the African American and Caribbean contribution to highlife dates back to the early 1900s (Shipley 2009; Shonekan 2012). In the Congo, and later in Senegal, Cuban music became very influential and popular (Shain 2002; White 2002). In the 1930s Cuba's rumba music was a major influence on the emergence of Congolese dance music, which would become popular across Africa (White 2002).

The music that emerged from African American and Caribbean communities in the 1960s through the 1980s would also find its way to Africa. The music from artists ranging from James Brown to Michael Jackson to Bob Marley would be a precursor to the wave of hip-hop music and culture that would impact the lives of many African youth in the 1980s and 1990s.

In addition to the legacy of retained African culture in African American and Caribbean music, twentieth-century African musical influences could also be heard in the music of the African diaspora in the United States. African musicians like Fela Kuti, Miriam Makeba, Lucky Dube, and Hugh Masekela became well known in the African diaspora in the United States. Many of these artists lived in America during the turbulent 1960s and 1970s and became involved in the civil rights and Black Power movements. This was especially the case of exiled South African artists like Hugh Masekela and Miriam Makeba. Makeba would eventually marry Black Power activist Kwame Toure (aka Stokely Carmichael). Fela Kuti was very vocal about his exposure to the Black Power movement of 1960s Los Angeles and its influence on his music. Fela Kuti would also influence the Black music scene in America.

As hip-hop grew in America, several artists would sample beats or vocal tracks from Africa. Afrobeat musician Fela Kuti is perhaps one of the most sampled African musicians in American hip-hop. A selection of some of the many artists to sample his music: Mos Def sampled "Fear Not of Man" for his song of the same name (D. Smith 1999); Missy Elliott sampled "Colonial Mentality" for "Watcha Gon' Do" (2001); Nas sampled "Na Poi" for "Warrior Song" (M.anifest 2012); the Roots sampled "Mr Grammarticalogylisationalism Is the Boss" for "I Will Not Apologize" (Trotter 2008); and J. Cole sampled "Gentleman" for "Let Nas Down" (2013). African American hip-hop artists Jay Z and Will Smith teamed up to produce the musical *Fela!*, which opened on Broadway in 2009.

The bridging of the gap across the Atlantic divide, between the United States and Africa, through hip-hop, has not been frequent, but the occurrences have been significant. There have been a number of collaborations between African and African American emcees. Much of this is due to the numbers of African emcees that migrated to the United States. In addition, several African American emcees are connecting with African artists in Africa. Collaborations between K'naan and Mos Def ("America," 2009), Wale and Pharrell Williams ("Let It Loose," 2009), M-1 and DJ Awadi ("The Roots," 2010), and Blitz the Ambassador and Chuck D ("The Oracle," 2011) have involved African and African American emcees on various projects. In fact, M-1 of the American hip-hop duo Dead Prez has been in two documentaries on hip-hop in Africa: *Ni wakati* and *United States of Africa: Beyond Hip Hop.*

Collaborations between African emcees from various parts of the continent have also led to linkages among urban youth across Africa. Early collaborations include, in 2000, the release of "Da Noize" by Kenya's Nazizi and Mizchif from Zimbabwe. With improvements in communications and technology we have increasingly seen more collaboration. In 2009, ProVerb (South Africa) and ModeNine (Nigeria) released "ProMode," Hip Hop Pantsula (HHP) (South Africa) and

"Boomerang": Hip-Hop and Pan-African Dialogues | 9

Naeto C (Nigeria) released "Boogie Down," HHP and Nazizi released "Daraja" (Künzler 2011b), and Professor Jay (Tanzania) and Kwaw Kese (Ghana) released "Who Be You."

In 2010, M.anifest (Ghana) and Krukid (Uganda) teamed up for a project entitled the African Rebel Movement and collaborated on the album *Two Africans and a Jew*. In that same year, Senegal's DJ Awadi traveled to thirteen African countries for his Présidents d'Afrique project. The project produced an album and the documentary *United States of Africa: Beyond Hip Hop*. The album features collaborations between hip-hop artists from different African countries, like "La patrie ou la mort" with Smockey of Burkina Faso, "Amandla" with Skwatta Kamp of South Africa, and "Uhuru" with Maji Maji of Kenya. Also in 2010, Dominant 1 (Malawi), the Holstar (Zambia), and Illuminate (Zimbabwe) released "Don't Stop Playing," and the Holstar and ProVerb released "Stepping Stone."

In 2011, ProVerb and Naeto C released "Higher," and Navio (Uganda) and Jua Cali (Kenya) released "Respect." In 2013, M.anifest and Camp Mulla (Kenya) released "All In," and Gigi LaMayne (South Africa), Sasa Klaas (Botswana), Devour Ke Lenyora (South Africa), Ru the Rapper (Namibia), and DJ Naida (Zimbabwe) released "No Sleep." In 2014, M.anifest and Proverb released "Proverbs Manifest," M.I. (Nigeria) and Sarkodie (Ghana) released "Millionaira Champagne," Sarkodie and Vector tha Viper (Nigeria) released "Rap Attack," and Khaligraph Jones (Kenya), Dominant 1 (Malawi), the Holstar (Zambia), and Raiza Biza (Rwanda) released "Fecko: Real African Poetry 2.0."

Defining African Hip-Hop

As the growth, influence, and content of hip-hop culture throughout Africa is being studied, so are attempts to define it. In the numerous interviews and conversations for this project, it became clear that several different positions were emerging on the topic. Most interviewees were asked to define African hip-hop, and the answers varied.

Some deny that hip-hop can be African, arguing that hip-hop is not an African music form, so all African hip-hop artists are just imitating American culture. Lliane Loots's (2003) piece on American hip-hop in South Africa claims that the impact of American hip-hop on Africans is negative. Loots (2003) compares the influence of hip-hop on Africans to Frantz Fanon's idea of cultural colonialism. This perspective deletes hip-hop's African past as well as its links to traditional forms of rapping and storytelling that exist in many African languages and cultures. Fanon's pivotal discussion of culture can be used to examine hip-hop in Africa (see chapter 3), but from the perspective of hip-hop as a tool for mobilization.

Some argue that hip-hop music is African only if artists are performing in local languages and over African rhythms. These arguments narrow the definition of hip-hop to simply a focus on music, ignoring the culture that surrounds African hip-hop. Hip-hop culture includes music but includes various other cultural elements. African hip-hop's influence is found in new slang emerging from various urban centers in Africa, and in the graffiti that colors African cities and towns. In addition, this argument ignores the contributions of the African diaspora to African music, such as *mbalax* (Senegalese dance music), highlife (West African dance music), or Afrobeat (Nigerian dance music), all of which were heavily influenced by the US diaspora.

There are those who argue it is about location. A fundamental principle of hip-hop is the idea of representation, of representing where you are from, your reality. The "locationists" argue that unless one's experience as an African emcee emanates from living in Africa, one cannot represent oneself as an African emcee. This perspective calls into question artists such as Nigerian American rapper Wale, disregarding whether or not Wale self-identifies as an African emcee. Wale's music is not considered African because his experience is not based on living in Nigeria. Some would also discount Somali-born artist K'naan as an African emcee because his perspective may not represent life on the streets of Mogadishu today; he has spent more than twenty years away from Somalia. This definition robs the African emcee of the power to self-identify as an African emcee. The emcee's representation of an African in the diaspora and all the identities and experiences that blend together is a representation of an African reality.

"Boomerang": Hip-Hop and Pan-African Dialogues | 11

The past thirty years have seen dramatic increases in the African immigrant population in the United States. Between 1990 and 2000 the number of Africans living in the United States jumped from 200,000 to 800,000; by 2013 the African-born population in the United States was 1.8 million (Anderson 2015). In cities such as New York, Minneapolis, Atlanta, Houston, and Washington, DC, which have been primary destinations, the increase has been even more significant. In Europe, countries like France and England had large African populations decades before the increase in African immigration to the United States. All these African immigrant communities form bridges between Africa and the West, and in many ways the African emcee informs each about the other. To deny African emcees their ability to represent Africa would be to reject an important part of the African experience.

African hip-hop is connected to the "notion of a global black experience of oppression and resistance" (Haupt 2008, 146). To understand hip-hop as a Black music form is sometimes a controversial position, although this characterization of hip-hop does not negate the connection nonblacks may have to the genre. There are hip-hop communities all over the world, many of them belonging to people who are not of African descent. But this does not mean hip-hop is not rooted in an African past. Stephanie Shonekan's article "Sharing Hip-Hop Cultures: The Case of Nigerians and African Americans" looks at the linkages between African and African American hip-hop and highlights the cultural links that exist in "all manifestations of Black music," referring to the progression of Black music not as a "continuum, but as a cycle" (2011, 11). Shonekan says that hip-hop is a Black music genre based on its roots in Black musical traditions and its role as a space to navigate and express Black identities and oppressions.

An essential element in hip-hop authenticity lies in truthful representation, in representing the culture and the environment from which the artist emerged (Forman 2002; S. Watkins 2005; Pennycook 2007; Hess 2009; Appert 2016). Authenticity in hip-hop is the degree to which artists remain true to hip-hop's core principles (see the next section). According to Catherine Appert, Senegalese "hip hop's very generic parameters allow for music that is grounded in Senegalese particularity and still definitively hip hop" (2016, 292). The same can be said for hip-hop globally. This study will use this definition of authenticity and apply it to hip-hop in Africa. Therefore, as long as an artist is representing his or her reality and experiences as an African, through hip-hop, it can be seen as African hip-hop.

When scholars consider hip-hop in Africa, they often include some of the talented artists who make up popular genres of urban youth music all over Africa: *kwaito* in South Africa, *bongo flava* in Tanzania, hiplife in Ghana, *kuduro* in Angola, *genge/kapuka/boomba* in Kenya. All these genres contain elements from hip-hop, reggae, R&B, house, and other music genres. Each has blended genres and influences to become its own genre, in much the way hip-hop did decades earlier. Artists like Yemi Alade, Davido, and P-Square (Nigerian), Obrafour (Ghanaian), Diamond Platnumz (Tanzanian), and Nonini (Kenyan) are extremely talented and have all become stars of urban pop music genres that emerged in their countries in recent decades. These artists are not necessarily hip-hop artists.

Boundaries between music genres are often fluid, making defining genres difficult. Mikhail Bakthin says that text belongs in the same genre when there are similarities "in theme, composition, or style" (1986, 87). While attempting to come up with a system of automatic music classification, Tao Li, Mitsunori Ogihara, and Qi Li (2003) and Nicolas Scaringella, Giorgio Zoia, and Daniel Mlynek (2006) concede the difficulty of the task. Li, Ogihara, and Li claim that a lot of "music sounds sit on boundaries between genres. These difficulties are due to the fact that music is an art that evolves, where performers and composers have been influenced by music in other genres" (2003, 282). Scaringella, Zoia, and Mlynek say that "musical genres are categories that have arisen through a complex interplay of cultures, artists and market forces to characterize similarities between musicians or compositions and organize music collections. Yet, the boundaries between genres still remain fuzzy as well as their definition making the problem of automatic classification a non-trivial task" (2006, 2).

Scholars in communication, computer science, and engineering have proposed methods by which music can successfully be automatically categorized into genres, including hip-hop. Such classification is helpful, and further examinations of how those methods could be

"Boomerang": Hip-Hop and Pan-African Dialogues | 13

used in hip-hop studies are needed. This book focuses on a variety of factors when defining hip-hop as not only a genre, but also a culture.

Hip-Hop Authenticity

That hip-hop would have a significant impact in Africa is not necessarily surprising. When hip-hop made its way to Africa, it caught on among the urban youth, who were attracted to the words, images, and beats of the music. The research tells us that the first attempts at performing hip-hop were often in the form of imitations and were not representative of local realities. Many simply imitated the cadence and style of popular American hip-hop artists. There are still artists who imitate Western musical styles, who incorporate images common in Western hip-hop, images foreign to their own experiences. For example, Haaken, Wallin-Ruschman, and Patange (2012), studying hip-hop in Sierra Leone, found that many hip-hop artists regularly used the word *nigga* because of their exposure to American hip-hop, but few knew anything about the history of the word or its current controversies. We will revisit the appropriations of African American and hip-hop culture more fully in chapter 6.

Many of the first hip-hop artists to break away from the pattern of imitation with their own unique styles helped shape hip-hop culture in their countries. In addition, the economic realities of the 1980s brought many African economies to their knees, and in the early 1990s these conditions would influence young artists across Africa to begin to transform hip-hop into an expression of contemporary African realities.

The foundations of hip-hop culture have been embraced in hip-hop communities throughout Africa, and in many cases there has been an understanding of the five elements of hip-hop as well as hip-hop values of authenticity, or "keeping it real." Hip-hop's five elements, recognized as the foundation of hip-hop culture, are the emcee (MC, or rap artist), the DJ, the b-boy or b-girl (breakdancer), the graffiti artist, and knowledge (of self) (Kitwana 2002; Chang 2005). The official website of the Universal Zulu Nation, a hip-hop collective that began in the 1970s in New York City, describes the five elements:

14 | *Hip-Hop in Africa*

1. Graffiti is the writing of language or the scribe that documents the history.

2. Emcee is the oral griot, the conveyer of the Message.

3. DJing is the heart beat, the drum of the art or movement; DJ comes from the Djembe drum.

4. B-Boy/Girl is the exercise and the human expression through dance or body movement to keep the body in proper health.

5. Knowledge is the reason why we are who we are where did our roots comes [*sic*] from, what is the beginning of Man and where are we today. How do we take the artistic expression of Hip Hop and find our purpose in LIFE! (UZN, n.d.)

In Kenya, Malawi, Senegal, South Africa, Tanzania, Uganda, Zambia, Zimbabwe, we see that hip-hop artists have embraced these hip-hop elements (Haupt 2008; Parris 2008; Mose 2011, 2013; Casco 2012; Charry 2012; Fenn 2012; Perullo 2012; Clark 2013; Kellerer 2013). In a 2011 interview, Ghanaian artist Edem indicated that hip-hop was about "staying true to yourself." In interviews with artists in Tanzania, several indicated that hip-hop was about representing the streets and keeping it real (Clark 2013). Malian emcee Amkoullel l'enfant Peul spoke in our interview about the importance of preserving the history of African hip-hop, as well as its connection with hip-hop's roots, in both New York and African cultures.

Hip-Hop and Representation

Universally the question of hip-hop authenticity has been a subject of debate, and definitions of hip-hop authenticity have varied. The link between hip-hop authenticity and an artist's relationship to poor, urban communities (ghettos) is based on hip-hop's emergence from the Black urban underclass, as a response to the wealth of the elite and corruption and racism among public figures. This brings us back to the idea of representation, a core aspect of hip-hop. Place and representation—where an artist represents—is almost as important as what an artist represents. Because of hip-hop's origins many still believe that in order to be authentically hip-hop one needs to be from the ghetto and espouse "ghetto" values, to speak to and represent "ghetto" culture (McLeod 1999; Forman 2002; S. Watkins 2005; L. Watkins 2012; Williams and Stroud 2014). The US hip-hop group Blahzay Blahzay captures the presence of these values in hip-hop in their 1996 song "Danger": "I rocks hardcore, even when I dress suited. / On some business shit my street is deep rooted." The idea of these lines and this belief is that even with money and when outside the physical space of the ghetto, being hip-hop means maintaining roots in ghetto culture.

These ideas are found throughout hip-hop in Africa, where gangster rap and also artists taking on "ghetto" identities have been popular. In countries like Malawi and South Africa gangster rap became popular and spawned several gangster rap artists (Haupt 2001, 2008; Fenn 2012). In the "ghettos" of Nima (or Boogie Down Nima, in Accra), Temeke (or TMK, Dar es Salaam), Dandora (Nairobi), Pikine (Dakar), Ajegunle (Lagos), Khayelitsha (Cape Town), and Soweto (Johannesburg), artists have emerged proudly representing their "ghetto" as a badge of authenticity. Groups like Tanzania's Niggas with Matatizo (problems) and Bantu Pound Gangsters reflect this celebration of the "hood" in their names. In South Africa many artists represent *kasi* (ghetto or township) identities. This is reflected in the names of artists like KasiTime, or songs like "Kasi Shit" by Q'ba, and with numerous South African artists identifying as kasi artists or kasi rap.

There is also the idea that "hip-hop must be a representation of the ghetto in order to be authentic," which serves as a defense mechanism. There is an inherent rejection of mainstream society, the same mainstream society that has marginalized individuals from the ghetto. Murray Forman (2002) and Byron Hurt (2006) suggest that the importance and celebration of ghetto representation in hip-hop comes from a lack of real power, and any power and strength one has is limited to within the ghetto and is not transferable. Mbali Langa suggests that artists attempt to "reclaim the word 'ghetto' as a marker of power and identity" (2010, 30). During an interview with South African emcee Yugen Blakrok, she expressed a similar sentiment, suggesting

16 | *Hip-Hop in Africa*

that in the face of the racism keeping Blacks out of the nicer areas, Black youth developed kasi identities that actually espouse an insincere preference for ghetto life.

Kembrew McLeod's 1999 study of hip-hop authenticity concludes that authentic hip-hop means representing yourself, your reality, and your culture, especially underground and urban cultures. It also includes understanding "hip-hop's cultural legacy" and core values. These ideas of hip-hop authenticity have been discussed by several authors (Forman 2002; S. Watkins 2005; Pennycook 2007; Hess 2009; Weiss 2009). Research examining hip-hop outside the United States has also addressed the topics of authenticity and representation within local hip-hop communities. Brad Weiss's (2009) research on Tanzania, Christopher Dennis's (2011) work on Afro-Colombian rap, Usama Kahf's (2011) look at Arabic hip-hop, and Caroline Mose's (2014) examination of hip-hop in Kenya are examples. In a project on hip-hop in Sierra Leone, Abdul Fofanah of the Moving to the Beat project discusses how "a progressive hip-hop identity centers on understanding its own historical roots" (Haaken, Wallin-Ruschman, and Patange 2012, 67). Fofanah goes on to discuss the importance of representing the streets, in embracing a global Black identity in which the marginalized have a voice (Haaken, Wallin-Ruschman, Patange 2012). Klara Boyer-Rossol (2014) finds similar sentiments among many hip-hop artists in Madagascar who she said had adopted a "Makoa" identity. The Makoa are descendants of the enslaved Africans brought to Madagascar who settled on the eastern coast of the island (Dina 2001; Boyer-Rossol 2014). Madagascar is a country whose population is a mix of the African and Asian settlers who came to the island, and as a result, among the population one finds a mixture of features that reveal these African and Asian origins. Thus, claiming a Makoa identity establishes the connection of these artists to a global Black identity. This claim of authenticity and Black identity is further emphasized when considering their claimed distinction from artists from the western part of the island, who are said to be descendants of Asian migrants to the island (Boyer-Rossol 2014).

In the 2006 track "Soldados Civis," the Angolan hip-hop group Kalibrados declares how they view and represent hip-hop:

RAP is attitude
. . .
Potent rhymes over fat beats
Waited too long
Now it's our turn
. . .
This is our love
And we take it personally
We heard
Want your respect
Criticize the country for the good of the nation
Our baggy pants is a matter of identification
We don't use uniforms but fight for the country
Guerrillas out of the woods
Civilian soldiers
Guerrillas out of the woods
Civilian soldiers.[1]

Representation in hip-hop allows artists to speak to a certain set of experiences and to "link an artist to a tradition of hip-hop from that region" (Hess 2009, xiv). While the ideal of keeping it real is important in hip-hop, what is "real" is not defined the same globally, and is dependent on local contexts. An additional consideration in hip-hop authenticity is hip-hop rhymes. Representation refers to the content of an artist's lyrics, but hip-hop music, like other genres, has rules and structures that distinguish it from other musics. Hip-hop music is defined by the presence of specific rhyme structures, and in order to differentiate hip-hop, and understand hip-hop lyricism, we need to look at hip-hop rhyme schemes.

Hip-Hop Flows and Rhyme Schemes

Emcees all around the world are diverse, and they utilize various rhyme styles and patterns in their lyrics. Rhyme patterns, or flows, can be performed over almost any type of music or beat, though there are distinct hip-hop beats. Hip-hop beats are often dominated by a heavy bass, music samples, and repetitive break beats. Many African artists rely on either hip-hop or African beats, which can share similar drum patterns.

Hip-hop's emphasis on rhyming "distinguishes it from almost every other form of contemporary music and from most contemporary literary poetry" (Bradley 2009, 51). The rhyme techniques and creativity are the primary determiners of an emcee's skill. But, unlike in other genres of music, hip-hop artists are expected to write their own rhymes. A hip-hop rhyme reflects both the thoughts and observations of the individual artist and a display of their lyrical prowess. Many genres of music have professional lyricists, but in hip-hop the focus is less on the ability to sing or play an instrument than on the ability to write rhymes. This is why the hip-hop cypher, or freestyle battle—in which artists are supposed to come up with their rhymes on the spot—is an important tradition in hip-hop culture.

Besides authenticity in content, in hip-hop authenticity in style is also important. There have been innovations in hip-hop lyricism, but an emcee's rap rhythm and flows are often cited as key (Alim 2006; Bradley 2009). Adam Bradley says it is rap's relationship to "lyric poetry" that distinguishes it from other genres. He points to "the dual rhythmic relationship between the beat of the drums and the flow of the voice" (2009, 31). H. Samy Alim defines the flow as "the relationship between the beats and the rhymes in time" (2006, 95). Alim (2006) says an artists flow must have a recognizable pattern, while the bars or lines must have recognizable rhyme patterns. For example, Alim (2003) looks at the multiple rhyme strategies used by American hip-hop lyricist Pharoahe Monch, in order to distinguish hip-hop lyricists from lyricists of other genres. Bradley (2009) points out that pop singers match their lyrics to the rhythm of the music, as well as to certain melodies and harmonies. Pop singers harmonize their voices with the musical melody. For groups, or individual artists using background singers, everyone's voice needs to harmonize together, as well as with the musical melody. This harmonization is not an element of hip-hop, primarily because hip-hop does not necessarily involve singing. Even in collaborations between hip-hop artists and singers, the singing on a song may harmonize with the music, while the rap portion focuses

"Boomerang": Hip-Hop and Pan-African Dialogues | 19

on being in step with the beat. We see a range of collaboration styles in songs such as "Call Waiting" with Ghanaian rapper Blitz the Ambassador and renowned Beninese singer Angélique Kidjo, "Gunshot" with Ghanaian rapper Sarkodie and Nigerian Afropop singer Davido, or "Juhudu za Masiojiweza" with Tanzanian rapper Fid Q and legendary Tanzanian *taarab* singer Bi Kidude. In each, the singing is in harmony with the music, while the rap is performed in time with the beat.

In addition to style and rhythm of flow, there are several rhyming patterns found in hip-hop lyrics, and it is useful to have a basic understanding of some of the rhyme patterns often used in hip-hop, as well as the basic stylistic structures of hip-hop music. Hip-hop songs often contain more words per minute than music of other genres (Mayer, Neumayer, and Rauber 2008). The structure of hip-hop verses often necessitates use of a greater number of words. A standard rap verse contains sixteen lines (or bars), though artists often experiment with this standard. Most hip-hop songs have three verses, so a standard song of four to four and a half minutes contains forty-eight lines of rap. Although it is an extreme example, the six-minute song "Rap God" (2013) by American rapper Eminem received a lot of attention because it contained over 1,500 words. Rudolf Mayer, Robert Neumayer, and Andreas Rauber (2008) compared hip-hop to genres such as country, pop, reggae, folk, metal, and R&B and found that hip-hop songs had significantly more words per minute. In a comparison of the top hip-hop and bongo flava artists in Tanzania, Fid Q and Diamond Platnumz, we see a definite difference in word count. Fid Q's "I Am a Professional" contained 531 words and "Bongo Hip Hop" contained 558 words, respectively. "Kesho" by Diamond Platnumz, by contrast, has only 200 words, and "Nimpate wapi," 230. As a whole, the songs in Fid Q's catalog average more than twice as many words as the songs of Diamond Platnumz.

In addition to word count, hip-hop songs must have a particular rhyme structure. A song cannot be considered a hip-hop song if there is no identifiable rhyme structure. There are various types of what are called end, perfect, or full rhymes, including monosyllable (masculine), dual-syllable (feminine), and antepenultimate syllable (triple) (Alim 2006).

An example of a monosyllable rhyme: "We taking it back to the raw / The harder they ball / the harder they fall" (Blitz the Ambassador, Ghana, "Dikembe!," 2013).

A dual-syllable rhyme: Mali, Koutonou, Malawi straight to Las Gidi / Cash no aba me spendi holidays with Figi / Adesa e be we don't wanna f***k'n city (Sarkodie, Ghana, "Dear Rap," 2014).

An antepenultimate-syllable rhyme: Siku hlasimlis'umzimba iben-gath'ufak'iVibrator / S'qhushumbis'iz'speaker uve kukhal'iHand grenator (Driemanskap, South Africa, "S'phum'eGugs," in Xhosa, 2009).

In these rhyme schemes, the rhyme falls on the last syllable(s) of the line. In addition to full rhymes, other rhyme styles include slant or half rhymes, which play with the pronunciation of words to create rhymes. Chain rhymes and monorhymes are similar in that they include repetitive rhyme patterns, sometimes using the same exact rhyme word for several lines. There are also internal rhymes, where the rhyme occurs in different parts of the line. There are numerous other rhyme styles and techniques. Artists may employ only one in a song, or they may use multiple rhyme techniques in a song. Here are some examples of the use of rhyme techniques by African hip-hop artists.

K'naan's (Somalia) "Does it Matter" employs the use of internal rhymes. With internal rhymes the rhyme occurs not only at the end of the line, but in the middle of the line as well.

> They don't expect me on this beat, the thunder on the street
> But I never turn the cheek, surrender or retreat
> You can bet that I am strong, trying to right what is wrong
> They say it won't be long, keep on singing your song
> But ayo you need a single, single to make a mingle
> Something that's kinda simple, I'd hate to call it jingle
> A single is a missile, takes you right to the middle of 106 and
>   park and maybe Jimmy Kimmel
> You'll need somebody famous co-signing for your anus
> Who you got on the album I don't see where the name is.

Ghanaian artist M.anifest mixes English, Pidgin English, and Twi in his lyrics. His song "Babylon Breakdown" uses more than one style; this excerpt highlights his use of both dual-syllable full rhymes

"Boomerang": Hip-Hop and Pan-African Dialogues | 21

and chain rhymes. In his full rhymes the last two syllables of the lines rhyme, and he uses the chain rhyme technique, repeating the same rhyme pattern in multiple lines:

> Black military represent for the ghetto youth
> Dem we slew them
> Pharisees and Babylon crew dem
> Free education, this generation could use 'em
> Shackles gotta lose 'em
> The pigs got egos, gotta bruise 'em
> A badge and a gun, try to confuse 'em
> Diallo never run, no gun, a wallet, why they shoot him?

In the song "Neo.Vadar" Yugen Blakrok (South Africa) provides a good example of hip-hop's emphasis on representation, as well as the use of hip-hop rhyme techniques. Yugen Blakrok's 2013 album *Return of the Astro-Goth* uses imagery that blends Asian symbols (similar to the US-based hip-hop group Wu-Tang Clan), African subjects, Black consciousness, and hip-hop lyricism. In the song "Neo.Vadar" Yugen Blakrok (seen in fig. 1.1 on the roof of her apartment building in Johannesburg) shows a lyrical style that uses the creative technique called slant rhymes. Unlike many full rhymes, in which the last words of a bar or line of rap have the same sound, slant rhymes have similar but not identical sounds.

> Planted these roots under the Transkei sky
> So when flowering, to shoot through the earth when the rains
>   subside
> Command them "Grow and bear fruit to feed the hungry and
>   wise"
> Divine sustenance, universal nature's benign
> But when the light behind the eyes fails to focus
> And threats of rebel armies on your horizon just swarming
>   like locusts
> My thoughts run with the speed of Hermes.
> Manifest these verses before the world of the mystic
>   submerges. (Bradley 2009)

22 | *Hip-Hop in Africa*

Figure 1.1. Yugen Blakrok in Johannesburg in 2016. Photo by author.

The song title "Neo.Vadar" is a play on Darth Vadar, the infamous Star Wars villain. The song blends science fiction, metaphysics, and Greek mythology and locates itself within a Xhosa community. In the song Blakrok places her herself firmly in the Transkei, a former Bantustan for the Xhosa in the Eastern Cape. Her lyrics are often more like streams of consciousness and contain a lot of symbolism, with references to spirituality and metaphysics, including a reference to the Greek god Hermes. Yugen Blakrok shows lyrical creativity in the use of symbolism and lyrical word to create a narrative that differs from the narratives created by her counterparts.

All three artists represent distinct styles of emceeing. The use of specific rhyme techniques by African artists distinguishes their music as hip-hop music, as separate from other music genres. While examples were given of English lyrics, similar defined rhyme techniques can be found in the music of hip-hop artists rapping in languages other than English.

In "Dans mon rêve," Senegal's Didier Awadi rhymes in French and uses chain rhymes to repeat the same word in more than two lines.

> J'ai fait le rêve que le peuple se levera
> Dans mon rêve cette fille se lèvera

Dans mon rêve ce fils se levera
Main dans la main la mere se levera . . .
Dans mon rêve Y'a pas d'homme qui est dominé
Dans mon rêve Pas de peuple qui est dominé
Dans mon rêve Pas de terre qui est dominée
Et l'état c'est la haine qui est dominée
Dans mon rêve des colons éliminés
Dans mon rêve Colonies eliminée.

Nikki Mbishi (Tanzania) rhymes in Swahili and uses internal rhymes in his song "Utamaduni."

Yo, vina punch na midundo, mafumbo na temithali
Za semi, zisome tungo, ni gumzo, jiweke mbali
Mi ni fundo we ni mwali nishike udumishe ndoa
Bila mishe niko poa nipishe nisafishe doa
Nadharia kwa kilinge, ninge hazitambi tena
Nishinde mbilinge, Mungu hazijui dhambi njema
Gongo La Mboto msoto hainyweki gongo ya moto
Maisha vitisho, mwisho wanaujua hadi Mrisho Mpoto.

While musical genres such as kwaito, bongo flava, kuduro, genge/kapuka/boomba, and hiplife may have derived from hip-hop, borrowing from R&B and reggae as well, they are not synonymous with hip-hop. Studies of hip-hop in Africa are newer than studies of hip-hop in America, the latter including the work of several scholars who have been actively involved in the culture. Studies that present research on bongo flava as Tanzanian hip-hop, kwaito as South African hip-hop, or hiplife as Ghanaian hip-hop are evidence of a need for further research and understandings of the spaces shared by hip-hop and other musical genres in Africa. This book will briefly touch on the relationship between hip-hop and other pop music genres in Africa, but a broader study may be needed. Research on hip-hop in Ghana leads to material on hiplife, which is often discussed as if it is synonymous with Ghanaian hip-hop. Hiplife is its own genre, much like highlife, Afrobeat, and others. Jesse Shipley has acknowledged the difficulty of defining hiplife, saying it is characterized "not by a particular rhythm or lyrical pattern" but by "a performative electronic orchestration of Akan-language practices and diasporic hip-hop" (2013, 132). Some say hiplife is Ghanaian hip-hop rapped in local languages, but Harry Odamtten (2011) indicates that hiplife is performed not only in local languages but also in English and Pidgin English. Both Shipley and Odamtten discuss the various genres that hiplife borrows from, including hip-hop, highlife, and reggae. The fact that Ghanaian hip-hop artists often produce both hip-hop and hiplife music adds to the ambiguity. Ghanaian emcees like Sarkodie have produced both hip-hop and hiplife. In a 2011 interview with Ghanaian emcee Yaa Pono, he said that he considered himself both a hip-hop and a hiplife artist, drawing a distinction between the two but easily moving between both genres. Given hiplife's dominance in Ghana, when I asked Yaa Pono why he performs hip-hop at all, his response was "because it satisfies my soul." Similar responses were given by other Ghanaian emcees who perform hiplife because of the genre's popularity and marketability.

Hip-Hop Subgenres and Hybrids

Musical genres are often influenced by other musical genres. In a sense, all musical genres are hybrids, developing out of a blending of musical styles and influences. In the emergence of hip-hop in the 1970s, we see the heavy influence of both reggae and Caribbean culture, as well as the Black Arts movement of the 1960s.[2] Hip-hop was influenced by contacts with other music genres and cultures as well but would merge these influences and develop its own identity. Similarly, hip-hop would both produce its own subgenres and influence the emergence of other genres.

Out of US hip-hop would come hip-hop subgenres, like gangsta rap, dirty south rap, and pimp rap in the United States (Lena 2006); out of South Africa came gangsta rap, spaza rap, motswako rap, and zef rap (UnderGround Angle 2009; Subzzee 2010b; Williams and Stroud 2013). In her studies, Jennifer Lena (2004, 2006) has identified thirteen rap subgenres in the United States, distinguishing them by looking

"Boomerang": Hip-Hop and Pan-African Dialogues | 25

at a combination of lyrical flow, lyrical content, style of background music, and rhythmic style. Artists participate in developing subgenres through experimentation, especially with samples and other elements that help distinguish where the artist is located and which subgenre they represent. According to Lena, sampling helps "the artist or group in signaling sub-genre identity. Through sampling practices, rappers tell listeners to which artistic circles they belong" (2004, 309). In South Africa's diverse rap scene, language is also a signifier of rap subgenre.

Hip-hop subgenres remain connected to broader hip-hop cultures and communities. Spaza and motswako rap artists in South Africa still use hip-hop rhyme techniques, while kwaito, its own genre, borrows elements from hip-hop music, as well as house music, and has its own rules of composition. In a study of hip-hop subgenres in the United States, Lena writes, "While the diversity of rap sub-genres over sixteen years of production is undeniable, an analysis of rap lyrics suggests strong similarities across sub-genre styles" (2004, 490). New genres of music emerge from blending elements of various music genres. As new genres develop their distinctive styles, dances, culture, and rules of composition, they also develop their own identity.

In Africa, hip-hop would influence the development of several new music genres. New, hip-hop-influenced, musical genres emerged in many countries in Africa in the 1990s. These new genres (hiplife in Ghana, bongo flava in Tanzania, and kwaito in South Africa) would often blend hip-hop, R&B, reggae, house, and African sounds. In the cases of hiplife and bongo flava, the songs are also performed primarily in local languages. They are popular in urban African club scenes and have directly competed with hip-hop for radio airtime.

In Ghana, hiplife emerged in the early 1990s (Odamtten 2011; Collins, 2012; Shipley 2012). Artists like Reggie Rockstone, along with groups like Talking Drums, were among the first hiplife musicians in the country. Rockstone, known by many as the godfather of hiplife, is also a hip-hop artist. In a photo taken at his home in Accra (fig. 1.2), he wears a T-shirt proclaiming "I am Hiplife." Ghana is home to an active hiplife and hip-hop community (sometimes referred to as GH rap, or Ghana rap), with many artists moving between the genres. Artists like Sarkodie, Reggie Rockstone, and Edem move between genres regularly.

26 | *Hip-Hop in Africa*

Figure 1.2. Reggie Rockstone in Accra in 2010. Photo by author.

Unlike in Tanzania and South Africa, both the Ghanaian hybrid (hiplife) and hip-hop deal with social and political issues. According to producer Panji Anoff, hiplife often takes a more humorous approach to social commentary, while hip-hop tends to be more aggressive in its approach. Kwaito and bongo flava are known as mainly dance music, lacking a lot of real political commentary. Hiplife, kwaito, and bongo flava have all been described as be their country's versions of hip-hop, but are actually their own genres, which incorporated sound from hip-hop and other music to create new genres. Today most are financially lucrative industries. Bongo flava is sung in Swahili, while hiplife is sung in Twi, Ewe, Ga, and other local languages. Kwaito is usually sung using one of the South African languages. Both kwaito and bongo flava contain lighter lyrical content, often avoiding many of the politics that South African and Tanzanian hip-hop often cover (World: The Global Hit 2007; Clark 2013), though in discussing early bongo flava, Lemelle (2006) suggests that it was initially political. Unlike in Ghana, in Tanzania hip-hop artists have fought to forge their

"Boomerang": Hip-Hop and Pan-African Dialogues | 27

own separate identity, distancing themselves from bongo flava, with only a few artists performing music in both genres. Ghanaian hip-hop artists often do both hip-hop and hiplife music. Likewise, in South Africa, Shaheen Ariefdien says that some hip-hop artists do kwaito in order to fund hip-hop projects. Shaheen Ariefdien is one of the members of pioneering South African hip-hop group Prophets of da City.

According to Shaheen Ariefdien, the reason hip-hop in South Africa remains strong is "because it doesn't imagine its life-force coming from a barcode" (pers. comm., August 11, 2011). Shaheen Ariefdien perceived the biggest threat to South African hip-hop to be hip-hop influences from outside South Africa, particularly the kind of hip-hop that a lot of conscious South African artists do not identify with ideologically. Indeed, South Africa does seem to be facing some of the debates facing American hip-hop. According to Lee Watkins (2012), the growing influence of purely profit-driven hip-hop music has created some divisions within South African hip-hop.

The subgenres of South African hip-hop include spaza, motswako, and zef rap. The three styles utilize the same hip-hop rhyme techniques, and these terms are applied to artists performing South African languages. Spaza rap contains lyrics that are performed in multiple languages, especially Xhosa, often representing ghetto life in South Africa (UnderGround Angle 2009; Subzzee 2010b; Williams and Stroud 2013). Examples of Spaza artists include Driemanskap, Middle Finga, and Kritsi Ye'Spaza. Motswako is said to have come to South Africa via Botswana, and also contains the blending of languages, especially Tswana (Subzzee 2010a). One of the best-known Motswako artists is Hip Hop Pantsula (HHP), while younger artists Chazz le Hippie and Missy RBK have emerged recently. Zef rap was a style started by White Afrikaans speaking hip-hop heads and is performed in Afrikaans (Williams and Stroud 2013).

In Tanzania, hip-hop is not as commercially viable as bongo flava: many hip-hop artists are critical of the pop genre and have turned into activists invested in maintaining and developing Tanzanian hip-hop culture. While hip-hop culture remains strong through the youth involved in the culture, the tensions between bongo flava and hip-hop may have had an impact on hip-hop's development and the willingness of hip-hop artists to experiment with sound. For example, many hip-hop artists in Tanzania have been hesitant to experiment by using beats and sounds that come from other music genres, exclusively using hip-hop beats, in an effort to stay "authentically" hip-hop. Meanwhile in Senegal, with a variety of youth music, hip-hop artists do not have a popular pop hybrid to compete with, though in recent years Senegalese hip-hop has begun seeing a trend toward dance music and more commercialized hip-hop, as discussed in the short documentary *100% Galsen* (Sene 2012).

As in Tanzania, some Senegalese hip-hop artists use only hip-hop beats, believing that using beats from other musical genres would affect the authenticity of their music (Appert 2016). According to Appert, mbalax beats are usually performed with socially and politically conscious lyrics in Senegal, though conscious lyrics are not always accompanied by mbalax beats. Also, as in Tanzania, Senegalese artists have a difficult time earning a living from their music (Keyti, pers. comm., August 2, 2009; Herson 2011; Clark 2013). Artists often have to rely on other business deals, paid appearances, shows, and touring to make a living.

Into Africa

As hip-hop spread globally, it made its way back across the Atlantic Ocean to Africa. Hip-hop arrived on the continent in the 1980s and brought with it a new sound and new styles of dance (e.g., breakdancing). Many young Africans first heard hip-hop as it trickled in via radio stations, house parties, and night clubs. As the music spread, it would often be those with relatives who traveled to the United States or Europe, or those with access to exchange students studying in their country, who would get the latest hip-hop cassette tapes. Copies of the prized tapes would then make their way around the neighborhood. Pioneering hip-hop artists like Zimbabwe's Doom E. Right, Tanzania's KBC of Kwanza Unit, and South Africa's Shaheen Ariefdien have all reflected on these experiences in their first contacts with hip-hop (Doom E. Right, pers, comm., August 26, 2011; KBC, pers. comm., September 1, 2011; Ariefdien and Burgess, 2011).

"Boomerang": Hip-Hop and Pan-African Dialogues | 29

In his 2007 memoir *A Long Way Gone: Memoirs of a Boy Soldier*, Ishmael Beah recounts his first contact with hip-hop music in early-1990s Sierra Leone. After hearing hip-hop for the first time, Beah and his friends became so absorbed by the music and the culture that they formed a hip-hop group. Though later forced into becoming a child soldier for the Sierra Leone military, it was his hip-hop cassettes and his skills as an emcee and dancer that initially saved Beah from being killed (Beah 2007). The civil wars in Sierra Leone and Liberia were infamous for their use of child soldiers. Often the boys forced to fight would be kept high on drugs (marijuana, cocaine) and plied with images and sounds of gangsta rap (Sommers 2003; Beah 2007). Armed with the lightweight, easy-to-use AK-47s, they were numb and ready to kill.

Elsewhere in Africa it would often be middle- and upper-class Africans who, with access to the appropriate equipment, formed the first rap crews. By the late 1980s African emcees grabbed the mic and began to transform hip-hop. Groups like Prophets of da City (POC) and Black Noise emerged to help pioneer hip-hop culture in South Africa. Both groups would be influenced by the music of American hip-hop groups like Public Enemy, X-Clan, and NWA as they told their own stories of life in apartheid South Africa (Ariefdien and Burgess 2011).

In West Africa the Senegalese group Positive Black Soul (PBS) emerged to help usher in hip-hop culture in that country. Along with rapper MC Solaar, PBS greatly influenced the emergence of hip-hop culture in Senegal. MC Solaar would go on to become one of the first African emcees to do a song with a major American hip-hop artist when he recorded "Le Bien, Le Mal" with Guru in 1993. Eric Charry provides a detailed account of hip-hop's arrival in West Africa via Europe. Charry is especially thorough in detailing hip-hop's history among francophone Africans. An important element in the growth of hip-hop in Senegal, for example, has been the migration of Senegalese immigrants into both New York and Paris, which would become important routes for hip-hop exchanges (Charry 2012).

The emergence of hip-hop culture varied all over the continent, but by the early 1990s several countries in Africa had flourishing hip-hop communities. In East Africa, groups Kwanza Unit and the

Figure 1.3. Zavara Mponjika, aka MC Rhymson, of the group Kwanza Unit in the Temeke district of Dar es Salaam in 2010. Photo by author.

De-Plow-Matz, and artist 2 Proud (now Sugu), were integral to the growth of hip-hop in Tanzania in the early 1990s. A photo (fig. 1.3) shows Kwanza Unit founding member Zavara Mponjika (aka Rhymson) in his old neighborhood of Temeke in Dar es Salaam. In Kenya, hip-hop artist Hardstone and the group Kalamashaka were influential in the development of hip-hop in that country. In West Africa, Reggie Rockstone and the group Talking Drums helped transform Ghanaian hip-hop, with artists performing in both English, Pidgin English, and various Ghanaian languages. Reggie Rockstone and Talking Drums also helped usher in hiplife, which came to incorporate various styles of music. There are hip-hop emcees, reggae musicians, and R&B singers who perform hiplife music.

These early pioneers of hip-hop in Africa helped transform the culture from an imitation of American hip-hop to something distinctly local. Some of these artists have stepped away from the spotlight and others are still active, while still others are transitioning into politics or organizing with NGOs to make a difference in social issues.

Hip-hop culture has five elements (the emcee, the DJ, graffiti, break-dancing, and knowledge of self). While the emcee has the largest visible presence in Africa, aspects of all the elements can be found in Africa. Knowledge of self as an element emerged last and is often cited only by serious hip-hop heads.[3] For most serious hip-hop heads, "knowledge of self is considered to be the fifth element of hip-hop, which informs the other elements" (Haupt 2008, 144). Many of the early African artists were attracted to not just the sound of hip-hop but the words. It was the honesty, and the voice of resistance, that also appealed to African hip-hop artists. Some of these artists understood the fifth element and incorporated it into a holistic approach to hip-hop culture.

In political science the phrase "all politics is local" could be similarly applied to hip-hop. All hip-hop is local. Emcees represent their contemporary local realities. Hip-hop scenes in various cities have their own distinctive styles and sounds. While hip-hop in Los Angeles was largely influenced by the funk music scene and gang culture there, hip-hop in Dakar was influenced by the mbalax music scene and Senegalese Islamic culture in that city. Hip-hop in Africa is a representation of local African communities and is influenced by local experiences and cultures. Hip-hop communities emerged nationally with very few connections with communities beyond their borders, and connections between francophone, anglophone, and lusophone countries were almost nonexistent. Aware of developments in the US hip-hop scenes, hip-hop communities in Africa developed in local contexts, largely a product of the music, culture, and history of the communities within which the culture developed.

The lyrics of those early African emcees encompassed the emotions and experience of entire generations of youth. The result was that artists not only speak to their national audiences, but contributed to global hip-hop dialogues as well. The goal for many artists was not just to speak to their local audiences but to represent their Africa to the world. For example, Senegalese rap pioneers Positive Black Soul (PBS) released their song "Africa" because they wanted to show the world "what Africa really is" (Appert 2016, 286).

African hip-hop artists also brought about conscious connections between hip-hop and African styles of rhyming and poetry, such as

32 | *Hip-Hop in Africa*

tassou (Senegal), *maanso* (Somalia), *ushairi* (Tanzania), that have existed for centuries in African cultures. K'naan, for example, has often reminded his listeners that Somalia is known as a nation of poets. Peter S. Scholtes quotes Senegalese hip-hop artist Faada Freddy: "Tassou still exists in Senegal . . . That's an ancient form of rap music." (2006, par. 4).

The process of indigenizing hip-hop culture was helped when many emcees began rapping in local languages. In countries like Ghana, Kenya, Liberia, Senegal, South Africa, Tanzania, and Uganda artists manipulated local languages and dialects and moved from producing English-only rap to also rapping in local languages. The importance of language use in hip-hop is crucial to understanding whom music speaks to, where an artist is coming from (Pennycook 2007; L. Watkins 2012). The language spoken by the masses has historically been assigned a low status (Devonish 1986). In fact, postcolonial policies to maintain colonial languages as official languages in much of Africa perpetuated the language inequality that developed, and the lower-class status assigned to the languages of the masses (Devonish 1986; Fanon 2004; Thiong'o 1986). Hip-hop's roots, however, are with the masses, with those very individuals whom society has assigned a low status. The languages utilized by hip-hop artists was taken from the language spoken on the streets, by the masses. The slang used in hip-hop has the characteristics of other spoken languages, in that it is constantly changing, and an in-group status is also assigned to those who are fluent in it. As a result of hip-hop's influence and popularity, in some countries hip-hop culture has promoted the status of indigenous and creole languages (and cultures) among the youth. In Ghana, for example, Pidgin English is assigned a low status but hip-hop artists have played a role in promoting its use among the youth. In response to the status of Pidgin English and street culture, Ghanaian artists Wanlov the Kubolor and M.anifest team up on the song "Gentleman" and proclaim, "I no be gentleman at all'o / I be African man original." Through the song the duo uses Pidgin English to assert a specific kind of Ghanaian identity, one that is rooted in the masses.

"Boomerang": Hip-Hop and Pan-African Dialogues | 33

2

"Understand Where I'm Coming From"

The Growth of African Hip-Hop and Representations of African Culture

Hip Hop. This isn't a hobby to me. This isn't something I just decided to try [to] do. I've been doing this my whole life. This is my life. It's in my DNA. Remember that.

—Gigi LaMayne, Tumblr post, January 7, 2016

HIP-HOP COMMUNITIES IN Africa emerged in the 1980s and 1990s and did not simply reflect what was happening on the ground but also constructed for us the realities for many urban youth in Africa. They also informed the youth and put their conditions into context, translating political speak into street language, and sometimes they provided instructions on confrontations with social and political institutions. By the mid-1990s and early 2000s pioneering hip-hop artists all over Africa were releasing politically and socially conscious music. Songs like Prophets of da City's "Ons stem" (Our voice, South Africa, 1991), Positive Black Soul's "Le bourreau est noir" (The executioner is black, Senegal, 1995), Kalamashaka's "Tafsiri hii" and "Ni wakati" (Translate this and It's time, Kenya, 1997, 2001), Kwanza Unit's "Msafiri" (Traveler, Tanzania, 1999), or Das Primeiro's "Liberdade" (Liberty, Angola, 2002) all pointed out hypocrisies in government, resurrected the words of past revolutionary leaders through sampling, and connected urban youth in Africa to global hip-hop communities. Many of these early artists were of a generation that was either engaged in liberation struggles (southern Africa) or the children of those who had engaged in liberation struggles. In an interview with Kama of Kalamashaka, the artist understood his role as both an emcee and an activist and saw the role of the emcee as similar to the roles of other intellectuals. Kama's grandparents were involved in the Mau Mau rebellion and he was himself politically educated but also rooted in hip-hop culture. During Kama's visit to Los Angeles he easily rapped along with songs from US emcee Redman's classic 1994 album *Dare Iz a Darkside,* engaged in substantive discussions of Mau Mau ideologies, and debated the ideas of Frances Cress Welsing.[1] Kama was representative of other socially conscious hip-hop artists. Several artists interviewed articulated the role of the emcee as street intellectuals, and several saw political education as a necessary process.

In a historical review of the growth of hip-hop as a form of cultural representation in Africa, this chapter focuses on the economic and political events on the continent in the 1980s and 1990s that led to the development and politicization of hip-hop culture in Africa, as well as at the diverse hip-hop representations found in select countries of Africa. I also look at the ways in which individual artists have shaped hip-hop in Africa as well as how they have contributed (festivals, conferences, award shows) to the development of hip-hop in Africa. The chapter details the ways in which hip-hop emerged as a tool to represent social dissonance and presents hip-hop as a cultural representation beyond the music, specifically the use of graffiti, media (film, magazines, radio), and fashion as forms of cultural representations within hip-hop culture.

Artists all over Africa have used hip-hop as a framework or vehicle to create certain narratives. It is within these narratives that the listener is able to discern historical, political, social, and economic dynamics within certain societies. Chuck D's famous quote that hip-hop is "black America's CNN" has broader implications through a cultural studies framework (Thorpe, 1999). In cultural studies even the news is a cultural representation, containing the perspectives and ideologies of the individuals editing the news stories. In many ways the evening news also represents certain cultural systems, and one's interpretation of the news is often shaped by one's own cultural connections. Through hip-hop, as through the evening news, reality is constructed and a historical record is created. Though different audiences translate or interpret cultural representations differently, based on their own social and economic background, those representations, be they hip-hop or the evening news, are no less legitimate realities for many.

Hip-hop, as a form of cultural representation, expresses the feelings, ideas, and concepts of the culture within which the artist lives. Hip-hop, as all cultural representations, has the power to shape, educate, and change society. There are definite similarities seen in cultural representations produced through hip-hop music all over the African continent. These similarities include expressions of hip-hop's core elements and culture and articulations of similar economic and political environments. Differences among representations in hip-hop in Africa come from the diverse environments that exist on the continent. These diverse environments are understood through an examination of hip-hop in various countries.

The chapter also deals with the ways in which African hip-hop artists produce and distribute music with the diversity of resources available to them. There are challenges and opportunities facing hip-hop artists in Africa, and the ways in which they are navigating those challenges and opportunities are important. African hip-hop artists have embraced new media and bypassed barriers imposed by mainstream or traditional media outlets. The internet has become a platform for videos, songs, lyrics, blogs, and articles written by hip-hop artists and content creators in Africa. On platforms like iTunes, Spotify, Pandora, ReverbNation, SoundCloud, Vimeo, YouTube, and others, the numbers of African emcees making their music available online has increased multifold since 2009, when my research on hip-hop in Africa began.

The chapter will finally explore the ways in which African hip-hop heads are exploring and using nonmusical representations in African hip-hop culture. Hip-hop culture goes beyond the music and finds expression in other art forms. Graffiti and breakdancing developed early on in many African countries, along with the music. Some hip-hop emcees had their start as breakdancers or graffiti artists. Later, with changes in technology and communication, more hip-hop heads used new media and social media to express hip-hop culture through images, films, and magazines. Additionally, distinctly African hip-hop fashion has become increasingly visible. The use of local textiles, slang, and graphics in fashion has led to more artists looking to African-produced fashions, leading to a fan base following their lead and fashion designers inspired to keep up with the changes.

Hip-Hop as Cultural Representation

Music and other forms of cultural representation (art, literature, film, etc.) may not simply be reflections of reality but indeed how reality is constructed. The constructivist approach to cultural representation posits that our understandings of reality and the world around us, including our concepts of self and other, are based on various representations. Representations create reality for us and reinforce or challenge the realities constructed by previous representations. According to the constructivist approach to cultural representation, "it is the social actors who use the conceptual systems of their culture and the linguistic and other representational systems to construct meaning, to make the world meaningful and to communicate about that world meaningfully to others" (Hall 2013, 25). Therefore, when we associate Somalia with lawlessness and piracy, while simultaneously associating America with lawfulness and security, it is because of the representation we have been exposed to about both countries. When Somali-born hip-hop artist K'naan, based in Canada and the United States, presents a representation of Somalia that challenges what we "know," his representations, especially when supported by further similar representations, can effectively impact our understanding of Somalia. Studies show that distorted media representations of Africa have often constructed in the minds of many in the West an image of an Africa plagued by disease, poverty, war, corruption, and famine (Schraeder and Endless 1998; Mengara 2001; Gallagher 2015). These representations are responsible for what Chimamanda Adichie (2009) referred to as the single story of Africa in her now-famous TED Talk. These representations have impacts on American and European foreign policy, on Western attitudes toward Africa and Africans, as well as on work done in Africa by NGOs and other international organizations.

This does not mean that all representations are interpreted in the same way. The realities constructed by one representation may be interpreted differently, depending on the cultural context from which the audience operates and their understanding of the cultural context from which the representation originates. A well-known example of the importance of understanding cultural context is the American *The Wire*, an iconic television series, especially within hip-hop culture. The story is told through the lens of an inner-city Black community in America in which hip-hop culture is firmly entrenched. The show challenged America's assumptions about the inner city, the people who lived there, and the government officials who worked there, in a way that was uncomfortable (Chaddha and Wilson 2010; Mittell 2010). Assumptions about inner-city African Americans, as well the appropriateness of the behaviors of government officials, have largely been shaped by cultural representations found in mainstream TV, film, and news media. Like the hip-hop culture represented in the show, *The Wire* challenged those representations by presenting a counternarrative to audiences that had already bought into a single story of inner-city African Americans. Understanding the representations presented in *The Wire* did not require one to have lived the experiences of West Baltimore residents, but it did require one to question, and even set aside, previously accepted representations in order to understand the cultural contexts within which the characters on *The Wire* operated. Because hip-hop culture featured prominently in the show, the program has become a cult classic with hip-hop heads around the world.

Cultural representations create reality, using coded language familiar to specific audiences and subcultures. In studying hip-hop, or any cultural representation, if one understands the context and the cultural codes of the system, then one can better understand the meanings of the representations. Within hip-hop culture in Africa, audiences inside and outside local communities unable to understand the cultural context of the artist may misinterpret the meanings of the representations. Understanding the cultural context requires a willingness to understand and to accept that previous representations may have constructed an incomplete reality, or a single story. African emcees are in the habit of presenting realities that contradict the single story of Africa. They bring with them complex cultures and histories and use creative wordplay to depict their realities. Hip-hop, wherever one finds it, is a form of cultural representation that informs the listener and constructs certain realities using coded language and the frameworks of hip-hop to speak to specific audiences. The social, political, and economic environments within which hip-hop emerged are significant to understanding its current use by youth across Africa.

Prelude to a Revolution

By the mid-1980s many African economies were facing difficulties, and governments found themselves in need of aid. African countries began talks or entered into financial agreements with international institutions like the International Monetary Fund (IMF) and the World Bank in order to help struggling economies (Konadu-Agyemang 2000a; Perullo 2005; Opoku 2008). As a condition of the loans provided by the IMF and the World Bank, many African countries were forced to adopt structural adjustment programs (SAPs) and to restructure their economies. Today SAPs have been replaced by poverty reduction strategy papers (PRSPs), but the latter come with similar conditions.

The SAPs mandated the adoption of neoliberal economic policies, which required countries to open their economies to foreign penetration, deregulation, a rollback of spending on public services, and privatization of public enterprises (Brydon and Legge 1996; Konadu-Agyemang 2000a; Shivji 2010; Liviga 2011). Life in urban Africa became extremely difficult. Residents faced widespread poverty, housing problems, high rates of underemployment and unemployment, and a decrease in access to healthcare and education (ECA 1989; Brydon and Legge 1996; Lugalla 1997; Bond and Dor 2003; Lemelle 2006; Mawuko-Yevugah 2010). In urban ghettos all over Africa, from which would emerge many hip-hop artists, problems included overcrowding, poor housing and sanitation, substandard healthcare and education, and high crime (Brydon and Legge 1996; Lugalla 1997; Ali 2002; Lemelle 2006).

The implemented neoliberal economic policies also led to the displacement, often through land grabbing, of rural peasants who would contribute to Africa's rapid urbanization and strain an already stressed infrastructure (Jumare 1997; Lugalla 1997; Konadu-Agyemang 2000b; Ali 2002; Weiss 2009; Manji 2012). The ranks of the unemployed also became filled with illiterate and semiliterate youth who increasingly turned to the informal market and illegal activities to survive.

The decline in standards of living due to rapid privatization and economic restructuring not only is the environment in which many hip-hop artists continue to emerge, it also is responsible for fueling and, in many cases, politicizing hip-hop in Africa. The economic environment inspired the development of hip-hop in Africa. Hip-hop provided youth with an opportunity to address the problems they were seeing around them. As in the United States, some of Africa's most notorious neighborhoods have given birth to some of the strongest hip-hop communities.

Today the continuation, and even acceleration, of repressive economic policies continues to spur youth activism around Africa and in some cases has led to harsher condemnations by artists as well as to artists taking to the streets in protest. The result of the SAPs and neoliberal economics has led to a transformation of the state in Africa, a state no longer accountable to its population but to international financial institutions. According to Firoz Manji, the main role of the state has been to "ensure an 'enabling environment' for international capital and to police the endless servicing of debt to international finance institutions" (2012, 5). The results have been increased strikes, protests, and numbers of economic refugees fleeing Africa. Pambazuka's (2012) publication *African Awakenings* details the increased uprisings throughout Africa. It is a critical examination of the use of social media to confront neoliberalism. Youth voices are an integral part of current waves of social protest.

Burkina Faso, Egypt, Senegal, South Africa, and Tunisia have seen some of the highest levels of mobilization in public protests in sub-Saharan Africa since 2010. In South Africa it is estimated that over eight thousand acts of public protest have occurred annually since 2005 (Manji 2012). More recently artists and activists have mobilized around the 2012 massacre of the protesting Marikana miners by South African security forces and the protests around the decolonization of education in South Africa during the 2015 #FeesMustFall and #RhodesMustFall protests. Between 2010 and 2012 thousands of Egyptians, Senegalese, and Tunisians, along with several hip-hop artists, took to the streets to protest the governments of then presidents Hosni Mubarak, Abdoulaye Wade, and Zine El Abidine Ben Ali, respectively (Manji 2012; Gueye 2013; Berktay 2014; Lo 2014; Wahlrab 2014). Protests would increase or emerge all over Africa. According to Manji, "During the first six months of 2011, protests, strikes and other actions took place in Zimbabwe, Senegal, Gabon, Sudan, Mauritania, Morocco, Algeria, Benin, Cameroon, Djibouti, Côte d'Ivoire, Burkina Faso, Botswana, Namibia, Uganda, Kenya, Malawi and Swaziland" (2012, 21).

While the Pambazuka publication does not address the role of hip-hop artists, in many of those countries hip-hop artists, along with other musicians, were contributing to the soundtracks of these movements, and in some cases were on the ground themselves. In a *New York Times* op-ed entitled "The Mixtape of the Revolution," Sujatha Fernandes (2012) highlights the activism of hip-hop artists in some of these social movements, some of which has gotten artists arrested. She says hip-hop artists and activists Thiat (Senegal) and El Général (Hamada Ben Amor) (Tunisia) "may be two of the most influential rappers in the history of hip-hop" (2012, par. 1).

After Egypt, Senegal, and Tunisia saw governments overthrown, hip-hop artists played a role in mass protests that broke out in Burkina Faso and the Democratic Republic of the Congo (DRC). In 2014 in Burkina Faso rapper Smockey was among the artists leading the grassroots group Le Balai Citoyen (citizen's broom), which led mass protests all over the capital, Ouagadougou. Balai Citoyen was a group of activists fighting the rule of President Blaise Compaoré, who had ruled Burkina Faso since the assassination of President Thomas Sankara, in 1987. Activists from both Balai Citoyen and Y'en a Marre (fed up) (Senegal) were arrested in the DRC in March 2015. They were invited by the Congolese group Filimbi but were seen as a threat by the

"Understand Where I'm Coming From": Growth of Hip-Hop | 41

Congolese government, perhaps because of their success in removing the presidents in their own countries.

Note that increases in social mobilization are not limited to Africa. The implementation of the same neoliberal economic policies has also caused protests in the United States, Greece, France, Bahrain, India, Columbia, Mexico, and other countries. Black Lives Matter, the Occupy movement, Anonymous, and the Arab Spring were reactions to these same global economic policies that are having disastrous impacts on the world's poor. Urbanization, land rights, workers' rights, police violence, education, healthcare, environmental rights, economic rights, and political representation are all subjects of protests in countries throughout the world.

No every country has seen the same level of response to neoliberalism. The social and political environment has differed across Africa. This has also influenced the evolution of hip-hop culture in Africa, which was shaped by numerous factors. To understand some of these major differences, we can examine a selection of Africa's largest and most-written-about hip-hop communities: Ghana, Senegal, South Africa, and Tanzania. Through them we can see the diversity of experiences in Africa represented through hip-hop. The realities constructed and the manner in which they were presented, however, varied. Hip-hop had arrived in Ghana, Senegal, South Africa, and Tanzania by the 1980s. This period saw the height of SAPs in Senegal and Tanzania; the rule of Jerry Rawlings, who came to power via a coup in Ghana; and increased pressures against apartheid rule in South Africa.

Politicization

Diverse arrivals and histories influenced the politicization of hip-hop in these countries. In Senegal, hip-hop was more confrontational than it was in either Ghana or Tanzania, for example. In apartheid South Africa censorship was a reality for hip-hop artists and activists who were aware of the death, disappearances, and forced exiles of other activists.

Through interviews with individuals within Ghanaian music circles, some believe the censorship experienced after the Rawlings

42 | *Hip-Hop in Africa*

coup, and during the Rawlings years, had lasting impacts on Ghanaian music, influencing self-censorship by many artists. Jesse Shipley (2013) argues that there is social and political content in Ghanaian music, but he provides another explanation for the impression that it is absent. Shipley says that the style of commentary in Ghanaian music is tied to the popularity of using proverbs in Ghanaian culture—the preferred, and less direct, method of social commentary.

Senegal, according to many scholars, activists, and musicians, has one of the largest hip-hop communities in the world, with three to five thousand in the city of Dakar alone (Künzler 2007; Herson, McIlvaine, and Moore 2009). In speaking to several Senegalese musicians and activists, many noted a tradition of direct criticism within Senegalese culture. In comparison to Ghana's preference for proverbs, in Senegalese culture there is often open and direct criticism of politics, and that has spilled over into hip-hop music.

While hip-hop came to Ghana in the wake of the Rawlings coup, it came to Senegal in the midst of a border conflict between Senegal and Mauritania, an economic crisis, and thousands of West Africans fleeing the continent in poorly constructed boats headed for Europe (Diouf, n.d.; ECA 1989; Okome 2002; Bailey 2006; Sy 2006; Charry 2012). One casualty of the economic crisis in Senegal was the closure of schools because of strikes. This event is often cited as a factor in the solidification and politicization of Senegalese hip-hop (Herson 2011). During a 2009 interview, Senegalese hip-hop veteran Keyti called the incident critical to politicizing Senegalese hip-hop.

In separate interviews longtime hip-hop artists Keyti and Xuman also said Senegalese cultural and religious traditions (Islam) have influenced the social and political content in the hip-hop music. According to both Keyti and Xuman, because of these cultural and religious traditions, in Senegalese hip-hop one does not find artists objectifying women, writings songs about alcohol or drugs, or crossing cultural taboos. Even music that is not overtly political, maintains a certain level of social responsibility. Xuman and Waterflow (Moussa Lo) both stated that artists that use explicit lyrics or content would risk losing their fan base and credibility.

Like in Senegal, in South Africa hip-hop became politicized early on, due in large part to both growing militancy in the antiapartheid

"Understand Where I'm Coming From": Growth of Hip-Hop | 43

Figure 2.1. Shaheen Ariefdien in Toronto in 2011. Photo by author.

struggles and the heavily political music of groups like Public Enemy, which influenced early hip-hop artists (Ariefdien and Burgess 2011; Ariefdien and Chapman 2014). For artists like Shaheen Ariefdien (fig. 2.1) of Prophets of da City, political hip-hop not only challenged apartheid but would later challenge neocolonialism or Western intrusion in Africa as well (Haupt 2008). The influence of these early socially conscious hip-hop artists profoundly impacted newer generations of hip-hop artists in South Africa. This has been reinforced by the presence of workshops, events, independent radio stations, and activists invested in supporting socially conscious hip-hop in South Africa (Haupt 2008; L. Watkins 2012). Hip-hop in today's South Africa, however, is challenged by the influence of gangster rap and commercialization, in some cases pushing socially conscious hip-hop out of the mainstream (L. Watkins 2012).

Tanzanian hip-hop has not been as confrontational as Senegalese. The country also did not undergo the censorship felt in South Africa. In Tanzania the use of an indigenous language, Swahili/Kiswahili, has meant hip-hop played a role in the politics of language in that country.

The vast majority of Tanzanian hip-hop is sung in Swahili/Kiswahili, a language central to the Tanzanian identity. Swahili/Kiswahili poetry and sayings are a valued part of the way Tanzanians communicate. According to Lemelle, in Tanzania "many of the signature aspects of rap music, including wordplay, risqué, or suggestive puns and lyrical rhyme, are deeply inscribed in Swahili culture, in the form of Swahili parables, proverbs, and allegory called methali" (2006, 238). Manipulating Swahili language styles, Tanzanian hip-hop pioneers like De-Plow-Matz, Professor Jay, and Sugu (aka 2 Proud, Mr. II) helped hip-hop's politicization in Tanzania.

Following a slump in socially conscious hip-hop in the mid-2000s, there has been a noticeable increase in confrontation in Tanzanian hip-hop. In 2011, Tanzanian artist Izzo Bizness released the song "Riz One," directed at the son of then president Jakaya Kikwete, Ridhiwani (aka Riz One). The song implores Riz One to tell his father to do something about the current living conditions in Tanzania. The song was shocking to some because it calls out Riz One by name. It was one of the few Tanzanian hip-hop songs to directly name a political figure, instead of insinuating and leaving it to the audience to understand whom the artist is talking about.

This compares to Senegal, when during the 2011 and 2012 uprisings against then president Abdoulaye Wade, a number of scathing hip-hop songs were released. Marame Gueye (2013) details the social activism seen by hip-hop artists, both on the ground and through their music. Senegalese artists like Kilifeu of the duo Keur Gui and Simon of Sen Kumpë released the song "Faux! Pas Forcé" (Don't push) in 2011, directed at then president Abdoulaye Wade. In the song they say: "Laye [short for Abdoulaye], do not look for alibis / Don't be like Gaddafi / If you do not want us to be like the people of Libya" (Gueye 2013). In 2012 a collaboration of artists in Senegal released the song "Doggali" (Finishing up a killing) in which they say,

> You have completed your term
> The whip must strike you
> The country needs other minds
> You must make way for them. (Gueye 2013)

"Understand Where I'm Coming From": Growth of Hip-Hop | 45

These songs represent the direct, more confrontational nature of Senegalese hip-hop.

The early 2000s witnessed a major decline in the production of hip-hop in Tanzania, due in large part to the popularity of bongo flava and some artists switching genres. Tanzania has experienced a resurgence in conscious hip-hop through the appearance of hip-hop collectives (like Okoa Mtaa Foundation, Ujamaa Hip Hop, and Tamaduni Muzik) and the recent popularity of open-mic events. Through weekly freestyle events like the Hip Hop Kilinge (cypher) hosted by Tamaduni Muzik, as well as hip-hop events put on at Alliance Française and the Nafasi Art Space, conscious hip-hop has been seeing a resurgence in Dar es Salaam. Tamaduni Muzik includes a collective of strong lyricists, like Nikki Mbishi, One the Incredible, Songa (fig. 2.2), P the MC, Nash MC, and Zaiid. In addition, the collective includes DJ Texas, hip-hop producer Duke Gervalius (fig. 2.3), and hip-hop writer Malle Marxist, all of whom are involved in creating a platform for hip-hop in Tanzania. In northern Tanzania, Okoa Mtaa has helped turn Arusha into a major East African hub for hip-hop. The group is a collective of artists that use hip-hop culture as a way to empower the youth. In additional to holding hip-hop festivals that focus on the five main elements, Okoa Mtaa uses hip-hop culture to "contribute in the social & economic development of East Africa" and to "use underground arts for social education that helps to create awareness and engagement in community positive changes" (Okoa Mtaa Foundation, n.d.). The group, as well as many artists in the area, has been heavily influenced by the work of the Arusha-based United African Alliance Community Center, a center run by former members of the Black Panther Party, Pete and Charlotte O'Neal. In an interview with members of the group Wanaitwa Uhuru ("they are called freedom") (fig. 2.4), a collective of seven to ten artists, they indicated that while conscious artists in Tanzania are still not united, they see these events as important to the survival of conscious hip-hop in Tanzania.

In addition to Okoa Mtaa, other countries in East Africa have claimed safe spaces within which to promote both culture and youth activism. In Nairobi, Pawa254[2] is a place where artists and activists meet regularly. Workshops, events, and trainings are held there. The

Figure 2.2. Songa at the New Msasani Club, home of the Hip Hop Kilinge (cypher), in Dar es Salaam in 2013. Photo by author.

Figure 2.3. Hip-hop producer Duke Gervalius in Dar es Salaam in 2014. Photo by author.

Figure 2.4. Members of the group Wanaitwa Uhuru in Dar es Salaam in 2014. Photo by author.

Pit in Nairobi also hosts regular events that promote hip-hop culture and the main elements in hip-hop: emceeing, DJing, graffiti, and breakdance. In Kampala, Uganda the B-Global Indigenous Hip Hop Gathering hosts a yearly gathering and has a space in the city for smaller, less formal events with Kampala youth. The B-Global, led by veteran Ugandan hip-hop artist Babaluku (former member of Bataka Squad), seeks "to empower and educate the youth to lay foundations upon which their communities can grow, build and be transformed, through engagement and practice of the Hip Hop culture" (B-Global, n.d.). Their gatherings often bring together Ugandan artists and artists from East and Central Africa.

The Hustle

There are thousands of African emcees living full-time or part-time on the African continent as well is in the diaspora. Many of these emcees give a new meaning to the word *hustle*. The hip-hop scene varies in Africa by country. Those artists based in the West have access to more resources but have a more difficult time breaking into the national scene. In Africa, talented artists have access to fewer resources but are in a better position to make a name for themselves nationally. Resources can include recording equipment, reliable internet access, media outlets (independent magazines, radio stations), and workshops where artists can network with others in the industry.

The transition from one's imagination to actually releasing an album and booking shows is universally difficult, but there are variations across Africa. In some countries, for example, artists have managers and promoters to assist in booking showings and managing images. In other countries many artists self-manage and self-promote. Access to resources also varies, with southern African artists having a clear advantage, followed by those in West Africa, where economic opportunities and relative proximity to the United States give the region a slight advantage.

While bootlegging is a problem globally throughout the music industry, weak enforcement of copyright laws in Africa makes it especially problematic on the continent. For African emcees distribution, especially internationally, continues to be a problem. Many albums released by African artists cannot be found in stores outside their own countries. Many have also not been able to get their music distributed via online outlets. Many of these artists still manage to develop strong fan bases in their home countries and internationally. Some, like K'naan and Blitz the Ambassador, have made inroads in the American hip-hop market.

Hip-hop is steadily evolving and new media and social media have been a crucial part of that evolution. Facebook, ReverbNation, SoundCloud, Twitter, Instagram, YouTube, iTunes, and even Wikipedia have all made information on music and artists more accessible globally. Many African emcees have videos on YouTube and pages on Facebook. Many use Facebook, Twitter, and Instagram to communicate with fans. While Facebook (1.15 billion) has more users than Twitter (215 million), both platforms allow artists to reach fans all over the world (Boorstin 2013). Online networking has meant African emcees are able to book shows all over the world and to collaborate with emcees based in other countries and regions. Some popular African hip-hop artists on social media have large numbers of followers, some with between 500,000 to 1 million followers on Facebook and Twitter, with many followers outside the artist's country of origin.

Of the African hip-hop artists with over 100,00 followers on both Facebook and Twitter we have also seen important rises in popularity in the past two to three years, due to a larger online presence by the artists and a greater online presence of their fans at home. Some artists have seen their followers more than double. For example, between 2013 and 2016 M.anifest's followers on Facebook rose from 79,000 to 540,000 and from 37,000 to 328,000 on Twitter; Wanlov's followers grew from 37,000 to 182,000 on Twitter; while Fid Q's followers grew from 29,000 to 138,000 on Twitter.

With internet-based companies selling users followers to inflate fan numbers on Facebook and Twitter, the number of likes and followers cannot be used as a precise measure of an artist's popularity or influence. However, with the exception of K'naan, the numbers of followers correlate with the artist's levels of activity on the social-networking platforms. K'naan seldom posts content on social media, but his exposure via the 2010 World Cup endorsement deals, as well as tours, can account for his many followers. The other artists regularly update their Facebook pages, post information and events, and send out tweets, often several times a week. Their fans also regularly engage with those posts by liking, commenting on, and sharing posts. Combined with frequent posts, the large number of followers draws in more followers who want to follow popular artists, a sort of bandwagon effect.

The impact of an artist cannot necessarily be gauged by the number of their fans. The hip-hop artists who were influential in mobilizing youth during the uprisings in Senegal and Burkina Faso, Kuer Gui and Smockey, respectively, each have fewer than twenty-one thousand followers on Facebook and fewer than five thousand followers on Twitter. These artists post infrequently on social media, sometimes less than once a month, though they have had significant impact on social and political change.

Hard copies of albums by Africa-based hip-hop artists are largely unavailable in the United States. While a comparatively small number of Africa-based artists have songs or albums available for sale online, digital downloads and online stores (iTunes, Amazon, ReverbNation, SoundCloud, BandCamp) have made it possible for African emcees to sell and distribute their music globally. There are few record labels that work internationally with Africa-based hip-hop artists. Most are American or European labels based in the West.

American record company Nomadic Wax was founded in 2001 to promote hip-hop music globally. Since then Nomadic Wax has released fifteen digital albums and eighteen mixtapes featuring artists from all over the continent, and the world. Nomadic Wax also produced the documentary *African Underground: Democracy in Dakar*, chronicling the impact of Senegalese hip-hop artists in Dakar. The fair-trade company has also produced minidocumentaries on hip-hop in Zimbabwe and Burkina Faso. One of Nomadic Wax's founders, Ben Herson, produces a series with MTV titled *Rebel Music* in which several socially conscious hip-hop music scenes and artists around the world are featured. The internet-based company Afrolution has produced two compilation CDs, *Afrolution Volume 1* and *Afrolution*

"Understand Where I'm Coming From": Growth of Hip-Hop | 51

Volume 2, featuring a variety of African emcees. In addition, their website features digital albums and mixtapes from a variety of African hip-hop artists. Established in 1997, Africanhiphop.com is one of the oldest websites dedicated to a platform for fans and artists of African hip-hop. The site features stories, interviews, CD reviews, and music.

New media have also given African emcees broader audiences via podcasts and internet radio programs that feature African hip-hop artists from all over the world. Programs like Hiphocalypse, hosted by Zimbabwean DJ Sensai T8, and African Hip Hop Radio, produced by Africanhiphop.com, featured songs by African emcees all over the world. Hiphocalypse is no longer being produced, but during its run, from 2006 to 2011, the show featured artists from all over Africa.

Television stations and award shows have also given recognition to emcees in Africa. The following television channels all feature music videos and programming that highlight African hip-hop artists around the world: M-Net (South Africa); East Africa Television (EATV) (Kenya, Tanzania, Uganda); Channel O (South Africa), MTV Base Africa (England). Since 2000 award shows such as the *Channel O Music Video Awards, MTV Africa Music Awards,* and the *KORA Awards* have recognized hip-hop by African artists both on the continent and abroad.

In 2008, Channel O started Emcee Africa, a competition that sought to find Africa's best emcee. Based on freestyle, battle, and performance skills, Emcee Africa aimed to celebrate the essence of hip-hop's origins. In Emcee Africa I the finalists included Snazz the Dictator (South Africa—winner), J-Town (Ghana), Rage Prophetional (Tanzania), Teeto (Nigeria), Young D (Angola), Big Mike (Kenya), and Adamiz (South Africa). Emcee Africa II kicked off in 2009 with Cibil Nyte (Botswana—winner), MarazA (South Africa), C-Real (Ghana), Point Blank (Kenya), and Black Jeez (Nigeria). The Emcee Africa competition has been judged by hip-hop veterans such as ModeNine (Nigeria), Professor Jay (Tanzania), Nazizi (Kenya), and Naeto C (Nigeria). According to the promoters, the motive was not only to find the "illest freestyle MC, but to initiate international awareness of the 'street life' surrounding social and cultural context of the localized music" (Kenyan Poet 2009).

Hip-hop festivals have also emerged throughout Africa, including places like Burkina Faso, Guinea, Mali, Senegal, South Africa, Tanzania, Togo, Uganda, and Zimbabwe. South Africa's Back to the City Festival, Burkina Faso's Waga Hip Hop Festival, the Ugandan HipHop Summit, and the Okoa Mtaa Festival in Tanzania have all placed a heavy emphasis on promoting African hip-hop culture and not merely a festival of performances. In Zambia hip-hop artists and activists formed the Hip Hop Foundation of Zambia in 2007 to "preserve the true elements of hip hop and promote local hip hop in Zambia and the greater world in which we are all part of" (Hip Hop Foundation of Zambia n.d.).

Hip-Hop Cultures

The five hip-hop elements took hold to different extents across the continent, but they are elements that have been studied and understood by artists all over Africa. The element of "knowledge" or "knowledge of self" is especially understood and embraced by socially conscious emcees, and it was cited in conversations with hip-hop artists in Ghana, Senegal, South Africa, Tanzania, and Uganda. The most visible element, the emcee, exists in all hip-hop communities in Africa.

A third element, the DJ, has existed in most African countries as well. But, as in other hip-hop communities, the role and prominence of the DJ has been transformed, due in large part to changes in music production and style. The emcee and his or her DJ were a team in the early years of hip-hop. As production changed and artists began working with multiple producers on projects, the role of the DJ shifted. The days of the emcee and the DJ coming as a set have long been replaced by the emcee and the set of producers he or she chooses to work with on any given project. This has given rise to hip-hop producers who spend more time in the studio and with electronic sound production than on the turntables. Hip-hop producers produce beats and are responsible for the final sound production of a track.

The other elements, breakdance and graffiti, have had varying levels of popularity across Africa. Graffiti can be seen all over Africa,

"Understand Where I'm Coming From": Growth of Hip-Hop | 53

Figure 2.5. B-boys from Kenya at the 2014 Okoa Mtaa Hip Hop Festival in Arusha, Tanzania. Photo by author.

though there may not always be a conscious connection between those doing the graffiti and hip-hop culture. Meanwhile, breakdancing (fig. 2.5) has waned in popularity around the world. It has largely been replaced by other forms of urban or hip-hop dance.

According to filmmaker and producer Ben Herson (2011) and hip-hop artist Waterflow (pers. comm., August 14, 2011), by the mid-1980s b-boy crews were emerging in Dakar dance clubs. During this time b-boys would be invited to perform during the shows of Senegalese superstars like Youssou N'Dour (Herson 2011). B-boy crews and graffiti artists would also emerge in South Africa, which continues to have a strong graffiti and DJ scene. According to Shaheen Ariefdien of Prophets of da City (POC), due to the lack of financial resources needed, breakdancing was the first element to become popular (Ariefdien, pers. comm., August 11, 2011; Notununu 2009). While other countries have seen a decline, according to Lee Watkins (2012) there is currently a rise in the popularity of DJing and breakdancing in South Africa. In Tanzania hip-hop organizations like Okoa Mtaa try to preserve the elements of emceeing, DJing, breakdance, and graffiti through their yearly Okoa Mtaa hip-hop festivals.

In East Africa breakdancing has the largest community in Uganda. According to Nicole Crowder, "break dancing is the second most widely spread hip-hop element in Uganda" (2015). Breakdancing and other aspects of hip-hop culture have been embraced by many Ugandan youth through community-based organizations (CBOs) and nongovernmental organizations (NGOs). There is a relatively large number of hip-hop CBOs and NGOs in Uganda that use hip-hop as a tool to engage the youth. Hip-hop emcees and breakdancers Sylvester and Abramz have been working to develop breakdance culture in Uganda. Through Breakdance Project Uganda, founded in 2006, Abramz works with youth throughout Uganda, including a partnership with groups in northern Uganda, which has been recovering from the violence perpetrated by the Lord's Resistance Army. The two breakdancers gained international attention after they were featured in the American documentary *Bouncing Cats* in 2010. The film starred New York breakdance pioneer Crazy Legs. In 2015, American hip-hop emcee Nas did a feature-length documentary on breakdancing globally. The film, *Shake the Dust,* also came to Uganda, where Ambramz and Breakdance Project Uganda were featured. Both documentary projects featured well-respected artists in hip-hop and helped establish Uganda as a respected location for breakdance and hip-hop culture. Globally, both DJing and breakdance have evolved since the 1990s and have incorporated new technologies and dance styles.

Graffiti

Graffiti has been an element of hip-hop culture from the very beginning, but the practice of writing graffiti on public walls predates hip-hop by over a thousand years, to ancient cities in Egypt, Greece, and Rome (Milnor 2009; Bagnall et al. 2016). Today's urban graffiti did not emerge from the world of fine art but as "the sole communication weapon of an oppressed people" (Kostka 1974). Urban street graffiti dates back to the 1960s and 1970s in the east coast of the United States (Ley and Cybriwsky 1974; Christen 2003; Werwath 2006). When hip-hop emerged, as a culture of resistance, the culture embraced graffiti

"Understand Where I'm Coming From": Growth of Hip-Hop | 55

as part of the new subculture. Graffiti culture has a long history of resistance to the state, and so many young graffiti artists were also drawn to hip-hop culture. Graffiti is a natural form of state resistance in many societies. In many countries unsanctioned graffiti tags are illegal, and graffiti artists doing unsanctioned pieces must evade the police or risk arrest. Traditionally graffiti artists, who were youth with little access to resources, would often steal the paint they needed to do tags or pieces on public spaces. These practices, along with the sometimes political nature of the pieces, are a rejection of state authority. It is therefore not surprising that some graffiti artists also participate in the musical elements of hip-hop. During a story on street art on CNN, they highlighted two graffiti artists that were also musicians, Shot B of Mozambique and Falko1 of South Africa (Said-Moorhouse 2013).

Little has been written on graffiti in Africa, in comparison to scholarship on hip-hop music in Africa. Much of the scholarship that has been published has focused on graffiti or street artists in South Africa, the graffiti movement in Senegal, graffiti on *matatu*s (buses) in Kenya, and graffiti and the Arab Spring in North Africa (Spocter 2004; Marschall 2008; Kidula 2012; Lennon 2014; Rabine 2014; Saber 2014; Waddacor 2014). In South Africa, Spocter (2004) traces the origins of graffiti in Cape Town to the 1980s in the community of Mitchells Plain in the Cape Flats area. This community is also considered the birthplace of South African hip-hop. Spocter (2004) examines the different styles of graffiti and aspects of graffiti culture in Cape Town, which the author says is meant to encourage public dialogue. In an interview with Voice of America, Johannesburg-based South African graffiti artist Sandile Radebe refers to graffiti as a sort of "coded language" in which artists become "social commenters" (Taylor 2013). Radebe also recounts the importance of graffiti culture during his childhood Johannesburg.

In Nairobi the matatus are famous for their colorful graffiti covering the entire bus. Matatu workers, mostly young men, operate buses that are the most common form of transportation for millions of Nairobi residents. In addition to having artists decorate their buses with graffiti, matatus often play hip-hop songs and videos. This makes them an important tool for the spread of hip-hop and pop music culture (Kidula 2012). While graffiti has long been a part of the Nairobi

56 | *Hip-Hop in Africa*

scene, in the run-up to the 2013 elections in Kenya, graffiti, like hip-hop, took on more political tones. Urban Kenya saw an increase of politicized graffiti tags in public spaces. Mokua Ombati (2013) studies a "graffiti revolution"—graffiti crews used the public space and graffiti as a tool of social activism.

In Tanzania, Wachata Crew, which formed in August 2007, are seen by many in Tanzania as the main representatives of graffiti culture in Tanzania. They have done both noncommissioned pieces (fig. 2.6) as well as commissioned pieces (fig. 2.7). In addition to holding graffiti workshops, Wachata Crew regularly participate in hip-hop festivals in Tanzania and in the United States. Wachata Crew operate in an interesting space. Many of their pieces offer social and political critiques of society and the state, however they do not have a hostile relationship with the government.

Figure 2.6. One of the early graffiti tags done by Wachata Crew member DMan. Taken in 2010 in the Namanga area of Dar es Salaam, the photo says "Hip-hop tuko pamoja" (Hip-hop, we are one). Photo by author.

Figure 2.7. This image was taken in 2014 at the University of Dar es Salaam. The piece, done ahead of the 2015 elections, features someone revealing the word "uhuru" (freedom), while the bottom tag says "kura 2015" (vote 2015). Photo by author.

"Understand Where I'm Coming From": Growth of Hip-Hop | 57

In Egypt the contemporary graffiti scene predates the revolution, but it was the graffiti of the revolution that sparked an increased international interest in that country's graffiti. Due to their political nature, many of the pieces were seen as helping ignite the revolution and expressing many of its ideologies (Lennon 2014; Saber 2014). One of the graffiti artists studied by Lennon (2014) had been largely influenced by American graffiti and the 1983 US hip-hop film *Wild Style*.(One of the first hip-hop films ever made, *Wild Style* centers on the graffiti and hip-hop scene in New York City.) Of Egypt's graffiti Lennon says, "The circulation of knowledge that graffiti represents in Cairo transforms physical space into contested sites as the walls' declarations reflect the larger political discussions of the day" (2014, 240). The graffiti tags during and since the revolution take on new political dimensions as the youth continue to challenge the state's legitimacy and push back against state repression. The government of President Abdel Fattah el-Sisi came to power in 2014 and, keen to avoid another revolution, has clamped down on any form of dissent, including graffiti.

In Senegal graffiti, as part of hip-hop culture, has existed for over a decade. While Senegalese hip-hop artists link hip-hop with traditional Senegalese rhyme styles and culture, many graffiti artists in Senegal also link graffiti with traditional Senegalese culture, as well as the "set setal (be clean/make clean) youth movement of the 1980s" (Rabine 2014, 89). In this context, graffiti is seen as part of a beautification project. Unlike in many cities, in Dakar, according to Rabine, graffiti on public spaces is not illegal and does not come with the negative associations with criminal or outlaw behavior. It is in fact often seen as beautifying the city. Senegalese graffiti artists, like Senegalese hip-hop artists, are conscious of their links to a broader hip-hop culture, as well as their place and responsibility in Senegalese culture. The country also hosts the annual Festigraff (Festival International de Graffiti en Afrique, International African Graffiti Festival). Festigraff began in 2010 and is said to be the first graffiti festival in Africa (African Urbanism 2014; Rabine 2014). Festigraff has brought together dozens of artists from around Africa to Dakar. Graffiti in Senegal, like the music, often has a political tone, with several pieces commenting on social or political topics. Both Egypt and Senegal experienced youth-led political movements that saw the removal of state leaders, and the graffiti art depicted and informed those events and processes.

Throughout Africa women in the graffiti scene are few. There are some female graffiti artists in South Africa, but by contrast there are no known female graffiti artists in Tanzania. Ricci Shryock (2015) did a feature on Senegalese graffiti artist Dieynaba Sidibe. The article places Sidibe as Senegal's first female graffiti artist. Shryock says that Sidibe gravitated toward "graffiti through an interest in hip-hop culture and slam poetry (par. 3)." Like GOTAL, the collective of female emcees in Senegal, the recent increase in women's participation in hip-hop culture has benefited from the attention Senegalese hip-hop has gotten from journalists and academics since 2011.

Hip-Hop Platforms

In many cities in Africa, hip-hop culture has found expressions outside the five elements of hip-hop. In parts of Africa, as in the United States, there is a relationship between spoken-word poetry and hip-hop. The structure of hip-hop lyricism often allows artists the agility of performing spoken word. It is not uncommon to see a hip-hop emcee performing at a spoken-word event. In researching platforms for artists in various countries, I found that several hip-hop emcees regularly perform at open-mic nights in their cities. In Harare, Zimbabwe, the Book Café has been around since the late 1990s. The Book Café hosts open-mic events regularly and has had many poets and emcees perform. In South Africa there are several poetry clubs where emcees and poets perform regularly. Several hip-hop emcees in South Africa, such as Miss Nthabi and Nazlee, have regularly performed on the South Africa poetry scene. In our interview Nazlee indicated that she got her start as a teenager on the slam poetry scene.

In Dar es Salaam poetry is popular and hip-hop artists are a prominent part of the poetry scene. When hip-hop artist Fid Q started the open-mic poetry event Poetry Addiction, which ran from 2012 to 2014, it was a platform where both emcees and poets performed. Following Poetry Addiction, in 2013 a group of African Americans and

"Understand Where I'm Coming From": Growth of Hip-Hop | 59

Tanzanians living in Dar es Salaam re-created the legendary Lyricist Lounge. The original Lyricist Lounge was started in the 1990s by local hip-hop heads as an open-mic event in New York City. The original Lyricist Lounge featured several socially conscious emcees like Mos Def, Common, and Dead Prez, hence the term is often associated with platforms for serious, socially conscious emcees. One of the founders of the Lyricist Lounge in Tanzania was a Queens, New York, native and promoter known as Fete Jen. Among the organizers is KBC (fig. 2.8), one of the original members of the 1990s pioneering Tanzanian hip-hop group Kwanza Unit.

Additionally, international cultural institutions such as the Goethe Institute (Germany) and Alliance Française (France) have supported many initiatives promoting spoken-word and hip-hop culture. On the Goethe Institute's website the organization details their Spoken Word Project, which highlights the spoken-word/poetry scene in cities across Africa, including Abidjan (Côte d'Ivoire), Bamako (Mali), Antananarivo (Madagascar), Johannesburg (South Africa), Kampala (Uganda), Luanda (Angola), Nairobi (Kenya), and Yaoundé (Cameroon). In most of these cities, the spoken-word scene is connected to the hip-hop scene, with hip-hop artists often performing with poets and at spoken-word events (Goethe Institute, n.d.).

As hip-hop culture became more recognized, media platforms began to open up in some countries. As social media and technology advances have made significant developments, artists also found new platforms online, allowing them to reach national and international audiences. Across the continent there are hip-hop magazines, radio stations, websites, YouTube shows, films, and fashion designers. Radio stations in many African countries began to offer airtime to local hip-hop through the 1990s and 2000s. In fact, hip-hop-only programming has become a part of the schedules of several stations in urban Africa. In Kenya, Ghetto Radio was established in 2007 and gives a lot of airtime to hip-hop music and news. The station markets itself as a voice of the ghetto and often features local and international hip-hop.

Figure 2.8. Kibacha Singo, aka KBC, of the group Kwanza Unit, in Dar es Salaam in 2014. Photo by author.

In South Africa hip-hop culture found a platform on community radio stations like Bush Radio. The show *Headwarmaz* is a weekly program that features hip-hop by South African and other hip-hop artists. South Africa's YFM also offers Hip Hop Thursdays, a weekly hip-hop program. Good Hope FM has *The Ready D Show*, hosted by former Prophets of da City member DJ Ready D. In 2016, *The Ready D Show* began to broadcast via video feed live on the internet and introduced a studio audience format in which a series of upcoming artists are featured. The show also features a DJ showcase and a hip-hop cypher in which emcees are invited to participate.

Hip-hop culture has also been expressed through various media platforms, such as hip-hop magazines like *Hip Hop World* in Nigeria, *HYPE* in South Africa, and *The Platform* in Zimbabwe (once edited by Zimbabwean emcee Black Bird). Online entertainment sites like OkayAfrica.com and ThisIsAfrica.me regularly features articles and coverage of hip-hop on the continent. The media personalities covering the hip-hop scenes often have connections in local hip-hop communities. In Tanzania, Ncha Kali was a DJ on Clouds FM, where he often hosted hip-hop programming. In addition, he recorded hip-hop tracks with Tanzanian artists like Fid Q and Lufunyo. Senegalese TV personality Guin Thieuss (fig. 2.9) works at one of the main television stations in the country, RTS. He hosts a hip-hop program there and has long-standing connections within the Senegalese hip-hop community. In Senegal two of the countries established hip-hop artists, Keyti and Xuman, launched *Journal Rappé* in 2013. The program is a short roundup of news stories done in rap verses. The videos are less than ten minutes and are posted to YouTube. Extremely successful, *Journal Rappé's* YouTube channel has almost 25,000 subscribers and their views for any given video average 50,000 views, with several receiving between 100,000 and 200,000 views. The show is also broadcast on Senegalese station 2S TV.

In 2014, *NewzBeatUganda* was launched using the same format as *Journal Rappé*, *NewzBeat* raps the news for listeners on Ugandan station NTV. Both *Journal Rappé* and *NewzBeat* address social and

Figure 2.9. Guin Thieuss during a visit to Los Angeles in 2010. Photo by author.

political issues. In one episode broadcasters reported on the controversial Anti-Homosexuality Bill, taking a controversial stand on the issue:

Uganda's anti-gay law is making news
Some countries have found it befitting to accuse
Uganda of treating gays as German Jews
Nothing to gain from this and more to lose. (Fallon 2015)

In 2011, Tanzanian hip-hop artist Fid Q launched the show *FidStyle Fridays* on YouTube. The show featured weekly interviews with various hip-hop artists in the country, many of whom received little radio airplay. Some of the episodes were aired on East Africa Television (EATV), but ended the show in 2012.

There has also been an increase of films on hip-hop in Africa, by African filmmakers documenting African hip-hop culture. These filmmakers have created a platform for hip-hop culture in another format. As African hip-hop filmmakers, they are placed in positions of telling their stories of hip-hop in their countries through film. Some of the documentaries include *Hip Hop Revolution* (South Africa, 2007) by Weaam Williams; *Counting Headz: South Afrika's Sistaz in Hip Hop* (2007), made in part by South African filmmaker Vusi Magubane; and *Hip Hop Colony* (2006) and *Ni wakati* (It's time) (2010) by Kenyan filmmakers Michael Wanguhu and Russell Kenya. Vusi Magubane's film is the first documentary film to focus entirely on women in hip-hop in Africa. The film examines their entry into hip-hop, the challenges they face, and their views on hip-hop in South Africa. Both Wanguhu and Kenya had ties to the hip-hop community in Kenya before making their films. *Hip Hop Colony* focuses on the emergence of hip-hop in Kenya, its ties to Kenyan popular music, and class and urban identity in Kenyan hip-hop. The second film, *Ni wakati,* was shot in Kenya and Tanzania and involved American hip-hop artists M-1 of Dead Prez and Umi of POW. The film focuses on the commercialization of hip-hop as well as the diaspora and African connections of hip-hop artists. The film highlights the Pan-African elements of hip-hop culture and the need for artists to recognize and nurture those elements.

64 | *Hip-Hop in Africa*

Two hip-hop feature films, *Coz ov Moni* (2010) and *Coz ov Moni 2 (FOKN Revenge)* (2013), were released by Ghanaian hip-hop artists M3NSA and Wanlov the Kubolor, collectively known as Fokn Bois. *Coz ov Moni* was marketed as the first African hip-hop musical. Each scene in the film is a song from the soundtrack played out in short interconnected skits. Fokn Bois have made a name for themselves because of their controversial lyrics, videos, and social media posts. Among topics like corruption and poverty, the two artists have spoken out about contradictions in religion, acceptance of homosexuality, love of sexuality, and frustrations with racism. They use comedy as an entertaining accompaniment to their social commentary. Both films focus on greed but include subplots that deal with crime, religion, and sex.

There have also been a number of minidocumentaries and short films posted on YouTube from all over Africa by both filmmakers and music video producers. Most of these films were produced after 2005, joining a similar number of similar films being made by American and European filmmakers.

Fashion

Like in the United States, African hip-hop culture has also impacted fashion. Young designers express their hip-hop cultural aesthetics through fashion. There are a number of designers producing graphic tees and other hip-hop-inspired clothing. Companies like Annansi Clothing (Ghana), Bongo Republic (Tanzania), GALXBOY (South Africa), Jamhuri Wear (Kenya), Jolof 4 Life (Senegal), and Kina Klothing (Tanzania) all produce popular T-shirts and other clothing that emphasize a hip-hop aesthetic. Jamhuri Wear gained notoriety when their products were worn by artists like K'naan, Emmanuel Jal, Dead Prez, Jay-Z, and Akon. Many of these designers use their fashions to represent African hip-hop culture while making social statements. Annansi Clothing teamed up with Sierra Leonean rapper Chosan for their popular "Bling Is Dead" T-shirts. They also sell T-shirts celebrating African figures such as Fela Kuti and Nelson Mandela.

Jolof 4 Life, a company started by Senegalese entrepreneurs living in France, Their brand became popular with the production of their "99 Jolof 4 Life" T-shirts. "Jolof 4 Life" referring to pride in being Senegalese, and the "99" representing the Senegalese people living in France. In France national identification numbers are given to everyone. For those born abroad, they are assigned the departmental code of 99 as part of their identification number. The "99 Jolof 4 Life" shirts signified migrant identities, which spoke to a presence in France while maintaining ties to home, made more pronounced by France officially categorizing them as foreign.

The most popular T-shirt created by Kina Klothing features the image of the first president of Tanzania, Julius Nyerere (fig. 2.10; the shirt is being worn by President Nyerere's granddaughter, Helena Nyerere). The image intentionally includes the Ghanaian flag in the background, symbolizing the linkages between Tanzania and Ghana in the struggles for African liberation and Pan-Africanism. Hip-hop culture in Africa has in many ways renewed the words and ideas of past leaders. This is especially true of artists coming from countries with leaders who held significant political influence in the region or the continent. Tanzanian artists often cite Nyerere; Ghanaian artists, Kwame Nkrumah; Burkinabé artists, Thomas Sankara, and South African artists, Steve Biko. According to P. Khalil Saucier (2015), Cape Verdean artists often cite Amílcar Cabral. Similar reimaging of African American liberation leaders has been expressed in American hip-hop culture's celebration of Malcolm X, Angela Davis, Assata Shakur, and members of the Black Panther Party.

Kwame Nkrumah, the first president of Ghana, and Julius Nyerere were both leaders at the forefront of African liberation struggles. Both their countries were and are home to numerous returnees from the United States and the Caribbean. Both men also gave land, resources, and support to various liberation struggles. The T-shirt with the image of Nyerere was worn by several hip-hop artists, including Fid Q on the cover of his album *Propaganda*. Kina Klothing's use of the image on a graphic T-shirt signifies the hip-hop generation as descendants of Nyerere ideals of Pan-Africanism and African unity—ideals that are continuously expressed in hip-hop culture and language.

66 | *Hip-Hop in Africa*

Figure 2.10. Helena Nyerere, granddaughter of President Julius Nyerere, the first president of Tanzania. Photo taken in Washington, DC, in 2012. Photo by author.

The problems associated with Western imperialism in Africa, which both leaders predicted, are seen in today's neocolonial policies, conflicts, and economic decay. In many ways African economies are more indebted to international financial institutions than ever before. The current economic, political, and social malaise has been the topic of many African hip-hop songs. Artists like Didier Awadi (Senegal), Kalamashaka (Kenya), and Godessa (South Africa) have all produced projects that blame both African governments and the international economic system for Africa's current problems. These artists and others have also recalled the ideas of past African leaders in their admonishment of current regimes. Awadi's 2010 release of *Présidents d'Afrique* includes politically conscious artists from all over Africa and the diaspora, and samples the speeches of past African leaders, to emphasize the message. Awadi's landmark project was intended as a message for the next generation, to teach them about their history and the dreams of the political and cultural founding fathers of Africa (Chale 2011). On the album several tracks feature the voices or words (or both) of African and African American leaders. Nkrumah on "We Must Unite," Nyerere on "We Are Also Praying," Sankara on "L'esclave" and "Woye," Martin Luther King on "Dans mon rêve," Malcolm X on "The Roots," Mandela on "Amandla!," Aimé Césaire on "Freedom," and Patrice Lumumba on "Ensemble."

Other artists have also remembered African leaders and important figures in their music. Kenya's Kalamashaka and their collective Ukoo Flani Mau Mau used the words, ideas and imagery of Mau Mau revolutionaries in their work. Kalamashaka's 2001 song "Ni wakati" features a speech by Malcolm X talking about the "Black revolution" in Kenya being carried out by the Mau Mau. In Blitz the Ambassador's 2004 song "Uhuru," the Ghanaian artist uses the Swahili word for freedom to express the need for liberation. In the chorus he chants, "Set my people free / Uhuru means freedom." In the 2007 song "Africa Represent," Ghanaian artist M.anifest proclaims,

> Ghanaian presence definin' the essence
> Ancestors blessed us beyond measure . . .
> In the name of Mandela
> Masakela, Makeba
> Oral traditions in a flavor you can savor
> We never gave up
> True warriors, vainglorious
> It's obvious the gift is upon us.

South Africa's Yugen Blakrok's 2013 album *Return of the Astro-Goth* contains a selection of a speech by Malcolm X in the song

"Constellations." In Tanzania, Fid Q's 2013 song "Siri ya mchezo" (The game's secret) references Steve Biko:

> I've come a long way but still respect where I'm at
> I wasn't that highly rated so it's the passion that gave me Steve
> Biko's teachings
> In my writings and in my speech, until fans screamed when
> I'm on stage
> Never believed that I truly had it till Hiphop came into my
> dreams.[3]

There are several examples throughout hip-hop of African emcees (as well as designers and artists) using the words, images, and words of African and African diaspora leaders. Some uses symbolize criticism of current regimes, some are meant to revive certain ideas in the minds of Africans today, while others seem to link Africa and the African diaspora to broader, global movements.

THIS CHAPTER seeks to provide background on the environments hip-hop emerged from in Africa, and to put into proper context the factors that influenced hip-hop's politicization. While there has been discussion of hip-hop's growth in other literature, it is important to understand and further emphasize the historical and contemporary interconnectedness of the socioeconomic environments throughout urban Africa, and how that has fostered the emergence of hip-hop artists as potential agents of change. Hip-hop as a culture and a method of representing African realities grew out of, and was influenced by, the economic and political environment of the 1980s and 1990s. Hip-hop culture provided youth with another vehicle with which to represent their realities and to verbalize their experiences. Improvements in technology and communication provided artists with additional opportunities to disseminate their music. This would prove important in countries where mainstream radio stations and record labels do not frequently play hip-hop music.

The move into different forms of media and the use of different platforms has resulted in qualitative and quantitative developments in the quality and amount of hip-hop music being produced in Africa.

"Understand Where I'm Coming From": Growth of Hip-Hop | 69

Additionally, hip-hop music cannot be divorced from hip-hop culture. Understanding the role of other hip-hop elements reveals the reach of hip-hop culture's presence within African cultures. Graffiti has a long history in Africa, as does filmmaking and fashion. With the development of hip-hop culture in Africa we have seen graffiti communities, who have a shared inclination toward state resistance, in alliance with socially conscious emcees. Additionally, hip-hop culture represented through fashion gives hip-hop heads additional ways to represent visually. The use of hip-hop-influenced slang, graffiti, graphic designs, and symbols provides visual representations of hip-hop culture worldwide, and hip-hop culture in Africa.

3

"Lettre à Mr le Président"

Social and Political Representations

IN SOME COUNTRIES hip-hop artists are among the voices calling for change, challenging the state and speaking on social issues. Their music offers representations of local social and political conditions, representations that often take the form of protest music. Several artists whose messages are deemed too political by the state are driven underground, and they find themselves in a tense relationship with the state, while other artists enjoy a degree of privilege and find themselves friends of the state. A lot is determined by the particular state, with African governments varying in their interactions with hip-hop and hip-hop artists varying in their challenges of the state.

This chapter will examine the social and political protest in African hip-hop music, in part using Frantz Fanon's 1961 theory on national culture. His theory surrounding protest literature versus combat literature in his seminal work *The Wretched of the Earth* provides a constructive lens with which to understand the relationship between culture (hip-hop) and social change in Africa. Fanon's book was originally published in 1961, during the anticolonial struggles in Algeria and throughout the world. The relevance of the text today is seen in its continued use in academia and among social activists and social justice groups. We will examine the applicability of its interpretation of the literature produced by the colonized intellectual to the music produced by hip-hop artists.

Fanon's discussion of national culture focuses on the important role of culture in national liberation. Fanon mostly addresses the colonized intellectuals, who have been trained by Europe but find themselves back home and needing to be integrated into the movement for national liberation. His essay details the stages the colonized writer must go through to move from assimilation, to protest, to combat. Our use of Fanon's theory will focus on similar growths in hip-hop in Africa. We will revisit hip-hop's phase of assimilation or imitation; we will also look at the relationship with the state as the artists have indigenized hip-hop music and begin to use it as a form of protest; and we will discuss the shift from protest music to combat music as artists take active roles in political transitions. Examples of the final combat stage have only been realized in a few countries, and the results have been mixed.

The growth of hip-hop culture throughout Africa, has forced politicians in Africa to at least acknowledge the influence of hip-hop culture. In some states politicians have tried to use hip-hop for their own political agendas, while others have tried to silence artists that produce music critical of the state. Hip-hop as a tool of protest has been a part of hip-hop's tradition since the genre's beginning. African artists have embraced this tradition and used hip-hop to present challenges to numerous social and political issues. A survey of hip-hop across Africa reveals intersecting social and political themes that are found throughout Africa.

We will finally examine the production of combat music in hip-hop in Africa, focusing on countries where the musicians have been integral in social and political transformations. We know that African emcees can often provide "soundtracks to social change," but in some cases the emcees are agents of social change. Their music provides historical accounts and narratives of social events happening in Africa. Like other genres of music that have their roots in confronting dominant power structures, hip-hop emcees can be important actors in societies undergoing social change. Ingram (2010) says "a rock-n-roll song may not be enough to start a political overthrow, but it can help set forces into motion which eventually coalesce into revolutionary struggle" (106). In Egypt, Tunisia, Burkina Faso, and Senegal we have seen artists playing active roles in the political transitions. In Angola, Cameroon, and the Democratic Republic of the Congo we have seen artists imprisoned and violently repressed by nondemocratic states fearful of revolutions in their own countries.

According to cultural studies theories of cultural representation, representations often play important roles in social mobilization. In their constructions of realities, emcees often influence the thoughts, actions, and worldviews of their audiences. Identifying with an emcee's lyrics, on a group level, has the power to transform youth and to threaten dominant power structures (Ingram 2010).

Protest versus Combat Literature

Many of the protest songs written by artists are directed toward both the state and the people. They serve as critiques of the governments, warnings to political leaders, and calls to action to the people. In this way, the music of these artists is a narrative of social change in their country and can also be an example of Fanon's "combat literature." The lyrics construct a narrative of the social and political changes occurring in a country, from a certain perspective. The lyrics' calls for action make them a tool for mobilization.

The stages that the colonized intellectual goes through, according to Fanon, include an attempt to assimilate into the culture of the colonizer. This often takes the form of trying to talk, behave, and dress like the colonizer. During the second stage there is a psychological break with the colonizer's culture, during which time the intellectual returns home. During this return, home is reinterpreted. The learned culture and knowledge of the colonizer will be indigenized, producing protest or precombat literature. During the final combat stage, the people are roused and the intellectual produces combat and revolutionary literature. Fanon says that combat literature "calls upon a whole people to join in the struggle for the existence of the nation. Combat literature, because it informs the national consciousness, gives it shape and contours, and opens up new, unlimited horizons" (2004, 173).

The figure of the hip-hop emcee, or what K'naan calls the dustyfoot philosopher, is in many ways a descendant of the colonized intellectual. The relationship between Africans and the colonizer's culture is fundamentally different than the relationship between Africans and hip-hop culture. Hip-hop culture is a culture of the colonized, or the oppressed. We may, however, draw parallels between the colonizer's culture and commercialized hip-hop. The commercialization of hip-hop culture, and its ties to American capitalism and culture of consumption, has resulted in the depoliticizing of most mainstream hip-hop. This process, which is promoted in Africa via the neocolonial project, has turned mainstream American hip-hop into a vehicle for marketing consumer goods and consumer culture. It is this commercialized, depoliticized hip-hop culture that becomes a tool of neocolonialism in Africa and the United States. Hip-hop culture is not the "colonizer's culture"; however, commercialized, mainstream hip-hop culture can be seen as a product of the "colonizer."

For many African hip-hop artists, the first stage is often a desire to assimilate to mainstream American hip-hop culture because that is what many artists come into contact with first. Via media content marketing, mainstream American hip-hop, and culture, many Africans are often first consumers of the American lifestyle, via a hip-hop aesthetic. Some Africans are introduced to hip-hop's political content early on, but the majority of African youth are introduced to hip-hop's commercial culture. For many African hip-hop artists, there is thus a first stage of wanting to emulate what they perceive to be "authentic" (African) American culture. Some artists remain in this first stage and simply want to reproduce what they consume from depictions of American hip-hop culture in the media. Other artists may skip the first stage completely and emerge in the second stage.

After the first stage of assimilation, artists localize or indigenize hip-hop to fit their own realities. During this second stage, artists learn from hip-hop's political past and hip-hop's roots in the urban Black ghettos of America. Hip-hop thus becomes something more than popular culture. It is at this stage that artists use hip-hop to protest or to provide social commentary on their environments. They speak to a myriad of topics, which will be discussed later. Perhaps most artists who move into this stage will remain at this stage. It is during the second stage that the relationship with the state becomes crucial. According to Fanon, protest literature is encourage by the state because it is seen as "an act of catharsis" that helps avoid full-on protest (2004, 173). Though this is not often the case in Africa, over the years various African governments have used anticorruption protest songs in their own propaganda and have attempted to harness the influence of protest songs as proof of their own incorruptibility. Former presidents Benjamin Mkapa of Tanzania, Abdoulaye Wade of Senegal, and Mwai Kibaki of Kenya and Presidents Yoweri Museveni of Uganda and Jacob Zuma of South Africa all used hip-hop songs and appearances by artists during elections as a way to appeal to youth.

We are alerted to an artist's move into the third stage, the combat stage, when the messages change. During this protest phase, the music is largely directed toward the oppressor, toward the government. During the combat stage the music is also directed to the people. This is an easily overlooked but important shift. During the protest stage artists are lamenting their struggles and complaining to those they deem responsible. They are calling out corrupt leaders and are protesting specific grievances. During the combat stage the artists also turn their attention to the people and produce songs meant to mobilize them. Of this stage Fanon uses the poem "African Dawn" written by Keita Fodeba, former minister for internal affairs for Guinea. Of the poem, Fanon says, "Understanding the poem is not only an intellectual act, but also a political one. To understand this poem is to understand the role we have to play, to identify our approach and prepare to fight" (2004, 167).

Few artists, hip-hop or otherwise, ever move into the combat stage. The move into this stage is always precipitated by other social and political factors. Those factors are largely tied to an artist's connection with activist groups, their relationship to the state, and an initial spark that turns the protest into a movement (Senegal, South Africa) or a revolution (Burkina Faso, Egypt, Tunisia). Both the protest and combat stages are important. During the protest stage artists begin to articulate the problems. They begin to frame the debate. There may never be a spark or an environment conducive to initiate a movement, but the cathartic and educational exercise of protest cannot be underestimated.

"Lettre à Mr le Président": Social and Political Representations | 75

Hip-Hop versus the State

With the broadening influence of hip-hop culture in Africa, African politicians have taken notice. As we will see, hip-hop artists in Africa address a broad range of topics and are often critical of government actions and policies. As hip-hop communities grew, and artists turned their attentions to social issues in their own countries, there were initial attempts to marginalize and censor hip-hop. There are still countries with stricter censorship of hip-hop music, but many politicians have attempted to use hip-hop's influence to win young voters. According to Daniel Künzler (2007), hip-hop has been banned or censored at times in Zanzibar (Tanzania), Nigeria, South Africa, and the Democratic Republic of the Congo. In addition, countries like Togo and Zimbabwe have harsher censorship regulations than their neighbors (Künzler 2007; Kellerer 2013).

The recognition and use of hip-hop by politicians reflect the fact that populations in many African countries are often more than 50 percent youth (under thirty years old). In the capitals of countries like Burkina Faso, Kenya, Senegal, Tanzania, and Uganda, the youth represent more than 50 percent of the population (Ntarangwi 2010; Mbaye 2011). The percentage of youth in national populations has grown significantly in many African countries in recent decades, and in most African countries the youth share of the population will continue to grow (Garcia and Fare 2008; Severino and Ray 2012). In addition, the first wave of Africa's hip-hop generation is now able to vote and is increasingly having an influence on politics in Africa. Several politicians have thus been attempting to harness the influence of hip-hop to their advantage. In the 2010 presidential election in Uganda, President Yoweri Museveni emerged with the rap song "You Want Another Rap." Museveni performed the song on TV and on the campaign trail in hopes of wooing young Ugandans. In 2009, Gabon's presidential candidate Ali Bongo Odimba brought American hip-hop artists Fat Joe and Jay-Z to perform in Gabon. Bongo, who had a brief career as a recording artist in the 1970s, also performed a hip-hop song during the sixth annual Gabon Hip-Hop Festival in 2009 (Juma4 2009; Ntarangwi 2010). In a brief look at two East African countries, Kenya and

Tanzania, we are able to see other examples of state engagement with hip-hop communities and youth activists using hip-hop to engage with the state.

Kenya

In Kenya the Kenya African National Union (KANU) ruled the country since independence in 1963, for several years as the sole political party in the country. Kenya's favorable status with the West allowed KANU to maintain power and suppress resistance, but by the time the 2002 elections came around KANU had fallen out of favor with most Kenyans and there was a sense that the time had come for KANU to go (Brown 2001; Murunga and Nasong'o 2007; Branch 2011). In 2002 a coalition of political parties formed the National Rainbow Coalition (NARC) to contest the upcoming elections against KANU's Uhuru Kenyatta. During the 2002 campaign NARC used hip-hop duo Gidi Gidi Maji Maji's song "Who Can Bwogo [defeat] Me?" Gidi Gidi Maji Maji performed the song at campaign rallies, and in both Kenya and Tanzania young people could be seen wearing T-shirts with the phrase "I am unbwogable" on the front. According to Joyce Nyairo and James Ogunde, "the song had long crossed the threshold of entertainment, to become a conduit of political expression and, indeed, a symbol of resistance and determination" (2005, 227).

Though NARC would fall apart within a few years after the election, the coalition did end KANU's rule and brought President Mwai Kibaki to power. There was debate as to whether or not NARC's use of a hip-hop song as its slogan translated into widespread youth support. Among many hip-hop artists, however, there was a hesitance to endorse any presidential candidate. The new NARC president, Mwai Kibaki, started his political career with KANU, so there was widespread belief that Kibaki's presidency did not really represent change.

In 2007 former NARC coalition partners Mwai Kibaki and Raila Odinga became the two main opponents in that year's presidential election. Kibaki's reelection sparked widespread violence between backers of Kibaki and backers of Odinga. The fighting led to the deaths of over twelve hundred people (Migiro 2011). Several hip-hop artists, like those with the group Ukoo Flani Mau Mau, released songs

"Lettre à Mr le Président": Social and Political Representations | 77

condemning the violence and calling for peace and political transparency. In the aftermath of the violence the group Hip Hop Parliament was formed as a collective of more than sixty mostly underground hip-hop artists in Kenya (Marsh and Petty 2013). The aim of the group has been to promote unity and political engagement in response to the political and ethnic violence of the 2007 elections (Marsh and Petty 2013). The group also engages with the youth to promote socially conscious hip-hop and youth involvement in social issues.

When the 2012 elections came, several hip-hop artists preemptively released songs calling for peace, while others released songs in support of candidates and performed in campaign rallies for political parties. Kayvo Kforce worked with the campaign for Orange Democratic Movement, while Abbas, Bamboo, and Chiwawa released and performed the song "My DNA Is TNA" during the election campaign of current president Uhuru Kenyatta and the National Alliance (TNA).

Artists in Kenya have generally had flexibility in their criticisms of the Kenyan government, with little concern over censorship. In their relationship with the state, there have been several artists that have performed during political campaign rallies in support of particular candidates. Conversely, performing at campaign rallies is generally criticized among artists that regard themselves as more politically conscious.

Tanzania

In Tanzania the relationship between hip-hop and politics has been even more intertwined. The ruling party Chama Cha Mapinduzi (Party of the Revolution, CCM) frequently used hip-hop to its benefit. In the 2005, 2010, and 2015 elections CCM hired several hip-hop artists to perform at campaign rallies and to mobilize youth voters. Hip-hop artists have also been hired to represent campaigns among the youth and to produce material in support of the ruling party. Hip-hop artists themselves have come out with songs that were both in support of the government and songs that were critical of the government. In some cases, hip-hop artists who have produced songs critical of the government have also performed at CCM and opposition party election rallies.

In the 2005 election hip-hop artist Mangwea (fig. 3.1) came out with the song "Mtoto wa Jah-Kaya" (Child of Jah-Kaya), in support of CCM

78 | *Hip-Hop in Africa*

candidate Jakaya Kikwete. Uta Reuster-Jahn's (2008) article on the 2005 election she translates a portion of the lyrics to Mangwea's song:

na mengi ya maana ongea kwa vijana	and many important things— talk to the youth
Ndiyo maana mwana nakufagilia sana	That's why I praise you much, man
Huna mpinzani si bara si visiwani . . .	You don't have a rival, not on the mainland nor on the isles
Mimi mwenyewe ni mmoja wa wale wenye kura yako	I myself am one of those who vote for you
Shahidi ukija geto ukutani picha yako	For evidence, if you come to my ghetto on the wall there is your portrait
Natamani kuona japo sarafu yenye sura yako	I also want to see your face on a coin

Figure 3.1. Albert Mangwair, aka Mangwea, was a hip-hop and bongo flava artist. This image was taken in Dar es Salaam in 2010, three years before his death. Photo by author.

Figure 3.2. Reproduction of the logo that appeared on shirts distributed by President Kikwete's campaign team. Image by author.

During the 2005 and 2010 elections, Mangwea's "Mtoto wa Jah-Kaya" emerged as a tagline on several T-shirts done in bold Rastafarian colors: green, yellow, and red (fig. 3.2). "Mtoto wa Jah-Kaya" was produced by Tanzanian rap artist Mangwair. Mototo is "child" in Swahili. "Mtoto wa Jah-Kaya" can be read as "child of President Jakaya" (Kikwete). "Jah," for Rastafarians, refers to God. This play on President Kikwete's name, the use of Rastafarian colors, and the recruitment of hip-hop artists was an attempt to appeal to the youth.

In the 2010 election, President Kikwete used several hip-hop artists in his reelection campaign. Many artists were brought in to mobilize the youth and to appear during campaign rallies. President Kikwete's son Ridhiwan, also known as Riz One, used his contacts in the hip-hop community to help design a campaign geared toward the youth. While the use of hip-hop was clearly a reflection of the voting demographics, it was also in reaction to the youth-dominated opposition party, Chadema (Chama cha Demokrasia na Maendeleo, Party for Democracy and Progress).

Tanzanian hip-hop artists Sugu and Professor Jay joined the center-right opposition Chadema Party and ran in parliamentary elections. Sugu (aka Joseph Mbilinyi, Mr. II) ran for and won a parliamentary seat in Mbeya, in southern Tanzania, in the 2010 and 2015 elections. In the 2015 elections Professor Jay (aka Joseph Haule) ran for and won a parliamentary seat in Mikumi, in central Tanzania.

Views on Sugu's performance during his term in office have been mixed. While he has supported media freedom and fought government attempts at censorship, he has also supported controversial private foreign investment initiatives.

Sugu's and Professor Jay's relevance goes beyond Tanzania. The first generations of hip-hop artists have increasingly decided to step into politics. US-Haitian hip-hop artist Wyclef Jean had a presidential bid in 2010 in Haiti, while US hip-hop activist Kevin Powell ran for a seat in the US Congress in 2008. Stepping into politics creates new opportunities for hip-hop artists and a culture that is still disregarded as *muziki ya wahuni* (thug music). For politically conscious artists, like Sugu and Professor Jay, holding political office also keeps artists accountable to the values they claimed to live by in their lyrics.

Hip-Hop as Protest Literature

Moving from attempting to assimilate or imitate an artist can transition into the second stage, the protest stage. The second stage is the artist "returning home." This is not necessarily a physical return. Like Fanon's colonized intellectual, it's a process that can happen regardless of physical location. Like the assimilated colonized intellectual, assimilated hip-hop artists who have immersed themselves completely in the adaptation of American hip-hop culture has disengaged from their own culture. The belief that American hip-hop culture is superior to one's own culture can manifest in artists attempting to dress, talk, and behave in the styles they see in American hip-hop videos played on MTV Base, Channel O, and other media. (For cultural misappropriations, see chapter 6, which includes a discussion of rappers who have appropriated American styles.)

In interviews with hip-hop artists in Tanzania, some were asked what made their music Tanzanian, aside from the fact that they were rapping in Swahili. For several artists there was an inability to conceive of hip-hop as being further localized and a belief in being as authentically (American) hip-hop as possible. This perspective was taken by several hip-hop artists interviewed, based on the continent

"Lettre à Mr le Président": Social and Political Representations | 81

or in the United States. The assimilation to, and imitation of, American hip-hop was an assimilation to mainstream hip-hop, with its emphasis on consumerism, sex, violence, and partying. The topics many of these assimilated artists discuss do not differ from the topics presented in mainstream American hip-hop. Additionally, these assimilated rappers can often be detached from any other types of hip-hop representations, with their entire frame of reference coming from mainstream media.

For artists who return home, or who begin in the second stage, we find an indigenization of hip-hop culture. Hip-hop becomes more relevant to home. During this period Fanon says that through the writings of the colonized intellectual, "old legends will be reinterpreted on the basis of a borrowed aesthetic" (2004, 159). The reinterpretation of Kwame Nkrumah, Steve Biko, and Thomas Sankara, or the reimagining of the Mau Mau rebellion or the Soweto uprising, are articulated in protest rap.

Like Fanon's discussion of protest literature, protest rap does engage the state. And as in the United States, protest rap can be encouraged by governments and seen as a method of deflating tensions. In some cases, governments directly embrace socially conscious hip-hop artists, even if the government has been targeted in their music. In Tanzania, Professor Jay's popular 2001 song "Ndio mzee" (Yes, sir/elder) was a direct criticism of the political leadership in Tanzania. The popularity of "Ndio mzee" and its description of a leader who makes false promises would be cited in a speech by the then president, Benjamin Mkapa. In President Mkapa's speech he is quoted as saying "I will eliminate 'Ndio mzee' from my administration. I will emanate these yes man [*sic*], these elders who just say I will do it or it can for you. I will eliminate them from my administration" (Barlow and Eyre 2005). The embrace of the song by President Mkapa, despite its commentary on his government, was an example of the government embracing socially conscious hip-hop, because it did not perceive it as a real threat.

Though he has produced several songs critical of the government, Tanzanian hip-hop artist Fid Q also made appearances in various campaign rallies for CCM. In 2010, Fid Q performed at appearances

82 | *Hip-Hop in Africa*

during President Jakaya Kikwete's reelection campaign, and again in 2015 during the election campaign of CCM candidate John Magufuli. Contrasting Fid Q's relationship with the state to his music, we see a government benefiting from the influence of Fid Q, though his influence comes from his criticisms of the government. In 2013, Fid Q released the song "Siri ya mchezo" (The game's secret). In it he is strongly critical of neoliberalism and government corruption.

> Long live the Party of Hooligans
> Long live . . .
> Neo colonialism gave us the Independence of a flying flag
> So we can witness the blasphemy of those with money
> Tanzania is a "swinger" whore
> They call her "available for all"
> Who manages to escape hangover by staying drinking all day
> The Big guys claim they can solve all their nations' issues
> They say you can't push a broken down vehicle by staying
> seated inside . . .
> There is no true Freedom in Africa
> Don't be fooled by the illusion
> And we are failing daily due to these political institutions
> Civilization has advanced now they killing us economically
> And the worst form of slavery is believing that you are free.[1]

The song is one of Fid Q's strongest condemnations of the state, of CCM, and of neoliberalism. He refers to CCM as the "Party of Hooligans," and is critical for leaders allowing the country's economy to be exploited by foreign companies. In spite of the song, Fid Q was again involved in CCM's 2015 campaign. The relationship hip-hop artists form with the state can impact their careers and their ability to get played on the radio and get their videos on TV. The relationship artists form with the state can also impact their credibility with their audiences and within the hip-hop community.

Through hip-hop, artists all over Africa have protested their governments, protested over human rights concerns, and protested conflict. Many African hip-hop artists have used hip-hop's tradition of social commentary as a platform to address their audiences, mostly

"Lettre à Mr le Président": Social and Political Representations | 83

urban youth. The belief in hip-hop as a tool, and as a living culture to be nurtured, has turned many hip-hop artists into activists fighting for the development of indigenous hip-hop culture, as well as for hip-hop as a space to allow artists to freely commentate on social and political issues. In the documentary *United States of Africa: Beyond Hip Hop,* South African emcee Zuluboy says that the role of artists is to hold their governments accountable. He says that artists, therefore, cannot take on that role if they participate in the political process or show bias toward a political party. He also asserts, "I'm a politician in my own right, as a lyricist and a person who creates and speaks to mass media, . . . and decides on what I'm going to feed people's ears and minds."

In South Africa pioneering hip-hop groups like Black Noise, Prophets of da City (POC), and Brasse Vannie Kaap (BVK) have actively continued to support the development of socially conscious hip-hop culture for years. Many of these early South African hip-hop artists participated in the voter education campaign Rapping for Democracy in 1994, when South Africa held their first democratic elections (Haupt 2001). Many of these artists have also engaged youth and younger artists through workshops and community programs. Adam Haupt's 2008 book *Stealing Empire: P2P, Intellectual Property and Hip Hop Subversion* chronicles the work of Black Noise and POC in South Africa. In addition, the book looks at the role of hip-hop activists with Bush Radio, a community radio station in South Africa. Bush Radio regularly held workshops titled Alternative Kerriculum for Mentoring Youth (ALKEMY). According to Haupt, ALKEMY used hip-hop "to engage youth about social, economic, and political realities, whilst also developing their creative writing and performance skills as hip hop MCs" (2008, 53). Emile YX? of Black Noise organized the annual African Hip Hop Indaba, which Lee Watkins (2012) describes as a platform for rappers, DJs, breakdancers, and graffiti artists. Ready D of POC hosts *The Ready D Show* on Good Hope FM, which provides a platform for up-and-coming hip-hop artists.

In Kenya the hip-hop group Kalamashaka had a hard time because of their political music. Instead of fighting and getting into the mainstream, according to group cofounder Kama, they learned the system and created their own space to get their music out (pers. comm.,

August 16, 2011). Kama says Kalamashaka gave out CDs/cassettes to matatu (public bus) drivers, underground clubs, and barbershops, who in turn played their music. By 1999, Kalamashaka had formed a large coalition of hip-hop groups called Ukoo Flani Mau Mau. Through this coalition Kalamashaka carried out community projects in their inner-city neighborhood of Dandora in Nairobi, including working with area youth on a number of projects, promoting hip-hop culture, and even building a studio for community-based emcees who cannot afford to record in more established studios (Wanguhu and Kenya, 2011).

With artists like Juliana Kanyomozi, Jose Chameleone, Bobi Wine, and Bebe Cool, on Ugandan radio there has been a definite promotion of R&B and reggae music over hip-hop. In the mid-1990s the hip-hop group Bataka Underground (later Bataka Squad) emerged to become one of the more influential hip-hop groups in Uganda. Inspired by the more socially conscious elements in hip-hop, group cofounder Silas (aka Babaluku) says Bataka Squad was one of the first hip-hop groups in Uganda to rap in Luganda, launching "Luga flow" (Silas, pers. comm., July 10, 2007).

In 2003 the group began an annual Hip-Hop Summit in Kampala (Saba Saba, pers. comm., December 25, 2011). Silas says that the group saw how their music impacted Ugandan youth, and part of their plat-form is speaking to the youth and supporting economic and educational opportunities for young people in Uganda (pers. comm., July 10, 2007). They are not simply a rap group, Silas points out; they want to see some real changes for youth in Uganda. In 2005 group member Silas founded the Bavubuka Foundation to work with youth in Uganda, particularly in the capital, Kampala. Silas says the foundation provides a space in which they conduct education and peace-building programs for youth in Uganda. In 2012 the summit morphed into the B-Global Indigenous Hip Hop Gathering, reconceptualized as a space for the promotion of indigenous languages and culture in hip-hop (B-Global, n.d.).

A survey of protest rap or socially conscious hip-hop in Africa found two issues that were addressed most frequently by a cross-national se-lection of hip-hop artists: corruption and migration. In each country surveyed we find a lot of music presenting various attitudes toward corruption within governments as well as corruption in relationships

"Lettre à Mr le Président": Social and Political Representations | 85

between African and Western states and institutions. Artists spoke of unfulfilled promises by their governments, stolen elections, police corruption and brutality, collusion with foreign powers, and the impact of government policies on the lives of the masses. Migration was also a common topic among African hip-hop artists. Migration from West Africa to Europe and the United States was more commonly addressed by West African artists, both francophone and anglophone. Migration into southern Africa was mostly addressed by South African artists.

Several additional topics were included in this study, not because of their frequent use but because of their broader relevance. Artists sometimes spoke on conflict. Hip-hop artists coming from countries engaged in conflicts often spoke on those conflicts in their music, placing blame on rebel soldiers as well as on government action, or inaction. The music produced by these artists also provided interesting insight into those conflicts. Discussions of human rights were also a theme of several artists, with artists speaking out on violence against women and minority populations. Violence against women was more commonly addressed by female artists, though several male artists also lent their voices to the topic. Violence against minority populations was most often voiced by artists coming from those populations. Artists also presented their perspectives on topics related to race and ethnicity. Race is more commonly discussed in American hip-hop, so a look at the topic in the African music was revealing. Given the racial dynamics in Africa, it was not surprising that many of the artists tackling race were based in southern Africa. Lastly, the topic of homosexuality in Africa has been extremely divisive. Most hip-hop artists in Africa have avoided the topic altogether, though it was helpful to look at commentary on queer[2] identities and politics from artists presenting ideas that went against the criminalization of homosexuality.

Corruption

In my survey of common topics among multiple artists in multiple countries, corruption was the most common topic. African hip-hop artists across the continent have talked about corruption in their governments and by representatives of the state (military and police). Many of the artists from West Africa have been very clear in their condemnation of the state. In Burkina Faso, Mali, and Senegal we find artists that have produced protest records, speaking on the government's role in socioeconomic conditions. Künzler's (2011a) article on hip-hop in Burkina Faso and Mali reveals a high level of anticorruption songs among hip-hop artists in those countries. Artists and groups like Mali's Amkoullel, l'enfant Peul, and Tata Pound, as well as Burkina Faso's Faso Kombat, Yeleen, and Smockey, have all been very vocal on issues of corruption, as well as their governments failing their responsibility to address poverty, healthcare, and education in those countries.

In Ghana, Blitz the Ambassador's 2011 song "Free Your Mind," from his *Native Sun* album, called out the World Bank and the IMF, "and the puppet politicians that's supporting their policies / selling out their own people to the government overseas." In 2014, Blitz released "Africa Is the Future," a collaboration with Oxmo Puccino of Mali, Oum of Morocco, and Blinky Bill of Kenya. In the song Blitz raps against Western and corporate exploitations of Africa, and for the need for Africa to look within the continent for solutions to development, "cause we never practice capitalism or socialism / we got 'Africanism,' and that is how we livin." Ghanaian artist A-Plus is known for his politically themed songs. He has released numerous tracks addressing corruption in Ghana, including "Freedom of Speech," "Letter to Parliament," and "Osono ate ahwe" (Political review).

In East Africa, several Kenyan and Tanzanian artists have also produced protest songs addressing corruption in their countries. Artists like Hustlajay Maumau and Fikrah Teule in Kenya, and Roma and Wanaitwa Uhuru in Tanzania are among several artists that have produced several anticorruption tracks. Hustlajay Maumau's "Africa Issues" looks at internal and external corruption affecting Africa. The song discusses the International Criminal Court's handling of the 2007 election violence in Kenya and the 1984 Wagalla massacre of ethnic Somalis in Kenya by Kenyan forces. The song is also critical of government misappropriation of foreign aid and the involvement

"Lettre à Mr le Président": Social and Political Representations | 87

of the United States in Africa, which he says is only in Africa to gain access to cheap resources.

Roma's "Tanzania" addresses leaders who steal government money and betray the country (Clark 2012a). His song focuses on the impacts of those betrayals on the people. Sima da Black Philosopher from the group Wanaitwa Uhuru released "Mr. President" in 2014, a direct criticism of the government:

> Degree holders but we still unemployed
> We educated but still uninformed
> We been living in poverty for just way too long
> They making billions out of the citizens
> Wao wanauza bamia[3]
> The air thick from the stress and the fear
> Maisha bora kwa kila Mtanzania[4]
> Justice is still a tale
> The traffic is still hell
> But when the moon falls you know daybreak will appear
> The revolution and you can lend a hand or an ear
> Mr. President, what is the future for Tanzania?

Sima said that the verse was inspired by the documentary *Darwin's Nightmare*, which he said tells of how the Tanzania government was complicit in the transport of billions of dollars worth of fish abroad, while local workers and local populations were often only able to get "leftover fish" (*mapanki*)" (Sima, pers. comm., January 2, 2016).

As for southern Africa, artists in Angola, South Africa, and Zimbabwe have also been vocal about corruption. As Africa's last region to gain independence, many artists have offered commentary on unfulfilled postindependence promises. While the 1960s was the decade of independence for most of Africa, many southern African countries did not get their independence until after 1970. Artists like MCK and Luaty Beirão in Angola (free in 1975), Ben Sharpa and Zuluboy in South Africa (free in 1994), and Outspoken and Comrade Fatso in Zimbabwe (free in 1980) were born during liberation struggles or immediately after independence and are far less removed from liberation struggle than their counterparts in other parts of Africa.

88 | *Hip-Hop in Africa*

In "Freedom Train," Outspoken talks about the journey to freedom that the Zimbabwean people fought for but only the elite have benefited from. In the song Outspoken asserts that the freedom train left the station in 1980, when Zimbabwe got its independence, heading toward democracy and freedom for all. The song concludes by proclaiming that the train still has not reached its destination.

In South Africa, Ben Sharpa's 2009 song "Hegemony," from his album *B. Sharpa*, deals with corruption at the hands of the police, the main institution of government enforcement among the civilian population:

> They don't care if he's a hero like Steven [*sic*] Biko
> Or high strung on a killing spree, like Asanda Baninzi[5]
> Cops all over the city ready lock you if you're dark-skinned
> Easy for the Boer to moer[6] you if you look poor and got comments
> I'm a hardcore hot-head—conform not to any pork chop[7]
> I mind control swine patrol in Jedi mode
> And bribe your whole ride with cold drinks.

The song is a condemnation of police corruption, as well as the relationship between the police and Black South Africans. South Africa's racial dynamics are inserted into this verse in Sharpa's statement on the role of race in the relationship between the police and the community.

In *United States of Africa*, Zuluboy reflects on the positions of African governments vis-à-vis international financial institutions and Western governments and asks, "What's the use of having power with no authority?" His question was posed in the context of African heads of state being in positions of power, but because of their relationships with Western governments and financial debt, they do not have real authority to exercise that power.

The protest songs produced by the artists studied were directed at corruption in the international community, within national governments, and within state institutions. Through these songs we understand perspectives on the impact and sources of government corruption. The songs comment on betrayals by governments to their people, and the economic and social inequalities that exist as a result. We see commentary on national government involvement with Western countries and economies, which have led to populations having

"Lettre à Mr le Président": Social and Political Representations | 89

decreased access to resources. We also see depictions of relationships between the state and the people in these protest songs. Through these songs we also see commentary on states that have been complicit in violence against their citizens.

Migration

As hip-hop emerged in Africa, in the 1980s, emigration out of Africa escalated, in direct response to a series of economic shocks brought on by economic restructuring (structural adjustment programs, SAPs). When examining debates on migration there is often talk in Europe and the United States of tightening borders. There is little discussion of the impact of Western-prescribed economic policies on the increased flow of migrants out of the developing world and into the developed world. Often in desperate need of economic survival, many Africans, especially the youth, are forced to leave home in search of employment. There are an estimated 4 million sub-Saharan Africans living in the West and thousands leaving every year (Adepoju 2010). Recently Al Jazeera aired a series entitled Surprising Europe, which looked at the lives of African migrants all over Western Europe.

With so many migrants leaving Africa for the West, African migration has been a popular topic among African emcees. In Ghana and Nigeria, countries with a large numbers of migrants in the West, artists MI, Reggie Rockstone, Wanlov the Kubolor, and Sarkodie have all written songs about Africans migrating west. In "Hustle," M-1 talks about the immigration hustle and trying to get to the United States. He criticizes migrants who ask, if they do not come home, what good have they done? Rockstone's song "Visa" talks about the difficulty of applying for and getting a visa from the US embassy, while Wanlov's song "Green Card" is a reflection of why one even wants a green card, given the myth of the West being a place of abundant economic opportunity. Sarkodie's "Borga" is a message to Ghanaians who live abroad (*borga*), many of whom return home with stories of prosperity in the West. Sarkodie is critical of Ghanaians abroad, and in figure 3.3 he is shown telling children from his hometown of Tema, outside Accra, to speak truthfully about the difficulty of living in the West.

Figure 3.3. Sarkodie with children in his Tema neighborhood, outside Accra in 2010. Photo by author.

In "Borga," Sarkodie sings,

> Do you think this it is easy? Stop we're really hustling
> Someone is in Canada he needs to go begging for his daily meal
> A lot of these borga are not truthful you would have known life in the West is ugly You're a tailor in Ghana and you make money
> You have food to eat, at the very least, you have somewhere to sleep
> You've saved money to get a visa
> You want to travel to America just to suffer
> Advice doesn't change a man unless he experiences it . . .
> Whose fault is it that you are suffering?
> Had it been you were in Ghana you would have commissioned schools and been hired by Tigo (mobile network) to be a manager
> Rather you are in the West sweeping the streets and after shake yourself cause you don't have a place to sleep.[8]

Several West African artists have also discussed the causes for and experiences of West Africans fleeing to Europe. Due to increased economic instability in West Africa and economic opportunities in North Africa and Europe, the late 1990s saw an increase in West Africans migrating north, either across the Sahara or by boat (IOM 2008; Abdellatif 2010). Many migrants head to North African countries, where they either settle or attempt to secure transportation into Europe. Those settling in North Africa often choose wealthier countries like Libya and Morocco. Many of these migrants take up low-paying jobs and often become a source of resentment for local residents. Before the attacks on sub-Saharan Africans during the toppling of the Libyan government in 2011, sub-Saharan Africans in Libya faced discrimination and violence. About 1 million workers from across West Africa, from Ghana to Niger, had settled in Libya, where they sought work and security (Hawley 2000). Then, in 2000 during violent backlashes by Libyan citizens, an estimated one hundred sub-Saharan Africans were killed, and thousands were forced to flee back to West Africa (Hawley 2000; BBC World Service 2000). In addition, West African migrants in Mauritania have also faced discrimination, and there are widespread accounts of sub-Saharan Africans living in servitude to wealthy Mauritanians (Watson 2001; Harter 2004). Much of this treatment has been fueled by ethnic and class discrimination and negative stereotypes of sub-Saharan Africans.

For those going on to Europe, the voyage is not without serious dangers. Between 1997 and 2001 an estimated 3,285 dead bodies were found on the shores of the Strait of Gibraltar, with an unknown number of bodies never being found (IOM 2008). In October 2013 more than two hundred migrants, mostly from Eritrea and Somalia, drowned when their boat caught fire and capsized near the Sicilian island of Lampedusa (BBC World Service 2013). The case sparked an international outcry, but it did not deter other would-be migrants from attempting the journey, based on the thousands that have died crossing into Europe from North Africa (mostly Libya) each year since 2013 (Taylor 2017). Compared to the thousands of dollars spent by migrants to be smuggled into Europe by air or boat, small canoes are often all that migrants can afford. A trip from Senegal to Spain costs an estimated $500 to $1,000 and takes over twelve days in rough waters to complete (Campbell 2010). Those choosing to cross the Sahara also find the route rife with dangers. In fact BBC reporter Paul Kenyon called the route across the Sahara "the most dangerous migration route in the world" (2009). Several migrants die trying to cross the desert with inadequate supplies or find themselves the victims of crime from local bandits along the way (Kenyon 2009; Campbell 2010).

Communities all over West Africa have felt the impact of large numbers of youth leaving African shores. Senegal, Ghana, and Nigeria have seen the highest number of migrants attempt the voyage (Campbell 2010). The North African countries most used for transit into Europe include Algeria, Libya, Morocco, and Tunisia (Campbell 2010). And recent years have seen the presence of migrants from as far away as South Asia taking similar routes through North Africa into Europe (Haas 2006; IOM 2008).

In Senegal, both DJ Awadi and the group Daara J have been vocal about these economic refugees. Through his studio, Studio Sankara (named after Burkina Faso's late president Thomas Sankara), Awadi has produced songs like "Sunugaal" (Our canoe/Canoe) released in 2006. The song addresses the plight of the migrants heading to Europe, putting the blame on the government for creating the conditions that have forced Senegalese to flee. In a 2006 BBC News article, journalist Joseph Winter translates an excerpt from "Sunugaal":

> You promised me I would have a job
> You promised me I would have food
> You promised me I would have real work and hope
> But so far—nothing
> That's why I am leaving, that's why I am taking off in this canoe
> Swearing not to stay here a second longer
> I would prefer to die than to live in this hell.

In 2010, Daara J (fig. 3.4) released "Unité 75," which dealt with the plight of West Africans in France, while the Senegalese collective VA Capsi Revolution released "Immigration Clandestine," which addressed the physical risks of migrating by boat. These songs were released on a special album entitled *Yes We Can: Songs about Leaving Africa* in 2010.

"Lettre à Mr le Président": Social and Political Representations | 93

Figure 3.4. Daara J performance in Washington, DC, in 2011. Photo by author.

The compilation features songs by various African emcees and is an ode to African migrants in Europe and the United States.

In 2011, French-born Senegalese artist Sefyu released "Malik and Boubakar," which details the lives of two African migrants in France living in the *banlieues* (suburbs).[9] The song discusses the tensions between Arab/North African migrants and Black sub-Saharan African migrants. Malick and Boubacar are from migrant families and the song depicts their rebellion in school as a rebellion against a system that continues to humiliate their parents. The song begins with Malik and Boubakar's arrival in France and ends with them dropping out of school, one ending up in jail and the other ending up dead.

In Burkina Faso the hip-hop group Yeleen and hip-hop artist Smockey have both produced songs addressing African migrants abroad. In a 2011 article on hip-hop in Burkina Faso and Mali, Künzler translates an excerpt from Yeleen's song "Le chemin de l'exil" (The road of exile):

> Over there, it will be cold and there will be nobody anymore
> Nobody, because over there it is everybody on their own
> . . .

You are going to forget your parents and only keep your
   studies in mind
You will bring along nice pictures and say "everything is perfect."

African hip-hop artists have also penned songs to address the influx of migrants to their region, specifically South Africa. Hip-hop artists have released songs to counter xenophobia in their countries. In 2010, Zubz released "Time to Heal" (for the Yes We Can project), in which he says,

See, ignorance is like a fertilizer for fear
Cultivating misconception, certifying for years
The notion that essentially, we're different
Separate but equal; tell me that you see the inference
There's no "Border Lines"; there's no "Yours" and "Mine"
There's just "Us"! What could be more divine?
Science has fortified this, they sing the tune too
Quantum Convergence? We call it "Ubuntu"!

In 2015, Driemanskap released "Anti-Xenophobia," which was not only critical of xenophobia but took a strong Pan-Africanist stance on the relationship between South Africa and other African nationals in the country.

At home, a Somalian is black
Xenophobia is wack
Nigeria is a place of Africans respect!
[Chorus] Blood (life) is scattered
Because of this xenophobia . . .
He lost his wife
Because of this xenophobia . . .
We are tired in South Africa
Because of this xenophobia . . .
Africans let this xenophobia end
In Malawi in Zambia
In Ghana in Ethiopia . . .
In Zimbabwe in Gambia
All over Africa.[10]

"Lettre à Mr le Président": Social and Political Representations | 95

Human Rights

During the research discussions of human rights, issues were found in the music of African hip-hop artists, most often by members of affected groups. For example, in the Democratic Republic of the Congo (DRC) and in Tanzania hip-hop artists N'Kashh and Albino Fulani, respectively, both released tracks condemning the violence against people with albinism in both countries. N'Kashh's songs include "Âme seule" (Lonely soul) and Albino Fulani's works include "One Man's Cry."

Human rights issues impacting women are more frequently addressed in hip-hop songs by African artists, and most often by female artists, though not exclusively. Violence against women is addressed most frequently in songs about female genital cutting (FGC) and domestic violence, though other forms of violence are also sometimes discussed. Songa (Tanzania) recorded the song "Beki tatu" about the mistreatment of domestic workers in Tanzania. Baay Bia (Senegal) released the song "Fistula" as part of an awareness campaign on treatment of women who have fistulas. (For a closer look at songs addressing domestic violence, see chapter 4.) A look at FGC revealed that the sensitive topic was discussed in songs by some Africa hip-hop artists.

In the 1990s the campaign against FGC became vogue among Western human rights activists. The voices of Western activists calling for an abolition of the practice brought international attention to the issue, but campaigns against FGC were often presented without the cultural context in which the custom was practiced. Additionally, actions and rhetoric often furthered tropes of the uncivilized African whom the West must save from herself. The result was mixed. While many states were pressured to enact anti-FGC laws, grassroots activists and community-based organizations that had been fighting for reform for years were often dismissed and accused of spreading Western propaganda. Hip-hop artists addressing FGC were few. In 2005, Tanzanian artist Witnesz (fig. 3.5) released "For the Blues"; then in 2015 Burkina Faso emcee Smockey released "Tomber la lame" (Drop the blade).

Most notably, Sister Fa from Senegal was vocal about her experience with FGC and had led a campaign via her music and activism

Figure 3.5. Witnesz Kibonge mwepec LA kisanii (Witness M. Sigbjorn LA kitaifa in Dar es Salaam in 2010). Photo by author.

through her organization Education sans Excision (Education without Cutting). Sister Fa's two albums *Hip Hop Yaw la Fall* (You are the one hip hop chooses) in 2005 and *Sarabah—Tales from the Flipside of Paradise* in 2009 contain tracks that address violence against women, especially FGC. Through her work, Sister Fa helped eradicate FGC in her home village of Thionck Essyl.

Discussions of human rights are also linked to conflicts, which tend to lead to escalations in human rights violations. The human rights impact of conflict on communities, nations, and the continent were addressed in songs that were about conflicts in Nigeria, Somalia, South Sudan, Uganda.

Conflict

The realities of conflict were seen in representations presented by hip-hop artists in songs that protested the impacts of those conflicts. There are two types of representations presented by artists, the first is by artists who have directly witnessed or participated in conflict. The second is by artists from countries where conflicts are occurring, though the artists may not be based in the conflict zones. This latter includes songs like "Osika" by Nigerian artist Blaise and "Invisible" by Ugandan artist Krukid/Ruyonga. Neither Blaise nor Krukid/Ruyonga are from the conflict regions in their respective countries, but both released songs adding their voices in protest of the conflicts.

Many artists released songs on conflict as a way to gain international attention, as a message to those in a position to end the conflict, and as a method of catharsis. In 2009, Sierra Leonean artist Chosan released "Blood Diamonds" and participated in the Bling Is Dead campaign as a means of calling attention to conflict minerals. In 2011 in the DRC a collective of hip-hop artists and other performers from the eastern part of the country released the song "Saisir l'avenir" (Seize the future). The eastern DRC had seen decades of violence and conflict; this record was the first time artists in the region have undertaken such a project in an effort to bring international attention to events happening in the DRC (Juma4 2011). In 2014, South Sudanese

98 | *Hip-Hop in Africa*

hip-hop artists Nelly Majestic and Manaz were part of a collective of artists that released "Let's Stand Together," a call for peace in the civil conflict in South Sudan. Senegal's Sister Fa released "Soldat" to draw attention to the conflict in her home region of Casamance. Other artists place themselves within the conflict and sometimes present protests of conflict from a first-person narrative. Two artists that fled conflicts, K'naan of Somalia and Emmanuel Jal of South Sudan, presented music that provided several narratives of conflicts in their countries. Their songs construct images of preconflict Somalia and preconflict South Sudan, and humanize the people in countries that have been primarily associated only with conflict. Both K'naan and Emmanuel Jal fled their countries as refugees at a young age, both ending up in Kenya and then going to the West—K'naan to Canada and Emmanuel Jal to England. As the most successful hip-hop artists, and perhaps the most popular musicians, from their native countries, both artists seem to have taken it upon themselves to represent their countries and the conditions there.

K'naan's music shares his memories of preconflict Somalia in songs like "My Old Home" and "Fatima." His songs take us through his youth in Mogadishu, as well as the outbreak of the conflict and its impact on him. In "Somalia," K'naan raps,

So what you know about the pirates who terrorize the ocean?
To never know a simple day without a big commotion?
It can't be healthy just to live with such a steep emotion
And when I try and sleep, I see coffins closin'.

In addition to narratives of the impact of conflict, K'naan's songs reflect aspects of the pain of survivor's guilt. K'naan constantly reminds his audience of the innocent lives that were lost in the conflict, by humanizing the lives of the friends and classmates he left behind. He provides depictions of a playful youth, interrupted by violence. In "People Like Me," K'naan talks about his cousin, with whom he survived a grenade blast, only to have to leave him in Somalia because his mother could not bring them both. In his song "Fatima," K'naan speaks of the death of a girl he loved as a child. We learn that Fatima was killed in the conflict, while K'naan managed to leave Somalia:

"Lettre à Mr le Président": Social and Political Representations | 99

Damn you shooter, damn you the building
Whose walls hid the blood she was spillin'?
Damn you country, so good at killin'
Damn you feelin' for persevering.

Emmanuel Jal was also a child soldier and in 2009 he released an album, book, and documentary all titled *Child Soldier*. In a 2009 interview Jal said he became exposed to hip-hop after he fled the war in Sudan and ended up in Kenya, and he was inspired by the stories of struggle that he heard about urban life in America (Clark 2009a). His song "War Child" tells of the death of his family because of the war, and in "Forced to Sin" he tells of his own experience as a child solder:

Left home at the ages [*sic*] of seven
One year later I lived with an AK-47
By my side
Slept with one eye open wide
Run
Duck
Play dead
Hide.

Several of Emmanuel Jal's songs, including "We Want Peace" and "Africa Awei," appeal for peace and condemn the conflicts in Sudan and South Sudan.

Emmanuel Jal talks mostly to the international community in his lyrics, while K'naan directs his lyrics more to Somalis themselves. At the end of the song "Soobax," K'naan explains, "I made a protest song and it's called 'Soobax.' Soobax means 'come out,' directly talking to the gunmen and the warlords of Africa. Letting them know that we can't, you know, the people can't take it no more, yeah and it's a- it's a soundtrack to a poor man's revolution in East Africa." The chorus of "Soobax" is

The people are dying, just come out
The troubles are filled, just come out
The blood has filled up, just come out
The floor is burnt, just come out
Just come out
Just come out.[11]

100 | *Hip-Hop in Africa*

Both K'naan and Emmanuel Jal offer protests of conflict that also offer additional narratives of those conflicts. Their songs go beyond calls for peace and provide intimate details of the human impacts of conflict. In the protest songs produced by K'naan and Emmanuel Jal the artists place themselves within the conflict and provide details of the personal impact of the conflict as well as indictments of the parties responsible.

Race

Hip-hop's treatment of race in America has tended to be very Black versus White, and very clear in addressing American racism in its various manifestations. African artists' voices on race and ethnicity have shown some similar themes, but have also departed in areas, reflecting the differing racial and ethnic dynamics in those countries. Songs addressing race were often reflections on either racism or reflections on racial identity within mixed-race communities. Songs that focus on race as a central theme were sometimes performed by Africans who come from multiracial backgrounds. For example, "Human Being" (2008) by Wanlov the Kubolor, who is Ghanaian and Romanian, is an introspective ballad about transcending race and seeing each other as human beings. Songs that focused on racism were sometimes done in solidarity with African Americans, like Sierra Leone's Chosan and his 2008 song "We are all Sean Bell"[12] or South Africa's Uno July, who often references Trayvon Martin[13] in several of his post-2012 projects, which he calls "Black Hoodie Rap" (pers. comm., July 13, August 4, 2016).

Songs that focused on racism also sometimes recalled legacies of racial struggles as themes. Slavery, colonialism, and apartheid have all been used as themes in music videos that depict Black resistance. In 2014, Ghanaian rapper Edem (fig. 3.6) released "The One" with Ghanaian-British rapper Sway. The video for the song depicts the enslavement of Africans in the Gold Coast (Ghana) by Europeans; a king is captured and leads an uprising against his European captors. The video creates a revised history in which the Africans are able to overpower their captors and regain their freedom. During a

Figure 3.6. Edem outside the Accra Mall in Accra in 2011. Photo by author.

phone interview Edem says in the song he intentionally used African drums, percussion, and traditional music to drive home the message of the song, which he said is ultimately about standing up to systems of oppression.

South African rapper Cassper Nyovest released the song "War Ready" in 2016, dedicating it to the youth who lost their lives during the 1976 Soweto student uprising. The uprisings were in response to the apartheid policy implementing Afrikaans as the medium of instruction. The video depicts student protestors violently clashing with riot police. The video, released forty years after Soweto, came in the wake of the #FeesMustFall protest. Parallels have been drawn between Soweto and #FeesMustFall, both of which saw students engaged in confrontations with the police over race-based power imbalances in the education system.

Reflections on racial identity came up as a topic more frequently among hip-hop artists in southern Africa. With communities historically divided along racial lines, the racial dynamics in southern Africa have always been unique. Quentin Williams and Christopher Stroud (2014) discuss the dilemma found in racial self-identification in South Africa. In South America there are multiple ways of categorizing someone, based on the amount of African, European, and indigenous ancestry they have. In the United States any traceable amount of African ancestry categorized someone as Black. In southern Africa communities were segregated based on the racial categories of Black, Coloured, and White. That segregation meant that while distinct Black and White South African cultures evolved, but so did a distinct Coloured South African culture. Hip-hop culture, as a product of Black culture, has created a space for artists to address race, especially in South Africa, where hip-hop first emerged in Cape Town's Coloured communities. There were early expressions of Black identities among many Coloured hip-hop artists, but there has also been people expressing differing identities.

Several Coloured hip-hop artists in southern Africa have addressed racial identity in their music. In 2013 the Namibian group Black Vulcanite released "Visions," which addresses race and economics. In the song AliThatDude raps,

> This is for all of my people struggling
> Trying to be a better man
> Rock bottom like sediments
> World of black and white
> I'm thinking like where do I fit in
> Wondered if I'd ever live to see a Baster president
> Corruption and incompetence evident in our governments
> Claim they for the people but do it for their own betterment.

The song refers to the artist's biracial background and the feeling of not belonging. In the song he also questions whether there will ever be a "Baster president" in Namibia.[14] The stressing of a Baster identity by AliThatDude is telling when juxtaposed with expressions of Black identities by some Coloured South African artists such as members of Black Noise and Prophets of da City. Both groups were made up of members who were considered Coloured in South Africa but intentionally embraced a Black identity. Künzler's (2011b) study of hip-hop in postapartheid South Africa revealed that Coloured hip-hop artists based in Cape Town often articulate both Black and Coloured identities.

"Lettre à Mr le Président": Social and Political Representations | 103

It was not surprising then that the research found different Coloured hip-hop artists articulating contrasting identities. Capetonian rapper Dope Saint Jude is considered Coloured but recognizes her Blackness. In our interview she said she sometimes prefers the term *Brown girl*, reflecting on the identity politics present in South Africa. In "Realtalk" she brings in the question of her identity: "I'm rapping like I'm Coloured but the Coloureds call me White / and the White kids call me Black / and the Black kids call me light." She also addresses her "Brown" identity in "Brown Baas" (Brown boss). In the video for the song, Dope Saint Jude is seen reading a copy of Steve Biko's book *I Write What I Like*. In the chorus she asks,

> Do you know what's it like to be Brown for a girl like me?
> Do you know what it's like to be baas for a girl like me?
> Do you know what it's like to be Brown for a Brown like me?
> Do you know what it's like to be baas for a Brown like me?

Conversely, in an OkayAfrica.com interview Capetonian artist Miss Celanious identifies as Coloured, saying that in her music she is "trying to promote Cape Town and Cape Coloured culture" (Jason 2015). Coloured South Africans can embrace a Coloured or Black identity, though both are their distinct communities (Williams and Stroud 2014).

In P. Khalil Saucier's (2015) book *Necessarily Black* the author reflects on racial identity among Cape Verdean communities in the United States. Saucier looks at hip-hop artists in Cape Verdean immigrant communities, finding artists that address American racism but that also articulate Black identities. This is important in a culture with its own cleavages among the country's largely mixed race populations.

The idea of Black consciousness, of identifying as African and not just Zulu, or Kikuyu, or Wolof emerged during the struggle for independence and has been further influenced by migration. Through independence struggles and movements for racial justice, African or Black identities have been articulated by youth globally. While many Africans continue to see ethnic or national identities as primary, hip-hop has been a vehicle for the further articulation of Black, African, or Pan-African identities.

104 | *Hip-Hop in Africa*

Homosexuality

Homosexuality has become part of dialogues around human rights on the continent. Resentment over what are perceived as imperialistic Western intrusions into African cultural values has caused divisions on the continent. The situation is somewhat reminiscent of debates in the 1990s over FGC in that activists fighting for the decriminalization of homosexuality are also often accused of spreading Western propaganda. The conversation around homosexuality shifted in the wake of public conversations around same-sex rights. The existence of homosexuality in precolonial Africa has been more vigorously denied, antihomosexuality bills (many written by colonial governments) were dusted off and strengthened, and the issue around same-sex rights became tethered to the idea of African sovereignty in the face of Western cultural imperialism.

The debate is taking place in hip-hop, as expected. Artists are positioned on different sides of the debate, and some artists have expressed the various positions lyrically. Most of the artists that have addressed homosexuality have reinforced many government positions on the "homosexual problem." Some of this research was conducted during the debate in Uganda over the Anti-Homosexuality Bill in 2013. In conversations with artists in Kampala most were opposed to the bill and saw it as a human rights issue, though almost none had verbalized this view publicly. There were similar views expressed with some of the artists interviewed in Dar es Salaam and Accra. There were, however, several artists who agreed with antihomosexuality laws and pointed to interpretations of religious doctrine.

Artists who have taken a public stance against antihomosexuality legislation are few. In 2010 the Ghanaian group Fokn Bois released "Brkn Lngwjz" (Broken languages), in which Wanlov the Kubolor refers to himself as "the non homosexual but I back freedom of choice fighter." In 2014, Nigerian hip-hop artist Sasha came out against that country's antihomosexuality laws: "Discrimination of any kind is discrimination. . . . Sexual orientation is not a crime, so nobody should have to go to jail for that" (Nation 2014).

"Lettre à Mr le Président": Social and Political Representations | 105

On June 11, 2015, Ugandan artist Slim Emcee published the following post titled "The Untold Yet Told Story":

> As for Uganda, aren't there hundreds that would want to come out and declare their status? If you doubt that, wait for the day the Ugandan government will set the LGBTIQ community free. The day gay parades will be legit. You will be shocked to know that your own father or mother, brother or sister, wife or husband, son or daughter or friend is part of that community you consider to be "unwanted."

On June 27, 2015, Slim Emcee published a post titled "Marry Who You Love Not the One Society Chooses for You." In the post Slim Emcee says:

> As the celebrations are ongoing in America, welcome to Uganda where it is illegal to even come out as a gay person. Where I believe that there are people who are silently part of the community but because they fear to lose their lives, be imprisoned or becoming outcasts within their communities they choose to keep their status secret and disclose it to only those that are in support of them.

The responses to Slim Emcee's posts varied, with many of the respondents condemning the idea that homosexuality has a place in Africa, and much of the support for Slim Emcee's posts coming from White commenters. The topic of homosexuality and sexual identity also has been expressed, in very limited ways, by queer hip-hop artists in Africa. Most expressions of queer sexualities by African hip-hop artists are from female emcees, with most of the more direct self-expressions of homosexuality coming from southern Africa (for more representations, see chapter 4). The topic of homosexuality is taboo throughout hip-hop's hypermasculine culture. Byron Hurt's film *Beyond Beats and Rhymes* explores the stigmas of homosexuality in American hip-hop communities. Therefore, it was not surprising to find similar stigmas in hip-hop communities in Africa. What was interesting was to find examples of hip-hop artists challenging antigay legislation in both African culture and hip-hop culture.

Hip-Hop as Combat Literature

After 2000 there has been an increase in mass uprisings globally. Due to social media and new technology, these movements are more visible globally than people's uprisings of previous centuries. This has given a global context to these protests, tying them to global concerns around economic inequality, labor, migration, gender, and corruption. Hip-hop artists in Africa have been speaking out on these issues for at least a decade before 2000. After 2000 several of those artists joined these uprisings through song, through their presence in the streets, through the creation of community organizations, and through their direct engagement with the state and law enforcement.

Success in Senegal and Burkina Faso

In Senegal we see a clear evolution of hip-hop as combat literature alongside the evolution of social mobilization in that country. Between the 2000, 2007, and 2012 Senegalese presidential elections we witnessed an increase in political participation by hip-hop artists. The tone of their music evolved from general political commentary on corruption to more direct and personal lyrical attacks directed at the president. In the 2000 presidential elections in Senegal, Abdoulaye Wade's Parti Démocratique Sénégalais (Senegalese Democratic Party, PDS) enjoyed widespread youth support. Incumbent president Abdou Diouf had been in power since 1981, and his Parti Socialiste du Sénégal (Socialist Party of Senegal, PS) had ruled Senegal since independence in 1960. There was a general sense, especially among the youth, that Diouf and the PS needed to go (Künzler 2007; Malone and Martinez 2010; Ntarangwi 2010). Hip-hop artists joined the push for change that the PDS represented. Abdoulaye Wade seized this opportunity and used the youth's frustration with the incumbent Abdou Diouf to gain votes (Künzler 2007). In addition to the abysmal state of Senegal's economy, Diouf's reported reference to hip-hop artists as "insane young people" did not earn him support in the hip-hop community (Künzler 2007).

Hip-hop artists may have helped Wade get elected in 2000, but they held Wade to task for promises made during the elections (Ludl

"Lettre à Mr le Président": Social and Political Representations | 107

2008). They especially held him accountable for the worsening economic situation in Senegal. With continued economic decline, hip-hop artists again mobilized in 2007 when President Wade came up for reelection. Much of this was captured in the 2007 documentary film *African Underground: Democracy in Dakar.* Though Wade won reelection, the film documents the increase in artists vocalizing opposition to the president. Artists spoke out on the economic decay, economic refugees fleeing Senegal, and corruption and greed within the regime.

In 2011 in Senegal hip-hop artists reacted to changes in electoral laws proposed by then president Wade. Artists and activists created the movement Y'en a Marre (Enough Is Enough) and, together with other activists, were successful in not only gaining international attention but also in getting the president to back down on some of his proposals (Fessy 2011; Gueye 2013; Fredericks 2014). The movement includes Senegalese hip-hop artists Fou Malade, Thiat and Kilifeu from the rap group Keur Gui, Simon from Jolof 4 life, and Matador.

When President Wade ran for reelection for a third term, violating the constitution, Y'en a Marre activists joined thousands of people in the streets of Dakar. In the studio they produced songs that were aimed directly at the regime (Gueye 2013; Berktay 2014; Fredericks 2014; Lo 2014). Unlike in previous presidential elections, Y'en a Marre focused on educating and mobilizing voters, through music and community outreach. Their methods included neighborhood voter registration drives in which they registered an estimated three hundred thousand voters (York 2015). In "Daas Fanaanal" (sharpening one's weapon the night before) Keur Gui and Fou Malade sing:

This is the sound of the alarm
Sharpen my weapon the night before!
My voter card is my weapon
Sharpen my weapon the night before!
It is what is going to wipe my tears! (Gueye 2013)

Their efforts helped prevent President Wade from winning a third term.

The 2012 elections also brought songs that were much more direct confrontations with the government. In some songs Keur Gui (fig. 3.7) refer to President Wade as "the Old Man," a "thug," or by his first

Figure 3.7. Thiat (*left*) and Kilifeu (*right*) of the group Keur Gui performing at the 2014 Trinity International Hip Hop Festival in Hartford, Connecticut. Photo by author.

name (Abdoulaye, or Laye) (Fredericks 2014; Gueye 2013; Lo 2014). The group expressed a willingness to die for their goals. In a tone reminiscent of Fanon's need for the oppressed to embrace the threat of violence, as opposed to a vow of nonviolence, Keur Gui infers that they are ready to shed blood. In the song "Faux! Pas forcé!" (Don't Push) they tell the government that they are not afraid of the military being called in, that they will sacrifice their bodies and "bear the clubs," and when the "blood flows" they will "lick it" (Gueye 2013). In the same song the artists remind Wade of events during the violent fall of Gaddafi in Libya (Gueye 2013).

Since the election of a new president in Senegal, Y'en a Marre continues to organize, forming collectives called the Spirit of Y'en a Marre with hundreds of members, and a minimum of ten women in each collective (Lo 2014). These collectives are not necessarily made up of other musicians. The collectives work locally to address local issues (Lo 2014).

The example of Senegal has resonated in other parts of Africa. In 2013, Senegalese and Gambian hip-hop artists Xuman, Djily Bagdad,

Thiat (of Keur Gui), and Ombre Zion released the song and video "Against Impunity" in protest of the regime of Gambian president Yahya Jammeh.

In 2013 artists and activists in Burkina Faso came together to form Le Balai Citoyen (Citizen's Broom), which was largely modeled after Y'en a Marre (Engels 2015). The name of the group was influenced by President Thomas Sankara's weekly street-cleaning actions (Engels 2015). Thomas Sankara has been referred to as "Africa's Che Guevara" (A. Smith 2014). He came to power via a coup in 1983. He was popular among the people, and his Afrocentric foreign policies, gender-progressive domestic policies, and Pan-Africanist policies made him a hero among activists all over Africa. His assassination, in 1987, had a similar impact as the assassination of revolutionary leaders in other countries, and he lived on in the minds and lyrics of artists around Africa. The group Balai Citoyen was cofounded by Burkinabe hip-hop artist Smockey, who has a long career of social activism and socially conscious music.

Balai Citoyen engaged the population by mobilizing protests of then president Blaise Compaoré, who had been president of Burkina Faso since 1987 and was often suspected to have had a role in the assassination President Thomas Sankara. The 2014 uprisings saw thousands in the streets of Ouagadougou and eventually led to the ouster of Compaoré, who fled the country while an interim government took power.

Movements in Progress

The movements in Burkina Faso and Senegal, as well as in North Africa during the Arab Spring, are examples of successful mobilization and political change. Much of the music the artists released were meant to speak to the people, to mobilize the people. While there are other examples of combat literature in hip-hop by African artists, not every movement has been successful. Some have stalled, while others remain in motion. After the success of Senegal and Burkina Faso, in March 2015 activists from both Balai Citoyen and Y'en a Marre traveled to the Democratic Republic of the Congo. They were invited to participate in workshops organized by the Congolese groups Lutte pour le Changement (LUCHA) and Filimbi. They were seen as a threat by the Congolese government, perhaps because of their success in removing the presidents in their own countries. President Joseph Kabila responded by arresting the activists, imprisoning the Congolese activists and deporting the non-Congolese activists (Lewis and Ross 2015).

In many countries in Africa, open criticism of the state and political leaders results in little repercussion, while in other countries artists directly confronting the state have faced arrest and imprisonment. In Guinea Bissau members of the hip-hop group Baloberos Crew were detained in 2009 over the lyrics in their song "Seven Minutes of Truth," which criticizes specific military leaders for murder and corruption (Livesay 2010). In Cameroon hip-hop artist Général Valsero got in trouble with authorities over his 2009 song "Lettre à Mr le Président," which was directly critical of the Cameroonian president Paul Biya, who has been in office since 1982. In perhaps an act of fan support, during a 2010 concert in Yaoundé posters of President Biya were destroyed by hundreds of Valsero fans (Tchakam 2011).

Spurred by the Arab Spring, in Angola the youth participated in a number of protests in 2011 over government corruption and repression, criticizing the rule of President José Eduardo dos Santos, who has been in power since 1979 (Al Jazeera 2011; Human Rights Watch 2011; Swank 2012; Pearce 2015). Angolan hip-hop artists MCK, Carbono, Explosivo Mental, and Luaty Beirão (aka Ikonoklasta) were active in these protests, enduring arrest and attacks from the police. In an OkayAfrica interview Beirão said of the protest:

> Sick and tired of this bullshit, we, the youth, decided to face up to our fears and took it to the streets in uproar. Since then, we've been prey to the Angolan authorities, thrown in jail, kidnapped, tortured, our houses broken into, our skulls cracked open AND YET, we have been refusing to fight back and resort to violence, keeping our protests peaceful in nature. (Swank 2012)

"Lettre à Mr le Président": Social and Political Representations | 111

In 2011, Beirão released the song "Cuka" in which he raps,

Hey Angolan
Don't do as we do
Wasting your time boozing!
That's what they want
That's what they want
If we're drunk and alienated, we won't notice them
Taking what's ours. Eatin' it to the bone
Asking us to let go
Picking my pocket
Picking your pocket
And filling us with more booze
They tell us to read, without ever sending us to school
. . .
There's no good excuse for mistreat
Don't put up with it 'cause you work hard!
If he pushes it, tear your shirt apart and fight.
. . .
Are we gonna come back and still vote for Dos Santos?
(SoundwayRecords 2012)

Many of the artists who participated in the protests faced problems with the state. In 2015, MCK had his passport confiscated by authorities when he attempted to travel to Brazil for a hip-hop festival (York 2015). In June 2015, Luaty Beirão was imprisoned with fourteen other Angolan activists (the #Angola15). After numerous attempts by human rights groups to secure their release, Beirão was put under house arrest in 2016. Since the arrest of Beirão and the other activists, Amnesty International was among the international groups continuing to call attention to the declining health of Luaty Beirão, due to a hunger strike, and for the immediate release of Beirão and the other detainees.

In South Africa in 2015 and 2016 hip-hop artists joined with activists of the movements #FeesMustFall and #RhodesMustFall. The campaigns saw thousands of young people protesting proposed fee

112 | *Hip-Hop in Africa*

hikes at the country's universities, the lack of Black faculty, and the presence of apartheid-era curricula and institutions. The demonstrations, the biggest student demonstrations since Soweto, in 1976, were a call for the "decolonization" of the education system (Baloyi and Isaacs 2015). During the protests several hip-hop artists collaborated to release the song "Must Fall" online. The track includes Java, Emile YX?, Linkris the Genius, Black Athena, Daddy Spencer, Crosby, and Khusta. In the song, Emile YX?, of the group Black Noise, says, "Our greatest minds are being mined and exploited like our mines / We're going hard like Marikana and get shot down by the swines." Emile YX? was a member of the hip-hop group Black Noise, which also spoke out against apartheid in the 1980s and early 1990s. This line in the song, and the tone of the activism in the country, consciously links what was happening with the students to the massacres at the Marikana mines. In both protests, the people confronted the state and were met with violent repression. In the case of the Marikana mines the confrontations led to the death of several people.

One of the students at the University of the Witwatersrand, who were heavily involved in the protests, Gigi LaMayne, released "Fees Will Fall" the day after her 2016 graduation (LaMayne 2016). The song begins,

How long are they gon' lie to us
And smile with us
Acting like they'll cry with us
Our parents barely get a wage but they slave for this nation
A Black child will never ever gain emancipation
I wonder if King Biko would agree to this shit
The forefathers of our land wouldn't sign to this shit.

Referring to the protests as "proletariat heat," LaMayne later declares that "the energy of the youth will be the truth and the way." In Cape Town, emcee Nazlee (fig. 3.8) participated in the protest. Nazlee, a University of Cape Town student and also a fallist,[15] penned a song for the protest. In the chorus she raps,

"Lettre à Mr le Président": Social and Political Representations | 113

Figure 3.8. Emcee and spoken-word artist Nazlee at her home in Cape Town in 2016. Photo by author.

All I see is cops out here
In the street
Swear it feels like 1976[16]
All I see is cops out here
In the street
Black bodies on the street
Black bodies on the street.

South Africa's history of protest is well known, and artists have always used their music as a form of protest and engagement with the state. In the #FeesMustFall and #RhodesMustFall movements, artists have directly engaged with activists and are seeing some success in getting South African institutions to halt fee hikes, revisit policies of outsourcing staff labor, and beginning conversations around decolonizing curricula and universities.

AS HIP-HOP COMMUNITIES evolve and mature in Africa, there will be continued engagements with political structures. Some artists will find their way into politics, while some will find roles as community activists. Politicians in Africa will continue to try to use hip-hop culture to their advantage, while simultaneously pushing for less politically conscious content. The struggles of American hip-hop artists are echoing in Africa as many artists are pushing to both maintain the essence of hip-hop and evolve the culture in an ever-changing African scene.

Facing greater commercialization and the continued influence of commercial hip-hop culture from America, several African hip-hop artists continue to assimilate to the style of commercial rap they see in major media outlets, like MTV. Many of these artists will not move toward producing protest rap. In discussing hip-hop in Africa with several individuals for this project there was a sense that the mainstream (radio, TV, major record studios, major concert series) was moving away from hip-hop and toward hybrid genres. This shift had in fact begun in the United States, and that Africa was following suit. Some point to the emergence of Nigerian pop artists like P-Square and D'Banj, and their collaborations with US artists, as evidence.

"Lettre à Mr le Président": Social and Political Representations | 115

Artists who do find themselves "returning home" and wanting to engage local communities more will often produce music that is more representative of home. They will also often produce protest rap.

There are thousands of African emcees representing Africa, both inside and outside the continent. Many of these artists are engaged in the production of protest music. Their protest music provides social commentary on politics, economics, migration, and human rights in Africa. Their representations of contemporary Africa construct realities of Africa that have resonated with African youth. Descriptions of poverty, street life, and a lack of opportunity paint bleak pictures of life for youth in urban Africa. These realities, for example, are often seen as push factors that cause migrants to leave their countries. African emcees create an image of Africans struggling to get a visa from Western embassies, to get a better life. They construct realities that show the desperation some have in using various means to find opportunity outside Africa. These realities constructed within African hip-hop correspond to films, literature, and news stories of the difficulties in securing visas and the lengths people go through to get to the United States.

The move toward "combat rap" or "combat literature" has happened in less than a dozen countries. Artists moving into combat rap are also often embedded in movements for social or political change. In some countries (Burkina Faso, Egypt, Senegal, Tunisia) those movements have been successful. In other countries artists are still engaged with the state in protest (South Africa) with many undergoing arrest and imprisonment (Angola, the DRC).

Hip-hop artists are not the only artists engaged in protest or combat with the state. Musicians of other genres, writers, fine artists, poets, photographers, and others are also engaging with the state. In South Africa, artist Ayanda Mabulu received a lot of attention for his nude depictions of South African president Jacob Zuma. In one painting Zuma is depicted raping South Africa, in another the president is in bed with Atul Gupta.[17] This art has to be seen within a broader movement opposed to President Zuma and the postapartheid government's abandonment of the people for its own financial goals.

116 | *Hip-Hop in Africa*

Our discussion of the use of hip-hop as commentary on social issues continues with examinations of the role of gender and representations of gender by women in hip-hop in Africa, as well as representations of African migrant experiences in hip-hop.

"Lettre à Mr le Président": Social and Political Representations | 117

4

"Femme de Combat"

Gendered Representations

ALTHOUGH WOMEN WERE involved in the growth of hip-hop communities in Africa, they did not begin to perform until much later. In some countries the first female emcees did not begin recording until more than a decade after the first male emcees began recording. When women did begin to perform and record, they added feminist voices to a predominantly male culture. While some male artists spoke to gender issues, many female emcees almost took it as a mandate that they must represent women's issues.

Looking at the lyricism of female emcees in Africa, we must translate the meanings of the words, the purpose of the text. This goes beyond language translation and is an analysis of the subtext understood through the artist's use of wordplay. In this example we will look at the use of braggadocio by female emcees in Africa. We will examine what the artist is trying to communicate through lyrics that appear to be only self-celebration and will reveal the role of braggadocio in an artist's empowerment and rejection of taboos around female aggression.

Female emcees use their voice as an opportunity to speak to gender oppressions and bring feminist voices to African hip-hop. An analysis of the message in the music of female emcees exposes feminist perspectives on major sociopolitical issues. This analysis also allows us to understand and discuss the positions of female emcees in Africa as valid voices on feminist questions.

The manner in which female emcees represent gender identities and sexuality in their music varies. Even as some women choose to act out the hypersexual images of women, they may simultaneously choose to assert their masculinity through their lyrics. Women, in fact, present their own "masculinities" and represent challenges to socially constructed gender identities in doing so (Clark 2014). A focus on the meanings of messages being conveyed provides an opportunity to expand ideas surrounding womanhood and sexuality in Africa. It also allows us to see the dialogue happening among artists as a representation of the varied notions on these topics among many African urban women.

During this study, I made a great effort to identify and find music and videos for female emcees from across sub-Saharan Africa. Many of the artists are known only locally or regionally and have little exposure outside Africa. In this research, I studied the works of over one hundred African female emcees. Though I found others, I limited the study to artists who were active or semiactive, with a greater focus on active artists. Their level of activity was determined by how recently and how often they had released music. Semiactive artists were those who had released fewer than ten songs since 2000. Active artists were those who had released at least ten songs since 2000 and had released at least one song since 2010. I studied female hip-hop artists in Botswana, Ghana, Kenya, Mozambique, Namibia, Nigeria, Rwanda, Senegal, South Africa, Tanzania, Uganda, Zambia, and Zimbabwe. Most of these artists are based in their country of origin, though some were also based abroad.

Braggadocio

Many female emcees in Africa have embraced the culture and tradition of emceeing. Like female emcees in the United States, many African female emcees focus heavily on gender issues: relationships, violence against women, women in society. Their music also sheds

"Femme de Combat": Gendered Representations | 119

light on other social and political issues, such as corruption, poverty, and health care. There is also a focus on the display of hip-hop lyricism among many of these artists, even those who move between genres. Many female emcees in Africa show lyrical creativity in their use of metaphors, symbolism, and wordplay as they utilize the different forms or styles of rap to tell stories, boast, and shed light on certain issues. Within hip-hop culture the mastery of various rap styles is seen as the litmus test for someone being considered a good artist.

Bragging about oneself is a key element in hip-hop lyricism. Most emcees have released songs in which all or parts of the lyrics tell the audience about the artist's skill as an emcee, warn competitors who may seek to challenge them, talk about their own clothes or physique, and claim ownership of material goods. Braggadocio is often controversial for several reasons. The items artists brag about owning are often out of the reach of most listeners. This embrace of consumer capitalism thus aligns hip-hop artists with the same capitalist infrastructures that hip-hop has traditionally striven to confront. Braggadocio is also sometimes tied to glorifications of violence, as artists describe their destruction of their opponents or their physical strength in repelling violent attacks. This glorification of violence is seen as partly fueling the popularity of "thug life" and gangsterism.

In women, braggadocio that extols sexual dominance and control is sometimes seen as undermining female empowerment and feminist values. Oware's (2009) article on "contradictory messages in the songs of female rappers" asks important questions on whether the braggadocio songs of female artists actually promote the exploitation of other women, thus "nullify[ing] the positive messages that are conveyed by female rap artists" (787). These criticisms are important, and need to include a consideration of the role of the music industry in promoting tensions between artists for the sake of record sales. Record companies are perceived to favor signing artists with morally questionable lyrics that glorify sexuality, violence, and materialism. So while artists often have more politically conscious music, they can feel pressure to perform morally questionable music in order to get and maintain record deals. We also cannot take agency away from the artists themselves, who may make a conscious decision to promote a particular message in furtherance of a specific agenda.

Braggadocio within hip-hop culture is also important in establishing an artist's credibility and authenticity as a serious hip-hop emcee, which is especially important for female emcees. Bradley (2009) notes that the origin of the poetic exchange predates hip-hop and cites the occurrence of the practice among women in parts of Namibia. Mose (2013) points out the importance of braggadocio in Kenya in giving an artist the credibility (street cred) and capital needed to be taken seriously and to be acknowledged as a "representative of a marginalized periphery" (112). Williams and Stroud (2013) discuss the verbal and linguistic skills that are needed and honed in braggadocio practice in the Cape Town hip-hop scene. Hip-hop culture, globally, is an unapologetically masculine and confrontational culture, with little tolerance for weakness. While female emcees seek to navigate that culture, it is even more crucial that they establish both their strength and their right to be there. As many of their male counterparts do not take them seriously, braggadocio is one way a female artist can claim her right to a position next to her male counterparts.

Across the continent female emcees engage in the tradition of braggadocio. For example, in underground Ghanaian emcee Eyirap's 2013 song "Rap and Me," the artist brags about both her skills ("I understand the game, so always I deliver") and her connection to hip-hop culture ("rap makes me whole / rap is all I need to live the life that I'm dreaming . . . go to where hip hop lives, that's where you'll find me all around"). A year later she released the even stronger, multilingual song, "Beast in the City," in which she declares,

> I am the dragon from Volta
> Not even the lion come closer
> Here is a message from Volta
> These little kangaroo rappers, shut up.

The Volta region of Ghana is home to the Ewe language, one of the languages Eyirap performs in. Senegalese artist Coumbis Sorra's song "Dou man ak yen" (It's not me and you) warns her competitors that

"Femme de Combat": Gendered Representations | 121

they are not on her level, that she will never lose, and in the hip-hop game she is number one.

Younger artists use braggadocio to introduce themselves to the hip-hop community, to establish their names and credibility. Gigi La-Mayne of South Africa, Mo'Cheddah of Nigeria, and Tifa Flowz of Tanzania all began their careers after 2010, in a hip-hop culture that can be hostile to women and for which entry requires an immediate show of strength and skill. In LaMayne's verse on the song "Yajika Lento," the artist seeks to establish her street cred, brag about her skill, and represent the neighborhood of Soweto:

I been running this race, ripping eyes wide open
My rhymes luring heads like a Zulu love potion
I could rhyme tighter than that, I'm better than that
Bas'biz iskeem samalahle[1] we were blazing them back like
  "Wassup"
So-we-to, the place I know
They ain't topping on my breed. Qhum iUFO[2]
Queen Hover on your pleins
One up from second place and we yelling "Aga! Mos ayjiki le
  train."[3]

Mo'Cheddah's verse on the song "Bad" also establishes her persona. Mo'Cheddah is known for her glossy videos with displays of expensive cars and clothes. The braggadocio in her lyrics is an attempt to establish her skills as an emcee as well as her ability to procure material items.

And I know you mad cos she bad
And I know you sad cos I'm back
Baby just relax, and
Emi[4] rolling, emi stunting
Emi onto the next, emi no long thing
. . .
Emi Mo
Cheddah, go getter
Emi so fly, eyin[5] no feather

122 | *Hip-Hop in Africa*

Emi, money long, third mainland bridge
Eyin coming soon, fourth mainland bridge.

Tifa's song "Wacha zako" (Stop that/Stop what you're doing) is a warning to competitors who may want to battle her lyrically. Battling has its origins in the early days of hip-hop and is a popular way for artists to quickly prove themselves, especially if they go after and win against more popular artists. In a traditional battle two artists take turns reciting their lyrics in front of a crowd, whose cheers determine the winner. Battles can also be "on wax," indicating a series of recorded songs released back and forth by battling artists. In that case, public opinion determines the winner. In the following song Tifa issues an open call to other female emcees who may want to battle her, yet a warning against those thinking about it. She compares herself to an invisible foe, dismissing their skills and preparedness for battle:

> Want battle with me, go prepare yourself
> . . .
> You're no match for me
> Mine comes from the heart, yours from the classroom
> . . .
> Your style is a fake copy and paste, I'm the queen of flows.[6]

Among more established emcees braggadocio also serves as a warning to competitors, signals the maintenance of their lyrical skill, and reaffirms their role in hip-hop. It can also help solidify their legacy. Kenyan emcee Nazizi has been performing since 2000 but has continued, through her career, to reaffirm her credentials (street cred) though braggadocio-laced lyrics. Her verse in the song "Hip Hop Halisi" (Real hip-hop) was done in 2009, long after she had made a name for herself. The song serves to remind the hip-hop community of her legacy.

> First Lady on the beat
> Pump it for my streets of Nairobbery town [Nairobi]
> We represent the girls
> And the boys

"Femme de Combat": Gendered Representations | 123

They joined with me
On this track is Ukoo Flani and me
N-A, Z-I, zi
From Mau Mau they got freedom, now we're free
To rock my crowd so they dance with us
They can't refuse instead they agree
That we the illest
For this crowd of artists
That's why we are chosen by the teenagers

. . .
Of Zimmer, South B, and Eastleigh.[7]

In the song Nazizi reinforces her self-appointed title of Kenya's first lady of hip-hop, a title she repeatedly uses throughout her career. This is common among artists wanting to establish their position at the top in their field, and their legacy in the history of hip-hop culture in their country. The song was performed with Kenyan hip-hop group Ukoo Flani Mau Mau, a group of predominantly male artists known for their socially conscious music. In the same interview with Kenya's AM Live, Nazizi talks about the importance of her establishing herself as a good emcee, not just a good female emcee (NTV Kenya 2014). In Mose's analysis, Nazizi is "harnessing her street cred and swag" (Mose 2013, 119). She does this lyrically, but also by performing alongside an established and respected male act.

Lyrical creativity and braggadocio often come together in the tradition of the hip-hop freestyle, or cypher. Bradley refers to the cypher as "rap's proving ground" (2009, 177). According to Alim, the cypher is where artists improve their skills in "rap delivery, reacting under pressure, and verbal battling" (2006, 98). In a cypher several emcees come together and take turns rapping, one after the other. The cypher serves as a test of one's skill, shows other artists in the community that you are a serious emcee, and provides a form of fellowship for the artists involved. And when artists from different hometowns come together, they represent where they are from. A look at female cyphers on YouTube reveals artists from all over the United States, including California, Florida, Minnesota, New York, Texas, and Washington, DC.

124 | *Hip-Hop in Africa*

It should be noted that cyphers can also be rap battles, where artists are in direct competition with one another, or just a space for artists to show their skills without competition. According to Bradley, "the battle in rap is not simply between competitors, it is also between the MC and the words themselves. Mastering language before it masters you is the first contest an MC must win" (2009, 177). While traditionally artists are supposed to make up their lyrics on the spot, it is not uncommon for artists to recite already written lyrics.

Hip-hop cyphers in Africa have given female emcees a chance, both by themselves and alongside men, to display their skills and promote unity instead of competition between the artists. In 2010 several female artists in Senegal, led by Toussa Senerap, came together to form the female hip-hop collective GOTAL (unity, in Wolof). Their 2013 song "Unity" uses the beats from the song of the same name by American female hip-hop artist Queen Latifah. The song is a collaboration among female emcees in Senegal and features GOTAL members Toussa Senerap, Anta, Lady Zee, and Venus. In 2011, GOTAL posted a cypher on YouTube entitled "GOTAL Freestyle Cypher in Ginaaw Rail, Dakar, Senegal: Senegalese Women Rappers in Wolof." Ali Colleen Neff (2015) looks at Toussa Senerap and other members of GOTAL in Senegal. In addition to Toussa Senerap acquiring a studio as a safe space for female emcees to record, Neff discusses GOTAL's use of weekly cyphers as a space for the emcees to develop their skills and offer mutual support. In Ghana in 2013 "Girls' Dorm Cypher" was released on YouTube, featuring Eyirap, Dein, Yayra, and Lila. In 2014 the video for "Gh Female Rappers Cypher" was released on YouTube, featuring Eno, Esbee, Abena, Porsche, Eyirap, Xcot, Mila, and Scrach. In both videos the women varied in their style and ability, and though some were more known for doing pop music, they used Pidgin English and Ghanaian languages in hip-hop wordplay to recite rhymes that focused on braggadocio.

All female collaborations have also highlighted the abilities of female emcees in Africa in hip-hop wordplay and braggadocio. In 2011, Nigerian female emcees Sasha, Muna, Eva, Mo'Cheddah, Blaise, and Zee released the video for the song "I No Send You." Some of these artists were already well known and others were new. Most of

"Femme de Combat": Gendered Representations | 125

the artists were also more known for their flashy, sexy pop songs; this collaboration signaled a temporary break to display their skills in hip-hop lyricism.

In 2013 southern African female emcees released "No Sleep," which featured Gigi LaMayne (South Africa), Sasa Klaas (Botswana), Devour Ke Lenyora (South Africa), Ru the Rapper (Namibia), and DJ Naida (Zimbabwe). The track was produced by DJ Naida, one of the few female hip-hop DJs in Zimbabwe. The track brings together very diverse styles and features younger artists. All of these cyphers and collaborations serve to give these artists the credibility they seek, as each artist effectively cosigns the credibility of the other artists.

The Messages

The underrepresentation of women's voices in hip-hop means that their issues are often not given prominence within hip-hop culture. Their economic, social, and political struggles may not seem as critical to larger movements. This means that the female voices that are present represent, for many youth, a primary source of exposure to challenges to gender oppressions—and for many, their primary source of exposure to African feminist discourse. The importance of women in hip-hop is that we often hear African feminist challenges to patriarchy and social constructions of gender in their music. Even when women do not challenge gender oppressions directly in their lyrics, they represent that challenge the moment they decide to be hip-hop artists.

Like other African feminist scholars and activists, female emcees often reject the ways in which African women are portrayed, by both Africans and Europeans. These sentiments are addressed in music by several female emcees in Africa. Their engagement in feminist discourse is important, and deliberate. In Senegal, Toussa Senerap identifies as a feminist and has consciously used feminism to inform her work (Neff 2015). In South Africa, artists like Q'ba, Dope St. Jude, and Gigi LaMayne have taken on the feminist label. Dope St. Jude's use of Cape Town's queer slang (called Gayle) in her feminist-inspired rap was the topic of an OkayAfrica article by Shiba Mazaza (2015). Gigi LaMayne identifies herself as a feminist, beginning her song "Genesis" with the line "This is what feminist freedom would really sound like." These representations produced by female hip-hop artists are what Layli Phillips, Kerri Reddick-Morgan, and Dionne Stephens (2005) call street-level feminism. These artists may not be part of a community-based organization or be directly engaged with feminist activists in their countries. The artists do engage with their own constituencies, presenting African feminist ideas to populations that may or may not further engage with other sources of feminist dialogue. For those that would otherwise engage with feminist discourse, the music of the artists can serve as reinforcement. For those who do not engage with feminist discourse, this is their primary exposure to African feminist thought.

In an interview with Kenya's *Nation* newspaper, Kenyan hip-hop artist Lness (Lydia Akwabi) articulates the importance of being a conscious artist: "I do music that intends to change women's place in society" (Garang 2009). In interviews with artists in East and southern Africa, most indicated the importance of using their music as a vehicle to talk about issues underrepresented in hip-hop culture. While their voices are few, many female emcees recognize the importance of producing representations that address gender oppressions. Female hip-hop artists in Africa produce messages around an array of topics; some of the most frequently heard are songs on the strength and challenges of African women and songs on topics related to violence against women.

The African Woman

The African woman praised in many hip-hop songs is the ideal of Mother Africa. She is often a mother who represents the country's values, who is dedicated to her people, and who is willing to sacrifice herself for the movement (Mose 2014). Female artists present their own representations of the African woman, sometimes addressing the multidimensionality of who the African woman is.

"Femme de Combat": Gendered Representations | 127

The members of Godessa were pioneers in South African hip-hop. In addition to their commentary about politics and economics, many of their lyrics promote female empowerment and criticize patriarchy. The group discussed self-images among African women, materialism, and sexism. The song "Social Ills" addresses hair in the "rainbow nation." Member Burni Aman says,

> Editorial like cartoon pictorials
> Individual development ain't affordable so this is in memorial
> Of people with hair in all the wrong follicles
> Probable cause as society flaws caught in the claws
> Can't be original of course.

This excerpt references Eurocentric concepts of beauty that suggest, through media representations, that certain hair types are considered "wrong." The politics of Black women's hair is an important subject for commentary, though it is often not a subject of hip-hop lyrics. Burni Aman's verse on the song "Femme de Combat" (2009) goes:

> This story begins at the feet of our mothers
> From our township streets and our gutters
> Who travel on taxis and trains to the suburbs
> Cleaning the filth that remains in the cupboards
> Leaving the children at the mercy of others
> Where little girls turning into women under covers
> Scrubbing the floors, known as Black and Coloured
> Women who work in factories where dreams are gutted
> Walk home tired to their households corrupted
> One parent alone she stands, no husband to hold her
> No money, education, means you destined to suffer
> The lines on her face make you think that she's older
> Though the stride in her walk has become very slow
> And she still carries the weight of the world on her shoulder
> She's older than the average policeman or soldier
> Therefore her story should be told and you should know her.

The song is a collaboration with Black Tiger, Thaïs, and René Mosele. Burni Aman's verse is not explicitly set during apartheid, but this may

128 | *Hip-Hop in Africa*

be intentional. The song is about Black and Coloured South African women who labor doing domestic work or in the factories, and the social costs that are often paid on family structures. Burni Aman's verse is her attempt at telling their stories.

Like Godessa in South Africa, Sister Fa was a pioneer for female emcees in Senegal. Also starting her career in 2000, she established a tradition of rapping about serious social issues. Her song "Milyamba" talks about the life of rural women in Senegal.

> Well-dressed this morning you go out and spend your time
> You don't take your time to walk slowly as in spring
> You do not give so much importance to the ones who say
> That the life in the countryside is difficult
> Because you little Sister live the easy life
> To go shopping you have your nice car
> You drive with it like a small nightingale
> Meanwhile me all morning I go to the rice fields
> With my child on my back I go kilometres
> Dressed in rags as if I had nothing else to wear
> To live happy I have to accept this work
> For it I use all my energy without any sorrow
> And to prove my braveness I start a simple croon.[8]

The song commends the strength and sacrifice of rural women while taking a more critical tone toward the "easy life" of young urban African women.

Neff discusses the song "Woman," in which Toussa Senerap talks about womanhood and the challenges of being a woman: "Close your eyes for five hours / And imagine the world without women / Everything would disappear" (2015, 473). Like Sister Fa's song "Milyamba," Toussa praises the work and struggle of women. While not limited to rural women, she focuses on the maternal aspects of womanhood and the relationship between women and Allah and between women and their sons. Mothers and all women are portrayed as a nexus that holds the universe together.

Some songs by female artists in Africa have been self-reflections, focusing on the lives of young women living in urban Africa. In

"Femme de Combat": Gendered Representations | 129

"J'déprime" (I'm depressed), Benin-born and Senegal-trained artist Moona explores the physical and psychological impacts of depression on women told from a firsthand perspective. Similarly, South African artist Nthabi's song "Fly" reflects on dealing with stress, spirituality, and thoughts of depression.

> It's just stress, pain, problems with love
> My heart breaks cause it feels as though God's given up
> On my mistakes
> I take
> Each day at a time
> And sometimes contemplate the different ways of taking my life
> But suicide is not the answer to this
> Whether I choose to slit my wrists
> Or take a couple of pills
> I need peace.

South African artist Skye Wanda's song "Yesterday" is an autobiographical reflection on growing up without her father's love as well as a message to young men fathering children on their own. Nigerian artist Blaise released "Lasan," a religious reflection on growing up as a troubled teen. She discusses her self-destructive behavior, criticisms of her looks, and the path she took to overcome her problems.

These songs offer some interesting reflections on struggle, loss, and even depression, which is often a taboo topic in many African societies. Discussions of depression in many African cultures, like elsewhere in the world, are often difficult to have. The songs the female emcees studies produced constructed some of the multidimensional experiences of African women. African female emcees present African women's experiences as mothers, daughters, lovers, saints, sinners, rural inhabitants, urban dwellers, challenged, poor, materialistic . . . and more.

Violence against Women

The decision to focus on violence against women is also common among female hip-hop artists in the United States (Phillips, Reddick-

Morgan, and Stephens, 2005). There are several types of violence committed against women, and while domestic violence is most often the focus of the artists in this study, other forms of violence against women were addressed. With the underrepresentation of the topic in music produced by male artists, many female artists have taken up the role of ensuring its inclusion in hip-hop culture.

In Senegal, where the majority of the population is Muslim and more conservative than their anglophone neighbors, much of the hip-hop has social or political content. Hip-hop in Senegal has a long history of social and political themes. And of course it is not unusual for artists to live their music, making their message part of their real-life actions (see chapter 3).

Senegalese artist Sister Fa has built a career on being outspoken on the issue of female genital cutting (FGC), both in her music and in her work. Sister Fa has also used her lyrics to speak out about FGC. Touring Senegal in an Education sans Excision (Education without Cutting) tour and working with NGOs to address the practice, her efforts have helped eradicate FGC in her home village of Thionck Essyl. Her work has also earned her several accolades, including an award from the organization Freedom to Create in 2011.

Senegalese artist Coumbis Sorra's "Farafina Mousso" deals with the treatment of women in society, as well as violence against women in domestic relationships. The song focuses not only on women in Senegal but is a broader message of women's struggles globally. Moona deals with domestic violence in her song "Désillusion." In "Revolution" she targets social divisions, including those erected in the name of religion, and calls for social change.

Several of the female artists I interviewed had songs that addressed women's issues. this was true of artists who produce primarily socially conscious music, as well as of artists who produce largely apolitical music. Several artists have dealt with domestic violence in their music. The first verse of Ugandan artist Keko's 2010 song "Alwoo" (Cry for help) tells of a woman in an abusive relationship who is unable to find support from her family. Kenyan artist FemiOne Shikow's 2013 song "Alejandro" is a verse-by-verse narration of an abusive relationship. Botswana artist Sasa Klaas's 2015 song "Freedom Calls" with

"Femme de Combat": Gendered Representations | 131

fellow rapper Scar takes us through an abusive relationship, with Scar taking on the role of the abusive boyfriend who has to face the consequences of his actions and Klaas being the abused girlfriend who struggles and emerges from the abuse.

In the songs "Hear Me Now" and "Daddy Issues," South African artist Gigi LaMayne deals with domestic violence from a daughter's perspective. In "Daddy Issues" LaMayne talks about witnessing her father abuse her mother and her father's absence in her life. Another South African emcee, Kanyi (on the cover), has a song entitled "Ingoma" from her 2012 album *Iintombi—Zifikile* that also deals with violence against women. Megan Jones describes the song "Ingoma":

> The song's densely metaphorical lyrics draw on isiXhosa *iimbongi*, a form of highly stylised praise poetry. Ritualistic scenes of dancing reveal Kanyi in the white clothing of *iqgirha*, a traditional healer. . . . Kanyi's aggressive rapping style and ferocious gaze unsettle the silencing of women and mobilises conventions of ritual to forge counter-voices. (2013, 41)

In the song's first verse Kanyi raps about a woman who chooses to stay in an abusive relationship. In an interview Kanyi says that the idea behind the song examines how the decisions we often make can be self-destructive. The song is not telling the woman to leave, but instead shows how her decisions to stay could ultimately lead to her death.

Violence against women is a global concern. Regardless of legislation passed, human rights, community, and women's groups have been fighting the various forms of violence against women. Blaise's song "Osika" was written for the young girls kidnapped by Boko Haram in 2014. This type of violence against women often gets attention and popular support because it is a terrorist act, in which the girls were randomly taken. Other forms of violence against women can often lack the same widespread popular support when questions of behavior and privacy are debated. This is sometimes the case with the struggle over FGC. Often communities are hesitant to change in the face of generations of cultural behavior. As with female emcees in the United States, violence against women is a common theme among female emcees in Africa. African women examine the violence within

132 | *Hip-Hop in Africa*

domestic relations but also violence through terrorism and FGC, as well as other forms of violence against women.

Sexuality

Expressions of sexuality among female emcees vary across the continent, from more conservative expressions found in predominantly Muslim countries like Senegal to more explicit expressions found in anglophone West Africa. Hip-hop and youth culture in urban Africa tends to reveal more liberal trends toward sex and sexuality than in rural Africa, but the extent of this varies. Across the continent increased, and more explicit, expressions of sexuality within youth culture correspond to global trends. Many gender and cultural studies scholars acknowledge the increased normalization of sex, sexuality, and hypersexuality via the media (Altman 2004; Attwood 2006). The increases in sexually explicit content and the skewed portrayals of women found in popular culture are consumed globally. The impacts locally differ, but young people in virtually every city in the world have access to sexualized images, texts, and sounds that play a role in shaping personal values, behaviors, and relationships. The artists in this study are both consumers and content creators, simultaneously being defined by and defining cultural representations of gender and sexuality.

In debates over the consumption and expressions of sexuality within hip-hop culture, the discussion of female agency often gets obscured in discussions of the internalization by youth of the sexism within a hip-hop (and popular) culture that celebrates highly sexualized roles for women, and in which women are often defined based on the desires of men. Several gender and hip-hop studies scholars address the negative social and psychological impacts exposure to hip-hop culture has on women (Peterson et al. 2007; Stephens and Few 2007; Kistler and Lee 2009). Female artists who express their sexuality in socially taboo ways are often seen as having internalized their own oppressions and as acting out the role given to them within hip-hop (and popular) culture (Cole and Guy-Sheftall 2003).

"Femme de Combat": Gendered Representations | 133

Other scholarship considers the agency and power of female artists who make the decision to display socially taboo expressions of female sexuality (Perry 2004; Pough 2004; M. Morgan 2005; Richardson 2007; Durham, Cooper, and Morris 2013). This scholarship considers that women may express a form of power via their own sexualized performances. Richardson (2007) discusses how female hip-hop artists and fans choose to navigate and find agency within a hip-hop culture that seeks to define them as whores, amoral women, and sources of entertainment.

Most of the scholarship on women's participation in hip-hop culture has come from US-based authors, who also link that participation to African American culture and historical experiences. Many of the frames used to examine African American women's participation in hip-hop cannot be used to examine African women's participation in hip-hop without adjustments for context because of differences in cultural and historical contexts. There are, however, relevant similarities between African and African American contemporary women's experiences. Historical views of Black womanhood and sexuality have sustained representations of the dichotomy of the sexually voracious and the asexual Black woman in the Western imagination (Ukadike 1994; Hill Collins 2002; Kramarae and Spender 2004). These familiar tropes are often played out in Western representations of African women. Cheris Kramarae and Dale Spender (2004) note that the image of the hypersexual African woman dates back to nineteenth-century Europe. This finding coincided with the presentation of Saartjie "Sarah" Baartman[9] as a representation of the abnormality of African women's bodies and sexualities. Baartman's ordeal, which is well known, was indicative of European attitudes toward African women as abnormal, exotic, and sexual. Cheris Kramarae and Dale Spender (2004) found that most news stories about African women published in the *New York Times* from 1985 to 1994 focused on sex practices, sexual anatomies, or sexuality as either primary or secondary themes (Kramarae and Spender 2004).

These representations have created an environment in which there is often complacency over violations against Black female bodies and silence over the policing of Black women's sexuality. African and African American women have been impacted by early European obsessions with, devaluation of, and sexualization of Black women's bodies, which have been tied to contemporary attempts to both control and exploit their bodies and sexualities in the United States and throughout Africa (Hill Collins 2002; Arnfred 2004; Nnaemeka 2005;; Gordon-Chipembere 2011; Harris-Perry 2011; D. Lewis 2011). These attempts to both control and exploit Black women's bodies and sexualities have resulted in reactions including resistance, acceptance, and denial by Black women in the United States and across Africa.

Unlike in the United States, however, female emcees in Africa operate in cultural and historical landscapes in which images of female sexuality in the media have been minimal, and in societies in which public expressions or displays of sexuality are either forbidden or are rare. While there are important variations across Africa, there are similarities in the values and ideas concerning female sexuality throughout the continent. Women in North, East, and Central Africa, as well as rural regions of southern and West Africa, grapple with perceptions of their morality and decency being tied to what they wear. Cultural, and sometimes legal, restrictions have sanctioned the policing of women's clothing in an attempt to prevent the corruption of their morals and, by extension, society's morals (Wipper 1972; Vincent 2008; Kwenaite and Van Heerden 2011; Lee 2011; Makoni 2011). A survival of the colonial era, single women living in urban centers in East African (Dar es Salaam, Kampala, Nairobi) are still more likely to be seen as loose and lacking morals in comparison to rural women (Mikell 1997; Geiger 1998; Haram 2004; Mose 2014). Cultural values determine acceptable expressions of female sexuality, while education systems and religious and cultural institutions enforce those values (Kambarami 2006; Oloruntuba-Oju 2007). Enforcement is often done through admonishment and public shaming, even through direct physical or sexual assault (Oloruntuba-Oju 2007; Vincent 2008; Kwenaite and Van Heerden 2011; Lee 2012; Makoni 2011; Shipley 2012).

This does not mean the avenues to expressing female sexuality publicly have not existed. There have been female musicians in various genres across Africa addressing topics of gender and sexuality through song. Naana Otoo-Oyortey (2007) and Abena Kyere (2012)

"Femme de Combat": Gendered Representations | 135

explore representations of sexual pleasure and fantasy by female musicians in Ghanaian music and proverbs. In East Africa, Tanzanian female taarab musicians use subtext to discuss sex and sexuality (Traoré 2007; Thompson 2011). In Kenya, female Gĩkũyũ artists directly attack patriarchy and gender roles in their music (Mwaũra 2007).

Urban women in Africa operate within a myriad of cultural, ethnic, and national codes that influence their participation in hip-hop culture. (Global) hip-hop culture also plays a defining role in that participation. According to Marcyliena Morgan, "Irrespective of style, hip-hop women share the same value of performance: hard, skillful, provocative, and intelligent rhyming . . . they represent the lives of women in hip-hop and the world" (2005, 428). Morgan points to the values of both noncensorship and representation within hip-hop culture, which have allowed women a platform from which to resist their silencing and policing. Expressions of sexuality by female artists in hip-hop range from symbolism hidden in lyrical slang to explicit proclamations.

In the West and across Africa, expectations of female modesty are enforced by portrayals of women as sexually deviant, with labels (*whore, prostitute, lesbian*) that are used to define that deviance. In discussions with male hip-hop artists, several were willing to give legitimacy to the music of their female peers, unless those female peers have presented themselves in appropriate ways. In other words, they were a version of Cheryl Keyes's Queen Mother trope. The Queen Mother, according to Keyes, is the female emcee who presents a persona embodying "Black female empowerment and spirituality, making clear their self-identification as African, woman, warrior, priestess, and queen . . . demand[ing] respect not only for their people but for Black women and men" (2002, 189–90).

Interestingly, female artists are often encouraged to emphasize their sexuality as a key to a successful music career. This commodification of female sexuality often occurs at the expense of the respectability of an artist when she relinquishes her own agency in presentations of her own sexuality. Female hip-hop artists in urban Africa, like their counterparts in the West, have to operate within environments that seek to police women's sexualities while stressing the need to market their sexuality. Female emcees in Africa can be

136 | *Hip-Hop in Africa*

encouraged to shed elements of their traditional cultures: those that oppress them as well as those that empower them. This can be done in the name of modernity and for marketability purposes but can disguise other oppressions, often cloaked in verbiage on sexual freedom and modernization. Presentations of female sexuality can, however, reveal strength and empowerment, when they are paired with agency. A female artists' expression of her sexuality can be a representation of power, especially when accompanied by lyrics that challenge certain gender constructs. Aisha Durham, Brittney Cooper, and Susana Morris (2013) note that female emcees outside the United States often dismantle respectability politics, legitimizing sex workers and women who enter into relationships and marriages out of financial necessity. The authors claim that some international artists "infuse transnational feminism into hip-hop feminist studies" (730). In Africa this has coincided with the work of young feminist activists and organizers who are contributing to conversations around sexuality, sexual orientation, and gender identity to African feminist discourses.

Recognizing expressions of female sexuality, sexual pleasure, and sexual identity by African female emcees as legitimate representations of African womanhood is important. We will look at artists that express their sexualities and sexual pleasures explicitly, those that challenge ideas of female sexuality, and artists that challenge attempts to control female sexuality. In an essay written for *Feminist Africa*, Athenkosi Sopitshi discusses views of female sexuality in postapartheid South Africa:

> [Some young South African women] had to be forced into a "good girl role" sexually. We acknowledged that we rarely derived any pleasure from this, and that we wanted pleasure—sexual pleasure, the pleasures of intimacy, and the pleasures of confidence in our bodies. We grieved over the frequency with which we seemed to accept the "good girl" role sexually, all in the hope of running away from being called whores or sluts. (2012, 131)

Several female artists expressed their sexualities in ways that challenge social conventions. In order to discuss the ways in which they do that, this study focused on artists in two ways: their aesthetics and

"Femme de Combat": Gendered Representations | 137

their lyrics. Aesthetics was evaluated based on the wearing of short skirts or short dresses, which was perceived as going against common social norms in many African cities. In many African cities the miniskirt has become a deeply contested battleground over the policing of women's bodies. African women in Kenya, Morocco, Namibia, South Africa, Swaziland, Tanzania, Uganda, and Zimbabwe have faced incidents including, public shaming, assault, and arrest for wearing miniskirts. Even when men and women do not participate in these incidents, Desiree Lewis (2011) says ideas of women's sexual behavior often allow for the justification of these violent acts. In wearing these clothes artists may be making a conscious choice to challenge social norms. Artists' lyrics were also examined for representations of female sexuality (discussion of sex, romantic relationships, sexual experiences, sexual desires, and sexual identity). The purpose of this exercise is to examine the broader meanings of these representations, to understand the constructions of African womanhood that they create for us.

Some female hip-hop artists in Africa present their sexuality in more explicit ways. Many present content that borrows heavily from Western popular culture and present gender constructs that seek to show power in expressions of sexuality. The following songs and videos are by artists who have built their personas around representations of female sexuality that challenge convention.

Ghana
Amaa Rae: "Wobejeimu"
Mz Porsche: "Do It J3"
Abena Rockstar: "Megye Wo Boy"
Eazzy: "Somthin Lost?," "Scream," "Emergency," "Rock Dis Party"

Kenya
Stella Mwangi (STL): "Stella Stella Stella," "Biashara"

Mozambique
Dama do Bling: "Me Luv It," "My Eish," "Bad Girl"

Nigeria
Sasha: "Emi le gan," "Only One"
Mo'Cheddah: "If You Want Me," "Bad"

138 | *Hip-Hop in Africa*

Zambia

Cleo Ice Queen: "Addicted," "Timi Mekoko," "Big Dreams"
Princess Mwamba: "Jungle," "Swag Walk"

In these songs and videos, the artists celebrate their sexuality, express sexual desire, and reject passive personas. Many of these artists have crafted images that market their sexuality as part of their persona, utilizing pop sounds, and glossy videos. For example, in most of her videos Eazzy's clothing challenges "acceptable" norms of women's dress and behavior in Ghana. Her songs often focus on self-praise, her physical appeal to men, and ways that men can please her. Stella Mwangi moves between styles in her songs and varies in how she expresses her sexuality. In the video for "Stella Stella Stella," she presents a sexy, confident, young, urban woman boasting about her sexual dominance and skill—a taboo for women in most societies. The song is also filled with braggadocio and depictions of Stella as a street-smart Nairobi woman.

In this excerpt from "Only One," Sasha represents female agency in relationships. Not only is she not passive in her dating, she ridicules men for the methods they employ to try to date her:

Everywhere I go I see d boys wanna try me
Still window shopping how jokers gonna buy me?
Know I'm looking good awon boys just dey eye me
Not the only one that has told me u like me
Why me? What u think I might be easy?
Wife me? Saying things u think will please me
Trust me . . . Its more than effizy
Its not about d money u have
. . .
I mean really
Psheww! Sash p first lady
Its going to take a whole lot more to drive me crazy!

In the song she presents a woman who has several pursuers, several men trying to make her happy. In the video we see her evaluate potential suitors, until she finally picks one she likes. The song ends,

"Femme de Combat": Gendered Representations | 139

I know you'll put me in a corner if I let you boy (oh my)
Put me in a corner boy
You'll put me in a corner boy?
My P is heavy you can't treat me like I'm one of your toys (oh my).

The end of the song is a blatant refusal to turn her selection into a submission. Even in her relationship she clearly expresses her confidence and refusal to be put into a corner, that is, controlled.

Looking at representations of female sexuality by female hip-hop artists across the continent, music produced by many female emcees in Ghana and Nigeria presented themes of sexuality in more overt or explicit ways than in many other countries studied. Of more than twenty-five female emcees studied in Ghana and Nigeria, over half presented their sexuality as a key component of their image or lyrical content. These artists were also more likely than other female emcees to cross genres, producing songs that blended hiplife and hip-hop (Ghana), as well as Nigerian pop and hip-hop (Nigeria). In fact, in looking at all the artists studied, there was a noticeable correlation between female artists who blended hip-hop and pop music genres and those who used sexual themes in their music and videos.

Nigerian music has been heavily influenced by its internationally successful pop music industry, with music giants such as Yemi Alade, Flavour, Davido, and P-Square. Nigerian's fast-paced pop music has influenced hip-hop music and culture within the country. Many Nigerian music videos have adopted the American formula and contain sexualized images of women and celebrations of female and male sexuality and experiences. In a discussion with Saratu Abiola, a writer for the *Guardian* in Nigeria, Saratu asserted that women are often given opportunities only if they align themselves with a male artist or group of artists or if they present themselves in a highly sexualized manner. Shonekan (2011) infers that in Nigeria there was in fact a depoliticizing of hip-hop and pop music, which may have been the result of an intentional effort to stop hip-hop's potential political influence.

In Ghana there has been a more conservative outlook on women's performance, though many of the female hip-hop artists do articulate sexually themed lyrics. They do this in the urban environment of Accra, a city that often seems to be negotiating a balance between conservatism and Western-style social liberalism. Hiplife artist Mzbel, sometimes referred to as the Lil' Kim of Ghana, was targeted for her decision to present her sexuality as a key component of her aesthetic and musical content. While her suggestive performances garnered her attention, a sexual assault on the artist led to debates among Ghanaians all over the world about Mzbel's culpability in her own assault (Shipley 2013). In Jesse Weaver Shipley's (2013) book on hiplife he details how the attack on Mzbel was seen by many as justified by her lewd behavior and performances. With few women in hiplife, Shipley explains that most of the women in the Ghanaian music scene choose to perform gospel music. If women are largely absent from the hiplife scene, they are almost nonexistent in the mainstream Ghanaian hip-hop scene. Most of the Ghanaian female emcees in this study are considered underground artists and have had little national and almost no international exposure. While many of these women choose to produce sexually themed content, their lack of exposure and visibility may be why, unlike Mzbel, they have been shielded from criticism.

There are female emcees who decide to use their agency to insert more African feminist frameworks into presentations of counternarratives. These counternarratives involve a consideration of overt expressions of sexuality. Using an African feminist lens, we know that attitudes toward women and sex often means that women's sexualities are often not seen as legitimate elements of womanhood but often as signs of sexual deviance. In the field of entertainment a women's sexuality is commodified and marketed, often at the cost of respectability. Some female artists choose to fight these constructs of African womanhood by challenging the use of their sexuality in expected or desired ways.

Mwangi and Wanjiru Mbure (2010) analyze Kenyan emcee Nazizi's 2004 song "Kenyan Girl/Kenyan Boy" using the lens of African feminist discourse. In the song Nazizi is the pursuer in the relationship, taking on what is considered a male role. In the video for the same song she presents a nonsexualized, yet unapologetically bold persona. Mwangi and Mbure discuss her image in the video, in which

"Femme de Combat": Gendered Representations | 141

she dons either dreadlocks or an African-print head scarf, with a T-shirt and jeans. They compare this to the hypersexualized women in US hip-hop videos. The South African video for Xhosa emcee Kanyi's song "Ungalibali" depicts female artists facing pressure to sex up their looks. The song features Kanyi meeting with record executives who proceed to put her in a dress, make-up, heels, and a wig. The video ultimately ends with her rejection of the persona, at the risk of her career. In our interview, Kanyi said that "Ungalibali" is about loving yourself, and not an indictment of women who project a more sexualized persona. Kanyi emphasizes that the message is "Don't forget your point of view. Don't forget yourself." Kanyi said she has always been conscious of what she wears because of the message or image it may give off. She felt it was important that people focused on her lyrics, not what she was wearing. She felt that it can become tricky when women (artists) want to be sexual, as it can easily be seen as a commodity, like they are selling sex. She revealed that her use of the cartoon character made in her image that appears on her album is a representation of herself. Through this character she can dress in ways that do not distract or take away from what she is saying, or do not allow a commoditization of her sexual persona.

The song "Me, My Girls and I" (2009) by South African emcees Burni Aman, Eavesdrop, Thaïs, Nilsa, EJ von Lyrik, Nthabi, and Shameema is a collaboration among female emcees. Burni Aman's lines capture the theme of the narratives these emcees produce:

> We got the rhythm swinging from the hips and back, ya'll
> This is that feminine energy, make you tap toes
> We don't engage in baring booty at a wack show
> We put the mind in the lyrics so don't ask "hoe."

Sexual Identity

Some female artists reject traditional ideas of gender and sexual identity by fully or partially adopting more masculine personas in their dress, style of rap, and stance. Artists like E.D.N.A. and Dein (Ghana), Toussa Senerap and Anta Ba (Senegal), Devour Ke Lenyora (South

Africa), and Chiku K (Tanzania) seem to reject conventional ideas of femininity in most or all of their music videos.

Neff (2015) claims that Toussa Senerap has deliberately refused to change her look to conform to traditional Senegalese Islamic gender constructs. Lenyora, unlike many other female rap artists, overtly inserts the questions of masculine and feminine sexuality into her lyrics. In "Somethings Gotta Give" she takes on a somewhat masculine persona:

> Fellaz and ladies catching emotion over my shit
> Wish they could catch a clue that I'm on that celibate tip
> Daring demeanor have them saying that "ugay lo"[10]
> I'm the man, motherfucker, thought I said so
> So I hang my pants low, put my hands on the biggest invisible
> nuts, gcwala, yi-dog lo[11]
> Limping in my stepping, guzu lak'dala, skhokho saizolo,[12] so I
> go harder, gcwala madzala.[13]

In her statement that both men and women are "catching emotion over my shit" it is not clear whether she is referring to her music or herself. Catching emotions or catching feelings is a slang term that indicates someone is falling in love with a person who has no interest in them. The next line in the song is a response to their emotions, in which Lenyora declares that she is celibate. This line suggests a reception of romantic feelings from both men and women. Later in the verse she takes on an overtly masculine demeanor with the line "I'm the man, motherfucker," and referring to her low-hung pants and her "invisible nuts." She does not seem to be identifying as a man, hence the word "invisible," but she presents a visual of a very masculine demeanor, even going as far as feminizing her male competition.

Other South African emcees that present sexualities that reject traditional gender norms and heteronormativity[14] include Cape Town emcees Dope Saint Jude and Nazlee. Both artists identify as queer. Nazlee informed me that she rejects gender-specific pronouns, and identifies simply as being queer. Dope Saint Jude's use of Cape Town queer slang and gender-bending imagery in her music are direct confrontations with heteronormativity. In the song and video she sets the

"Femme de Combat": Gendered Representations | 143

audience up by announcing her intention to diverge from the "norm." She presents lyrics that directly express her rebellion of heteronormativity. In the first verse she raps

> It's the hour to be bold
> Will you play or will you fold?
> Throwing shade to make you cold
> Buy your shit before its sold
> Your aesthetic's getting old
> And your style is too defensive
> And you're trying to hold me back when you know my shit's progressive.

She goes on to insert feminist and queer dialogues:

> You listen to my rhymes looking like you constipated
> 'Cause your brand of feminism to my world is so outdated
> Please update it, for the rappers, for the fly girls, for the others
> For the girls who like to fuck, for the sisters, for the mothers
> For the mothers with the baby daddy and baby mama
> For the girls who also boys, please update it, make it smarter
> I'll be doing fine if you keep your shit in line
> Pussy power, pussy time, pussy doing just fine.

Dope Saint Jude references feminism, "girl power" movements, transgender identities, same-sex relationships, and female sexuality in just eight lines of rap. She also uses misogynistic mindsets in rap and manipulates them. The line "straight boys, gay boys, all turning into dykes" is suggests lesbians being turned "straight." The line "I had five boys and they all my side bitches" mocks the hypermasculine elements in hip-hop that value the conquest of women, or "bitches." This is reinforced through the video, which shows an old black-and-white TV playing a video of male American hip-hop artists performing with video models featured prominently in the background.

Devour Ke Lenyora, Dope Saint Jude, and Nazlee are female artists who live in South Africa, and benefit from an environment in which they find more liberal views on sexuality. South Africa gives these artists more room to explore gender and sexuality. There are still social taboos that often impact the expressions of sexuality that may be considered deviant (Gunkel 2010; Sopitshi 2012). Other female artists use subtext to create representations of sexual identity. Some artists in the study produced music that insinuates struggles with sexual identities, or social perceptions of their sexual identity.

IN LOOKING AT the representations of women in hip-hop there are challenges, but there are clear contributions women can and do make to the culture when they do decide to participate. Few women are compelled to emcee, and fewer still decide to face the challenges of making it their career. This absence of a larger presence of African women's voices within hip-hop weakens hip-hop's ability to call itself a true voice of the people. If hip-hop is to convey the story of a people, without women, part of that story is missing. While it is important that hip-hop contributes critique to public policies and social discourse, the danger is that if women's voices are missing, then challenges to policies and social practices that oppress women are neglected within that critique. The presence of women's voices also helps shed light on the contradictions with regard to gender within hip-hop. Female emcees often critique the misogynist lyrics of other artists and create representations that challenge that misogyny. This is sometimes done in partnership with male artists, through public engagements, interviews, or social media.

This chapter revealed how women's representations reveal the ways in which African women use their agency to create space within hip-hop cultures for feminist voices. In the focus on lyricism we examined women's contributions to hip-hop culture in Africa from an analysis of their use of braggadocio. Braggadocio in rap serves many functions. In this chapter we saw how female artists use the tradition to establish their reputations and credibility. While the criticisms of braggadocio are important, it was necessary to focus on it as a method by which women create space in hip-hop culture. The celebration of materialism, the ridicule of female competitors, and the use of explicit language may be agency on the part of the artist in determining the best methods by which to establish herself, or it may be manipulation

"Femme de Combat": Gendered Representations | 145

by labels or managers (or both) seeking to exploit and capitalize off of the artist. Either or both certainly apply to various artists. The question is not *if* braggadocio is an important method of establishing credibility in hip-hop, but the types of braggadocio artists employ. Hip-hop braggadocio, for example, can be considered unladylike. But it is also a way to establish strength, and the aggressive lyrics and boasting in braggadocio lyrics result in women intentionally challenging assigned gender roles to insert themselves and their voices into hip-hop culture.

The social messages presented in the lyrics of these female artists distinguish them from their male counterparts. The female artists were much more likely to offer diverse representations of African women's experiences. Female artists presented more discussions of issues affecting women, like violence against women, health, and self-esteem than their male counterparts. These discussions also tended to be more diverse. For example, Godessa's treatment of the politics of Black women's hair belongs with the larger conversations happening on the topic within academia and among Black and African feminist groups. It is a topic that may have found its way into the lyrics of male hip-hop artists, but the importance of a feminist voice is obvious. Again, the inclusion of women's voices in hip-hop allows for discourse around issues directly affecting women. Male artists do, however, address women's issues, through music and activism. Many male artists have addressed issues like domestic violence, FGC, and other forms of violence against women. If there were only male voices, however, there would be an underrepresented, one-sided representation of these topics in hip-hop music.

Female emcees were also more likely to offer representations of female sexuality that showed female agency than their male counterparts. Male artists in Africa varied in the ways in which they presented female sexuality. There were sometimes representations of Black women that were similar to what is found in a lot of mainstream American hip-hop music. Many representations furthered misogynist depictions of Black women and Black female sexuality. Many of these songs serve as representations of male commentary on female sexuality. In these commentaries the good woman/bad woman dichotomy is played out in depictions of African women that emphasize expected gender roles for women and reinforce social policing of women's bodies. It is important to note that there were male artists who presented complex, diverse, and thoughtful stories of women and female sexuality, but these representations were in the minority among the artists studied for this research. Female sexuality in hip-hop, especially in Africa, the motherland, is a contested space. As we have seen, there is much debate over the representations of sexuality of Black women, by Black women. The goal in this research was to show the ways in which women on the continent chose to engage, or not engage, their sexuality within their music. The research revealed the complexities and challenges African women face when deciding to make space for their sexuality.

Female artists in Africa represent their communities, womanhood, and hip-hop in varying and legitimate ways. They navigate cultural environments in which they find support and challenges. But we cannot separate the female emcees in Africa from those environments. These African women are influenced by traditions of resistance and womanhood at home, as well as traditions of resistance and womanhood in African American hip-hop. We cannot dismiss them simply as representations of the influence of Western culture or US hegemony in Africa. Their representations contribute to our understandings of Africa. They are African women and their music reflects the cultures, politics, and people of Africa. These women also navigate hip-hop culture, where they also find support and challenges. But we also cannot separate the female emcee in Africa from hip-hop culture. We cannot assume that female emcees in Africa are not true representations of hip-hop. These artists choose hip-hop culture—with its aggression, vulgarity, and confrontation—as the conduit through which to represent their experiences.

"Femme de Combat": Gendered Representations | 147

5

"Make You No Forget"

Representations of African Migrant Experiences in African Hip-hop

TWO SONGS SPEAK to the relationship between Africa and its migrants: "Dear Africa" by Blitz the Ambassador, of Ghana, and "Dearest Child" by Kimba Mutanda, of Malawi. "Dear Africa" is a letter to Africa from a child who left home years ago. "Dearest Child" is a letter from Malawi to the children who left home years ago. Both songs are more spoken-word pieces than hip-hop rhymes. They both depict the continued ties to home, the economic conditions that cause many migrants to flee, the stress of life in the West, and the idea of return. In "Dear Africa," Blitz says,

> Dear Africa, it's just me, your son. I pray this letter finds you better, I hope you're doing fine. I can't believe that ten years have gone by since I last packed my bags, got a cab and said "bye." Only can imagine the feeling watching your kids go. Must have been heartbreaking, where did the years go? But you'd be proud to know I never stopped reppin' you, every show, every track, every last interview.

In "Dearest Child," Kimba Mutanda writes as his country, Malawi:

> Dearest Child, I decided it's better if wrote this letter in English, because some of you were pretty young when you left

and you might not remember your mother tongue . . . a lot of your cousins and friends have jumped on planes to chase dreams that they've seen on DStv screens. It makes no sense to me. They say they've lost faith in your uncle Chilembwe's pocket money and would rather get cash that's green, or be paid by a woman they call Queen. Her name's familiar . . . we might have met before. But I think the last time I saw her was in 1964. . . . Dearest child, I'm gonna post this to your last known address. I hope the stress of living illegally in a foreign place hasn't prematurely wrinkled your face . . . I miss you. But don't let my emotion be a weight on your spirit. These words should be like a sad song that makes you feel warm and confident when you hear it. Remember, my main concern is that you're happy. From the bottom of my warm heart, yours eternally, your mother, Malawi.

These songs articulate the ties between migrant and home. They address the economic conditions that led to migration, the stress of long periods of separation and of the idea of return. The relationship between migrant and home is the central theme of these songs, and of this chapter. This chapter examines the role of migration in African hip-hop, and argues that African migrant hip-hop artists in the United States present representations of African migrant experiences, ties to home, and shifting transnational identities. African emcees who migrated to the United States present their own representations that differ from African artists who have only lived at home, or from African American artists who have lived only in the United States. In looking at the growing African population we need to understand the origins of the population growth. Increased African migration to the United States is linked to changes in both American and European immigration laws. It is also linked to the social and economic crises that occurred throughout Africa in the 1980s and 1990s (see chapter 2).

More recently, post-2000 African migrant experiences differ from the experiences of previous waves of African migrants to the United States. It is this population that many of the artists discussed in this chapter represent. It is important to look at the similarities and

"Make You No Forget": Representations of Migrant Experiences | 149

differences in the ways in which post-2000 migrant artists tell the migration experience, as compared to what we see in the poetry and literature of earlier African migrants. Through their music these post-2000 African migrants provide their own experiences of alienation, ties to home, and transnationalism.

These post-2000 migrant hip-hop artists also present additional considerations in the debate over Afropolitanism, a term that has recently emerged as a cultural identity for contemporary, mobile, transnational African migrants. Such transnational migrants have sometimes been called hypermobile or hypertransnational, referring to the fact that they are not tethered to one location (Liu 2011; Kilkey and Merla 2014; Ley 2013, Pottie-Sherman 2013). These artists bring together Afropolitanism and Pan-Africanism in a way that challenges the classism found in Afropolitanism, while acknowledging the need to recognize shifts in what it means to be African and to be a Pan-Africanist.

Migration

Since the 1980s the number of Africans migrating to American cities has grown exponentially. Despite continued migration to Europe, the numbers of Africans going there began to decrease in the 1990s, after peaking in the postindependence period through to the 1970s and 1980s (Weil and Crowley 1994; Guiraudon 2002; Opoku-Dapaah 2006). Soon European countries enacted laws that curbed the number of immigrants who could legally enter their countries. France, for example, began refusing the renewal of residency permits, deporting undocumented immigrants, and denying automatic citizenship to the children of immigrants who were born in that country (Guiraudon 2002; Okome 2002).

During the same time the United States began to liberalize its immigration policies, beginning with the Immigration and Nationality Act of 1965. Among other things, the act eliminated national origin, race, or ancestry as bases for immigration to the United States, abolishing the national origins quota system. The act also established a seven-category preference system for relatives of US citizens and permanent resident aliens in an effort to promote family reunification. This means that immigrants in America have been able to sponsor the immigration of relatives. The liberalization of US immigration laws, in conjunction with tighter immigration laws in Europe, is credited with the shift in focus for African immigrants from Europe to America.

And the increase in African immigrants to this country has been dramatic. For example, there were only 80,000 African immigrants living in the United States in 1970 (USCIS n.d.; Anderson 2015). The number of African immigrants living in America more than doubled, to 200,000, in 1980 and then grew to 364,000 in 1990 (USCIS n.d.; Anderson 2015). There was then another large spike, to 881,000, in 2000, and then to 1,380,000 in 2013 (Anderson 2015). These dramatically increasing numbers have sparked a lot of research and discussion on the growing African immigrant presence in this country.

Understanding the migration of Africans to the United States is crucial when looking at African hip-hop artists here. Some of these African artists have moved into traditionally African American enclaves, such as those in Atlanta, Houston, New York, and Washington, DC. In the Bronx borough of New York, where hip-hop emerged in the 1970s, one finds a large Ghanaian population and a neighborhood in the borough known as Little Accra (Beekman 2010; Halpern and McKibben 2014). Likewise, areas of Harlem are referred to as Little Senegal, and sections of Washington, DC, and Los Angeles have been dubbed Little Ethiopia.

Many of the hip-hop artists living in the United States live in close proximity to African Americans, in predominantly Black cities or predominantly Black neighborhoods. Their music is a reflection of these experiences. Many of these artists have produced music that is indistinguishable from much of the hip-hop produced in the States, including artists such as Just Lyphe (Zimbabwe/south-central Los Angeles), 2C (Liberia/Atlanta), Say'hu (Gambia/Charlotte, NC), and Big Sow (Ghana/Worcester, MA). Other artists blend African American and African sounds to create music that is African but that also reflects diaspora experiences. These artists have included Blitz the Ambassador (Ghana/Brooklyn), M.anifest (Ghana/Minneapolis), and Dumi Right

"Make You No Forget": Representations of Migrant Experiences | 151

(Zimbabwe/Washington, DC). Many of the African emcees living in the United States immigrated here at a young age, often under the age of twenty-five, which may account for the blended sounds. The literature suggests that younger migrants (college age and younger), as well as second-generation migrants, have stronger assimilation patterns in their host communities (Apraku 1991; Arthur 2000; Rong and Brown 2002).

Some African emcees migrated at a young age with their families, others came over as students, and others on immigrant visas. Many are among the majority of African migrants to have arrived after 1980 (Rong and Brown 2002; Diouf, n.d.; Wilson 2003). Others arrived later for school and are among the post-2000 migrants from Africa to the United States. Many of these African migrant experiences have been depicted in the lyrics of artists such as M.anifest's "Coming to America," K'naan's "15 Minutes Away," and Krukid's "Black Immigrant." Wale, the son of Nigerian immigrants, penned the song "'Cause I'm African" for his 2006 mixtape *Hate Is the New Love:*

> The pain of an immigrant
> I know it cause I been in it
> Payless nigga, my friends had Timberlands
> . . .
> That's African, tell me what you niggas know
> House smelling like fufu, my niggas at the door
> That's cold, but I'm African
> Some of ya'll niggas never had it as bad is this
> I rap like magic, my town on my back
> Got the backing of a continent.

These hip-hop artists often have representations of both host and home in their music. In songs about home, artists often reminisce about life in Africa—for example, 2C's "Liberian Girl" or Krukid's "City Life," in which he constructs images of the daily lives of the residents in Kampala, Uganda:

> And skewers spin rotisserie meat on a spit outside
> Locals stay, gettin' high though
> But stone-cold women

And even the major roads got potholes in them
Clubs open at dusk and don't close 'til dawn
And drunks stagger home as the cock crows in the morning.

In constructing these representations of life back home, the artists provide a visual for listeners of life in urban Africa. Songs like Minista of Agrikulcha's "Sweet Mother," K'naan's "My Old Home" and "Somalia," and Chosan's "Blood Diamonds" have depicted struggles and social issues back home, often juxtaposing them with life in the United States. Saucier's (2015) study of second-generation Cape Verdean migrants also talks about songs that celebrate home and Cape Verdean identities, even for those who have never been to Cape Verde.

K'naan

K'naan (fig. 5.1) was born in Mogadishu, Somalia, and left because of the civil war there. Fleeing the conflict in Somalia in 1991, K'naan arrived in the West at the age of thirteen, arriving in New York and then moving to Toronto (Cowie 2009). During his adolescence and early

Figure 5.1. K'Naan's 2009 performance at the Kennedy Center in Washington, DC. Photo by author.

adult life, K'naan lived in Somalia, Kenya, Canada, and the United States; which impacted his sound and lyrics. He mostly performs in English but has several songs in Somali as well. K'naan became exposed to hip-hop while in Somalia through records he received from family members in the United States (Cowie 2009). K'naan, in fact, credits hip-hop music with aiding in his mastery of the English language (Essence 2009). In "The African Way" (2006), K'naan talks about his introduction to hip-hop as a youth, saying he understood it as "the new poor people's weapon." In the same song he goes on to say that he was "a lyricist before I even spoke a word of English." K'naan used hip-hop as a tool to fashion for us an alternative story of Somalia, one that contradicted the story constructed by mainstream Western media.

In "My Old Home," from the album *Dusty Foot Philosopher*, K'naan remembers the food, sights, smells, and sounds of the Somalia of his youth. He paints an image of Somalia that celebrates the culture and people, but one that is often left out of media images of the country.

> Kids playing football with sand and a sock
> We had what we got, and it wasn't a lot
> No one knew they were poor, we were all innocent to grieve
>   judgment
> The country was combusting with life like a long hibernating
>   volcano
> With a long tale of success like J-Lo
> Farmers, fishers, fighters, even fools had a place in production
> The coastal line was the place of seduction
> The coral reef make you daze in reflection
> The women walked with grace and perfection
> And we just knew we were warriors too
> Nothing morbid, it's true.

He talks of an age of innocence for a young boy who grew up in a Somalia on the verge of implosion. The image of preconflict Somalia starkly contrasts with assumptions made about Somali society in the Western press. This is not the Somalia of Hollywood films like *Black Hawk Down*. The verse challenges the images of Somalia that have been constructed for us. In the song he describes that implosion with the line "And one day it came / Spoiled the parade like rain." K'naan describes the impact of the war on the people when in the chorus he says,

> Goodwill is looted, in my old home
> Religion is burned down, in my old home
> Kindness has been shackled, in my old home
> Justice has been raped, in my old home
> Murderers hold post,[1] in my old home
> The land vomits ghosts, in my old home.

Even in discussing the war, K'naan depicts the conflict as happening to the Somali people, against their will, not with their endorsement. K'naan's music contains several representations of life in Somalia, constructing images of the country that is often more multidimensional than the representations found in Western media outlets.

K'naan's music is also a representation of an African migrant that is connected with home, with their migrant community in the host country, as well as with other diaspora communities in the host country. K'naan's music frequently references the Somali community in the United States. In the song "I Come Prepared," with Damian Marley, he sings,

> I came solo I ain't even bring my army
> The type of niggas that are always ruining the party
> You know those socially inadequate Somalis
> Who walk in uninvited and you're VIP.

This excerpt plays on the reputations of Somali youth among some other African diaspora communities. The US media has run stories of young Somali men either traveling to Somalia to join al-Shabaab or getting involved in illegal activities in the United States. Among East African communities in Columbus, Ohio, which has a sizable Somali community, the young Somali men are often seen as troublemakers, who are often said to begin many of the fights at African parties held in the city. These lines are more a nod to Somali migrant populations and the reputations of Somali men among some African migrant communities.

"Make You No Forget": Representations of Migrant Experiences | 155

On his albums *Dusty Foot Philosopher* (2005) and *Troubadour* (2009), K'naan often presents the realities of life in Somalia while juxtaposing it with glorifications of the gangster lifestyle in mainstream US hip-hop culture. While in Somalia, K'naan's family lived in an area of Mogadishu called Wardhiigley, known as the River of Blood (Cowie 2009). This experience likely influenced songs like "Hardcore," in which he examines the glorification of the gangster lifestyle in African American hip-hop. In "What's Hardcore," K'naan raps,

> We begin our day by the way of the gun
> Rocket-propelled grenades blow you away if you front
> We got no police, ambulance, or firefighters
> We start riots by burning car tires
> They looting and everybody start shooting
> Bullshit politicians talking about solutions
> But it's all talk
> You can't go half a block without a roadblock
> You don't pay at the roadblock, you get your throat shot
> And each roadblock is set up by these gangsters
> And different gangsters go by different standards.

In the song K'naan transposes American ideas of gangsterism with Somalia's warlord-ruled society. This includes describing a war-torn Somalia devoid of many of the basic institutions even inner-city Americans benefit from, such as fire and rescue services. K'naan describes a society in which young boys brandishing AK-47s and chewing khat[2] control different parts of the city. But he also describes a society in which people live, work, and adjust to life without many of the basic structural and institutional protections in the United States. "What's Hardcore" is written from the perspective of a migrant but uses African American Vernacular English, which indicates a level of integration into African American culture.

K'naan does this again on the album *Troubadour* in the songs "T.I.A." (This Is Africa) and "Does It Really Matter?" Both songs provide reflection on the place of Africa in the diaspora imagination. In "T.I.A.," K'naan sets up the song by telling "rappers" he's taking them on a field trip, and he proceeds to describe "ghetto" life in a depiction that is meant to speak to the entire continent. In the two lines: "My Nigerian niggas would call you Pussy / My Somali niggas are quick to grab the uzi."

K'naan's use of the word *nigga* and description of aggression by young African men is claiming a space for urban African (male) youth in global hip-hop/ghetto culture. Within hip-hop culture, as discussed in previous chapters, strength, overt claims of masculinity, and bravado are often valued. In the same song K'naan, after claiming space for an African presence in hip-hop/ghetto culture, he distinguishes that space from others with the lines

> Around here we only bumping Fela Kuti
> Tupac, or Bob Marley, Lucky Dube
> So we don't really give a fuck about your groupies
> This Is Africa, Hooray.

In the tradition of hip-hop representation, in "T.I.A.," K'naan is representing the entire continent, claiming it as a space where hip-hop and ghetto culture exist, in a distinctly African sense.

In "Does It Really Matter?" K'naan again attempts to claim a space for African voices within hip-hop culture. The song questions whether it matters where an artist is from, if their "flow is hot," or where it is from "if the beat is hot." In the second verse K'naan connects prominent African American rappers with the locations they represent. He says that he could have been from Chi-Town (Chicago), like fast-rhyming Chicago emcee Twista "with a flow so sick it'll blow you to bits." Or he could have been from New York like pioneering emcee Rakim: "with my pen / I could get paid in full[3] / with praise and tools." He then says he could be from Los Angeles

> like Dre and Snoop[4]
> Rolling in my six-four with fresh case jewels
> And I'm riding on them niggas unless they cool
> And I got border troubles like them esés[5] fool.

He could be from "the dirty[6] like A-town[7] or MIA."[8] But he declares in the end, "I'm from Africa, where they say 'K'naan, boom-aye.'"[9]

Throughout K'naan's music he claims both African and diaspora spaces as his own. His music and lyrics represent Somali, African,

"Make You No Forget": Representations of Migrant Experiences | 157

and African American experiences. Much of this is captured in the video for "Soobax" on *The Dusty Foot Philosopher* album. The artist filmed the video on location in Nairobi, Kenya. The video is situated in a matatu station, where various buses are tagged with graffiti in the background. The crowds in the video are mostly Kenyan and Somali youth, with shots of young men dancing interspersed. Somali women dance prominently in the background of some of the scenes. The video takes us around Nairobi, where the viewer is shown images of life in the city's slums/ghettos. Most of the song is sung in Somali and infuses Somali rhythms.

In 2010, K'naan's 2009 song "Wavin' Flag" became the official anthem of the 2010 World Cup. This boosted his fame globally and turned K'naan into an international star. This stardom was followed by a disconnect with his core audience, witnessed on his 2012 album *Country, God or the Girl*. The album had a heavily commercial sound, was worked on by several pop music producers, featured several pop music collaborations, and resulted in a sound that, for many, signaled a sharp departure from K'naan's previous music. In *Country, God or the Girl* the artist's representations of Somalia, Africa, and the Diaspora were muted. In a revealing *New York Times* article, K'naan (2012) discusses the pressure of the music industry, and the censorship he faced in trying to create music that was representative of him and his experiences: "I had made an album in which a few genuine songs are all but drowned out by the loud siren of [the industry's] ambition." K'naan's 2012 album and article are important to this study in that they provide understandings of how representations can be co-opted. The article is also an important statement on the impact of mainstream media houses on the content of the media we consume.

Of the dozens of African emcees actively recording and performing in the United States, the majority rap in English. The artists who are second-generation migrants (like Wale) largely exclude representations of Africa from their mainstream music. Others remain outside the mainstream industry. Those who record their music primarily in African languages, like Saba Saba (Luganda), Wakazi (Swahili), and Waterflow Wagëblë (French/Wolof), see their primary audience as being outside the United States.

Post-2000 Migrants

The presence of African hip-hop artists among African immigrant communities in this country has provided new opportunities to understand changing migrant experiences and environments. Post-2000 migrants from Africa arrived in an environment affected by heightened security in a post-9/11 era, often resulting in a more vigorous enforcement of immigration laws and increased anti-immigrant sentiment. They also migrated during a time when improvements in technology, communication, and social media allowed for an altered relationship with both host and home. The hip-hop artists among these migrants have provided social commentary on their experiences, as well as on their place at home and in the diaspora. Their music has narrated the experiences of post-2000 African migrants and their increased internationalization.

These artists, through their music, provide a new and important link between the new African diaspora and home. By understanding hip-hop music as cultural representation, as a method by which African migrant experiences are constructed and depicted, we are able to examine the contributions of African hip-hop artists to our understandings of African migration experiences, feelings of alienation, and ties to home. A constructivist view of cultural representation asserts that our knowledge of everything is shaped by representations (Barker 2012; Hall 2013). Whether it is through a news broadcast, a history book, or a poem, our understandings of the world and how we identify with that world are shaped by representations. These representations construct for us the meanings that our understandings are based on. In addition, all representations emanate from a cultural system. So, while humans share many similar ways of processing certain cultural clues, our own cultural background (system) determines how we filter and process certain representations. When we understand the cultural system, we are better able to decipher the meanings being represented. This research, therefore, attempts to put in proper context the systems within which these artists operate, so that we better understand the meanings of the words and symbols they use.

"Make You No Forget": Representations of Migrant Experiences | 159

An examination of African hip-hop music and the cultural systems these artists use to construct narratives of African immigrant experiences also tells us a lot about who these artists are speaking to and what they want their audiences to know. When we examine the music of Ghanaian artists Samuel Bazawule (aka Blitz the Ambassador), Kwame Tsikata (aka M.anifest), Emmanuel Owusu-Bonsu (aka Wanlov the Kubolor), and Ugandan artist Edwin Ruyonga (aka Krukid, now Ruyonga), we see the ways in which their music depicts certain realities for African migrants in the United States. This depiction informs its audience of African immigrant realities, while at the same engaging fellow migrants, and would-be migrants, in conversations around those same realities.

Immigrant Chronicles: Coming to America

My people came on boats and planes
Some with passports, some stow away
Not knowing the future so we pray
In sha' Allah, things will be better
That's what we say when we write our letters.

—M.anifest, "Coming to America"

The migration patterns of Africans primarily revolve around desires for self-improvement (Arango 2000; Takougang 2003; Moore 2013). International migrants go in search of economic and educational opportunities that they believe they can find outside their home country. But several texts discuss the experiences of African migrants who come to the United States only to find economic, social, and legal hardship (Arango 2000; Takougang 2003; Dosi, Rushubirwa, and Myers 2007; Obiakor and Afoláyan 2007; Gonzalez 2007; Stebleton 2012). Studies by Dosi, Rushubirwa, and Myers (2007) and Stebleton (2012) focus on African college students studying in this country and the difficulties they face, including economic problems, socialization issues, and the struggle to maintain their status and stay in school. Stebleton found that African students often face discrimination and racism, which

160 | *Hip-Hop in Africa*

serve as barriers to "acculturation and acculturative stress" (2012, 54). These studies reinforce narratives created in the music of the four artists in this section, all of whom came to the United States to pursue a university education, and all of whom speak of the financial stresses and discrimination they experienced.

Songs with themes of immigration are not uncommon for a variety of musicians, poets, and artists. Many artists begin their narratives of the migrant experience prior to their departure from Africa.[10] The four artists in this section begin with their visions of life here, their expectations for their American lives, and the process of securing a visa to travel. The artists' imaginations of America as a land of opportunity were a large part of their decisions to migrate. Their music reflects the difficulties in getting the visa and the naiveté of many visa seekers about the realities of the United States.

In his first album, *Raisin in the Sun* (2005), Krukid begins with a conversation between two Africans reflecting on how much better life in the United States must be—a land rife with opportunities. The skit is a satirical look at visions of the American dream in Africa. This sentiment is revisited later when Krukid suggests that he beat the odds in being able to travel to the States. Two years later, in *Black Immigrant Mixtape* (2007), Krukid revisits his decision to migrate. He discusses migrating from Kampala, Uganda, to Champaign, Illinois, saying that he often felt "like a Black immigrant sneaking in past the government." On his album *Afr-I-Can* (2007) and since his return to Uganda, Krukid has continued to express the failure of the American dream for many African migrants.

Blitz the Ambassador (fig. 5.2) also reflects on his preimmigrant experience, lamenting in his song "Dying to Live" (2009) that he landed at "JFK with a duffle bag and a dream." In "Native Sun" (2011) Blitz portrays an almost depressing image of visa applicants: "we were all looking for a way out / Across the border / Lining up for visas like sheep to the slaughter." The use of this simile can be seen as both a comment on the visa application process and Blitz revealing his own naiveté about America when he applied for a visa.

M.anifest's second album, *Immigrant Chronicles: Coming to America* (2011), has five songs that address his immigration experience and

Figure 5.2. Blitz the Ambassador at a performance on the campus of the University of California, Los Angeles in 2010. Photo by author.

is almost an ode to African immigrant struggles in the United States. "Motherland," "Suffer," "Blue," "Motion Picture," and "Coming to America" all take the audience through his decision to go to America and the culture shock he experienced after arriving there.

M.anifest's lyrics present the harsh irony of thinking one has arrived, only to find a different type of suffering. In "Motion Picture" (2011) M.anifest sings,

> young dummy
> Thought it was the land of milk and honey
> Hunger pains in my tummy
> Why is everything about money?

The sense of disillusionment, combined with economic hardship, creates stresses for many African migrants. The economic stresses are tied to emotional and financial commitments in both the United States and Africa. In "Coming to America" they lead many to seek degrees, and others to commit crimes, such as internet and email scams. Similarly, in Wanlov's "Green Card" the artist says,

We fought to get off the slave yard
Now we fight to get us a green card
Why do we work for this stuff so hard?
How you living and you working graveyard?

All the artists discuss migrants trying to elude immigration officials in America, struggles to pay bills, and being forced to work low-wage jobs because of a lack of proper documentation. Again in "Green Card," Wanlov talks about running out of money and being told he needs to get a job. Because of his lack of papers (student visa holders are often not allowed to work off campus), he has only two options: work with someone else's papers or get paid under the table.

While most literature deals with Africans' experiences after their US arrival, several songs have focused on the visa process. The consular section at the US embassy in Ghana is often viewed as more difficult to navigate than other US consular sections in Africa, especially in its treatment of applicants, a lack of assistance in understanding procedure, and a seeming disregard for the applicants' wait times. The treatment of visa applicants in Ghana has also been a topic discussed in the Ghanaian press. Pascal Kafuabotsi (2015) writes, "Complaints have also been made about how unfriendly the interviewers are, to visa applicants . . . they shout and scream at applicants as if they are third class humans." In an op-ed in the *Guardian*, Nana Sekyiamah (2013) cites the high refusal rates at the US embassy in Accra. Ghanaian immigration lawyer Opoku Acheampong (2015) claims, "Ghana ranks as one of the countries with the highest B visa[11] refusal rates in the world," a rate higher than that of Nigeria.

Negative experiences at the consular section at the US embassy often become the migrant's first official experience with United States immigration, as reflected in Blitz the Ambassador's "Native Sun." Ghana-based Ghanaian musician Reggie Rockstone also talks about the difficulty of getting a visa from the US embassy in his song "Visa." And in "Green Card," Wanlov the Kubolor (fig. 5.3) says,

Stand for days
At the American consulate
They're running late

"Make You No Forget": Representations of Migrant Experiences | 163

Figure 5.3. Wanlov the Kubolor in the Osu area of Accra in 2010. Photo by author.

Push back your interview date
So you won't stay
They ask for a bank slate
Meant to bring one
Forgot
Now they close gates
Bills ain't paid
Money spent on visa fees
You crying
Landlady standing vis-à-vis
C'est la vie, mon ami
Ask Uncle Kofi
Maybe he's got connections at the embassy.

Wanlov has been extremely outspoken about his own immigration experiences: the difficulty of getting a visa, his detention, and his recent problems securing a visa. The introspective piece "Laredo" (2007) relates his experience with immigration and law enforcement officials in Texas, where he was studying at the time. The song starts with Wanlov getting pulled over by the police and later being handed over to immigration officials. Wanlov, whose legal immigration status had expired, was taken to a private detention facility in Laredo, which he describes as no better than a prison where people are stranded with little or no resources. Wanlov is one of the first hip-hop artists from Africa to depict their experiences in a US immigrant detention facility. Wanlov had the resources to secure bail and was able to leave the facility. He later decided to go back to Ghana rather than stay and fight the immigration case. In the song he reflects that he could not believe that he was locked up simply for not paying school fees.[12] In the song he goes on to talk about the slow deportation process and the money being made off the detainees.

All the artists' experiences in this study reflect a post-9/11 environment, where stricter, sometimes repressive views of migrants often result in them being criminalized. Many languish in detention centers waiting for trial. Some border states, like Arizona and Texas, have seen stricter enforcement of federal immigration laws but much of

"Make You No Forget": Representations of Migrant Experiences | 165

the vigorous enforcement can be attributed to states, municipalities, and corporations that make money from detaining migrants (Flynn and Cannon 2009; Veney 2009). While many African migrants are detained for being "out of status," there are a growing number of African migrants from Ghana, Nigeria, and Somalia who are flying into Latin America and then traveling to the United States by land. Many of these migrants are detained in border state facilities in places like Arizona, Texas, and California. Being detained by immigration is a traumatic experience for migrants, but it is not the only stress they face.

Alienation

Grant Farred presents the concept of "out of contextness" to describe the diaspora experience as a sense of not having a home and of not being completely at home in any location after prolonged absences: "to live diasporically is to recognize the condition of living without the possibility of a singular context" (2010, 263). He points to expressions of "out of contextness" found in literature and music from diasporic artists who express feelings of being alienated from their homeland and feeling distressed in their host culture. Several scholarly works since the 1990s have also taken up the topic of alienation among contemporary African immigrants in the West (Nwadiora 1995; Arthur 2000; Rong and Brown 2001; S. Lewis 2006; Burns 2009). James Burns's discussion of the works of Ghanaian performers articulates these feelings of "out of contextness" or alienation. Burns asserts that for Ghanaian musicians of the postcolonial generation, "a new subject for the blues became the difficulties faced by Ghanaians living abroad" (2009, 128).

The music of African hip-hop artists in the United States further constructs the experience of "out of contextness" or alienation, specifically among post-9/11 young, male African migrants to the United States. There are important similarities to the depictions of alienation found in colonial (Léopold Senghor's "A la mort" in 1938) and postcolonial (Syl Cheney-Coker's *Concerto for an Exile* in 1973) poetry written by earlier African migrants (Soyinka 2001; S. Lewis 2006; Oripeloye 2012). These earlier migrants describe similar feelings of loneliness, frustration with racism and discrimination, and longing memories of home.

Sylvia Bâ (1973) looks at the experience of alienation articulated in the poetry of West African and West Indian migrants, especially Senghor, for whom exile is a major theme (Bâ 1973; Jaji 2014). Senghor's work often deals with the "constant ordeal of the Black man in a White world" (Bâ 1973, 28). Like the hip-hop artists in this study, Senghor also dealt with the physical separation from family and culture. Bâ (1973) translates excerpts of Senghor's poems "Hosties noires" and "Chants d'ombre," in which Senghor's laments are similar to the words penned by African hip-hop artists living in the Unites States.

> Bless you, Mother!
> I hear your voice when I am left to the stealthy silence of this
>   European night
> Prisoner of my cold, white, tightly drawn sheets, of all the
>   woes that weigh me down inextricably
> . . .
>   . . . the anguish
> That makes me cry out at midnight down to my trembling
>   imprisoned toes.

The emotions expressed by Senghor can be felt in K'naan's "Voices in My Head":

> The shit that I'm in and the pain, I'm literally going insane
> I'm frightened, my heart and my head have been fightin'
> I'm certain that it's hurtin' the rest of my body
> Them voices as loud as Manhattan come chattin'

These two African artists, of two different generations, spaces, and time, experience and express similar feelings of alienation. Bâ looks at the creation of the Negritude movement by poets like Senghor as an attempt "to rejoin the family, to re-establish contact with the land, to understand and be understood restored the exile to his original integrity" (1973, 42).

There are also important differences in the types of alienation experienced by colonial and postcolonial (early-twentieth-century and mid-twentieth-century) artists and poets. Improved communication, new technology, and social media have all had an impact on the ways in which migrants reconnect with home. Many twenty-first-century African migrants are arriving in cities with already flourishing African communities. These communities have religious and civic associations, grocery stores, restaurants, and clothing shops, which may lessen the difficulties of separation for many. Many migrants are therefore able to maintain an existence between these two communities through social media and improvements in technology. Improved technology (email, Skype) and social media (Facebook, Twitter) are therefore allowing "migrants to be both in Diaspora and at home" (Nzegwu 2009, 361). This does indeed change, but does not eliminate, the feelings of alienation among African migrants.

In his song "Motion Picture," M.anifest describes the emotional impact of being an African in a hostile land: "In Ghana I was a human being'o / Here I'm an alien, a martian Mandingo." M.anifest's "Blue" and Wanlov's "Smallest Time" also deal with the profound sense of alienation they feel as African migrants in America. The hook for "Smallest Time" shows mourning: "My people I dey greet you / Africa I miss you / I dey come o." In "Smallest Time," Wanlov goes on to say,

> Then my mind be say I dey go some better yard
> I never know say there hard
> Sometimes I got so lonely
> Wanted to see my family
> Spent money on phone calls
> Voices helped me cross those pitfalls
> Oh chale, where my posses dey
> I don't know if I can make it through another day.

"Blue" is told in the voice of the immigrant longing for home, for the food and culture of his people. M.anifest reminisces over eating kelewele and fufu,[13] and of walking barefoot. He talks about seeing images of Ghanaian food and culture in his dreams, and even talks of missing hearing the cock crow in the morning. The chorus, which is sung in Pidgin, laments on the overwhelming feelings of nostalgia, and the blues, for home. In the song "Blue" by M.anifest the artist says,

I got dirty feet that I tap on this dirty beat
Many men never heard of me
But certainly if they follow my trajectory
They would find that I'm royalty
And the younger me
Wants to climb on a mango tree
And I miss me feeling free
And I miss me eating that Kelewele
Girls shaking their wele right in front of me
And I miss me walking barefooted and innocent
Talking pidgin, Ghanaian citizen
Pounding of fufu, I miss the beat
And I miss them calling me Dadabee, (Haye!)
Home is where my heart is
Torn from home, could be so heartless
Visual memoirs of a travelling artist
Case of the blues I got it the baddest.

In their songs Blitz the Ambassador, Wanlov the Kubolor, and Krukid have all used the sound of the cock crowing as a symbol for home. The sound, familiar throughout Africa, ties them to their memories of home. Other symbols include food, music, and familiar landmarks. In M.anifest's video for "Coming to America," shot in Minneapolis, he presents himself as an outsider, as a new arrival who is different from everyone else. In one scene we see M.anifest on a commuter train wearing African clothing and jewelry, and holding a "Ghana-must-go" bag. He is clearly showing himself as an outsider, as someone in a foreign culture surrounded by people who do not look like him. Of the symbols he uses to separate himself from everyone else, one of the most impactful is the "Ghana-must-go" bag, an instantly recognizable item for many Africans. These large, cheap (less than $10) plastic bags with checkered patterns are called many things throughout Africa. Anyone traveling in Africa will find them tied atop long distance buses, holding a market seller's goods, or used as storage in people's homes. While they can be bought in America, they are mostly found in shops that cater to immigrant communities, making the use of the bag a salient symbol for otherness in America.

Within the music of these migrant artists there are feelings of alienation, but importantly there is also a rejection of assimilation, of losing one's Africaness, which is a dominant theme, particularly with Wanlov, who raps primarily in Pidgin. Wanlov's "Asem," partly in Twi and partly in Pidgin, paints an image of his daily life in America. He talks about the stereotypes of Africans and those who judge him based on his looks. "Choptime" tells his listeners to "forget your fork, your spoon, your knife," suggesting that he is more comfortable eating with his hands. "Gentleman" is a collaboration between Wanlov and M.anifest. In it both declare their pride in an African identity, but do so while holding that identity up against more so-called refined European aesthetics. The chorus is sung in Pidgin and declares: "I no be gentleman at all'o / I be African man original." The song signals the retention of an African identity, of African culture and aesthetics in the face of pressures to adopt a more "civilized," Western, or gentlemanly identity and demeanor. In the song Wanlov declares, "In our simplicity we are elegant / So to us your coat and tie are irrelevant / Give up my culture for your religion? I can't."

In the face of alienation, there is a definite rejection of assimilation. Many see the goal for many migrants as partial or full assimilation into American culture, often considered the natural progression for African migrants navigating host and home (Shaw-Taylor 2007; Moore 2013). For all of the artists studied, there is an emphasis on representing their national (and continental) identities, and rejecting assimilation.

Using hip-hop culture, with its roots in urban Black America, the artists are able to reemphasize African identities. A foundation of hip-hop lies in representation—representing who one is, where one is from. Location and origins are at the core of a hip-hop artist's identity. Representation within hip-hop therefore means linguistically, lyrically, and ascetically an artist represents a particular location. In hip-hop, artists often talk about where they are from, give stories of their hometown, and boast of coming from a certain city. Thus, hip-hop may have provided African artists a tool to assert both Pan-African and African identities. For example, all the artists use hip-hop/African American vernacular to express African immigrant experiences; to discuss alienation, struggle, and ties to home.

Ties to Home

Studies have found that familial and community ties are strong among African (and other) migrants (Dosi, Rushubirwa, and Myers 2007; Stebleton 2012; Okome 2012). These ties come with responsibilities that include sending money home, calling home regularly, and helping relatives planning to travel to the United States (Stebleton 2012; Okome 2012). Ties to home have impacted the decisions of many immigrants to return home (Okome 2012). Other factors include economic and legal problems in this country and economic opportunities at home. Okome's (2012) look at reverse migration among African immigrants suggests that economic opportunities at home drive a lot of reverse migration. Okome points in part to economic opportunities, family ties, and feelings of nostalgia to explain return. The artists in this study fall into that pattern, though at least one, Wanlov, has been open about his immigration problems as a partial cause for his return to Ghana.

While critical of social and political issues in both the United States and their home countries, the artists in the study paint a much more positive image of their ties to home. Krukid's album *Afr-I-Can* is his last before returning to Uganda. On it, he seems to reclaim his Ugandan roots, and delves a bit more into the immigration experience. Even though he acknowledges that he chose to leave Uganda, he still laments on the pain of not being with his family. He expresses values of "we are, therefore I am" in talking about the support system that exists within his family and community in Uganda. In almost a prelude to his return to Uganda, he also reflects on life and the importance of his journey.

All the artists talk about the importance of buying phone cards to call home and of the need to send money home. Krukid's song "Family" talks about calling home and feeling helpless when he hears about problems back home. Wanlov's "Smallest Time" reflects on spending money on phone cards just to hear familiar voices. Wanlov directs the lyrics of this song to Africans living in America who are also missing home. In "Suffer" (2011) and "Coming to America" (2011), M.anifest also speaks of ties to home. "Coming to America" goes into the pressure to send money home and adjusting to life in America, including the difficulties of adjusting to school, language barriers, "phone cards, long distance, broken hearts." Blitz the Ambassador's "Call Waiting" features Benin-born, US-based artist Angélique Kidjo. The song is a telephone conversation between a son (Blitz) and his mother (Kidjo). The son talks about the money he sent, the difficulties in paying rent, and his plan to permanently return to Ghana. The song depicts the pain of separation for mother and son, with the son offering serious contemplation on returning home.

The decisions to return home were forecast in the music of the four musicians. For example, after his arrival in the United States, Blitz released an album and two EPs. In all those projects, he sang almost exclusively in English. In his 2011 album *Native Sun*, he includes more African rhythms as well as verses and whole songs sung in Twi. *Native Sun* was a conscious move toward a more Ghanaian sound, something that is also reflected in Blitz's lyrics. All four of the artists have since returned home, either permanently or temporarily. All four have also tapped back into the local music scene, where they started their careers before leaving for America. Wanlov was the first to move back home, returning to Ghana in 2007. Krukid returned to Uganda in 2011 and M.anifest moved back to Ghana in 2012, while Blitz the Ambassador travels between Ghana and the Unites States regularly.

Since their return to Africa the music of the artists reflects almost a reimmersion into their home cultures. This is heard in lyrics and accents that celebrate home, as well through collaborations and projects with local artists. In Krukid/Ruyonga's (fig. 5.4) postreturn songs "Pearl City Anthem" (2013) and "Here I Come," he sings lines like "oh UG how I missed you" and "man it's so good to be home." In reference to his earlier song "City Life," he sings about what has and has not changed in Kampala. "City Life," "Pearl City Anthem" and "Here I Come" are a celebration of life in Kampala, of a typical urban scene in Africa. Upon returning to Ghana, Wanlov the Kubolor linked up with M3NSA, a Ghanaian hip-hop artist based in London, to form Fokn Bois. Wanlov always performed in Pidgin, and continues to do so. He has, however, become known for always wearing an African wrapper around his waist and never wearing shoes. Wanlov has expressed a rejection not only of Western values but also of what he sees as Westernized African values.

172 | *Hip-Hop in Africa*

Figure 5.4. Ruyonga (formerly known as Krukid) in Kampala in 2013. Photo by author.

While the three who have permanently returned have embarked on numerous local projects, they do contribute interesting questions on the possibility of return. All may still be seen as outsiders by some in their home country, and all have found that simply returning and declaring your intentions to stay have not been enough to gain full acceptance. Wanlov and M.anifest have embarked on projects in other parts of Africa and Europe as well. Blitz the Ambassador maintains a home in Brooklyn, New York, but has also toured and done projects throughout Africa, Europe, Asia, and Latin America. This leads to the final discussion of this research. Some may argue that these artists have not simply returned home, that they have become part of, and represent, a growing number of transnational Africans. Through their music they construct identities that are rooted in Africa but that express transnational experiences. They use Twi, Pidgin, or Luganda, along with African American dialects. They use African rhythms, jazz, and hip-hop beats in their music. They often use hip-hop/African American idioms to construct African experiences, and do all this in a manner that reflects ownership of African and hip-hop culture.

"Make You No Forget": Representations of Migrant Experiences | 173

Afropolitan Dreams

> I represent African with a spectacular street vernacular.
>
> —M.anifest, "Represent"

The artists in this study represent a growing number of transnational Africans. Their experiences are similar to what Thomas Owusu (2006) found in his study of transnationalism among Ghanaian migrants in Canada. In this sense transnationalism is looked at as ties maintained between host and home countries. According to Owusu, transnationalism describes most African migrant experiences, which are defined by regular communication with, and travel to, home countries. This transnationalism includes regular remittances, participation in social and political discussions at home, and plans to return home. Owusu study found that 75 percent of respondents had returned to visit Ghana, with many returning several times.

There is no question that a discussion of transnational Africans necessitates examinations of class. Many migrants are working jobs that do not provide the needed income to regularly travel home, nor do they have the immigration papers that would allow them to return to the United States if they leave. Though all the artists in this study came from middle- to upper-income families, while they were in the America there was a definite loss in status. Their experiences and conditions were similar to other migrants. After developing successful music careers, these artists gained access to resources in order to travel, and to become more transnational. Now, most of the artists travel regularly between not only their home and host countries, but other countries as well. They have developed transnational, global, "Afropolitan" identities.

The term Afropolitan, often used to describe Africans who are transnational (or cosmopolitan, can be traced to Achille Mbembe's (2001) article "Ways of Seeing: Beyond the New Nativism," which was an introduction for a special edition of the *African Studies Review*. Mbembe does not use the term Afropolitan but discusses Africa's renaissance and cosmopolitanism. He credits much to the emergence of cosmopolitan culture in postapartheid South Africa, which attracted migrants and influenced other African metropolises. The term itself was coined and popularized by Taiye Tuakli-Wosornu's 2005 article "Bye-Bye Babar." Tuakli-Wosornu focuses her discussion on the manifestation of that cosmopolitanism in the arts, culture, and fashion. Later Mbembe (2007) and Chielozona Eze (2014) would provide an academic context for the term.

There are several definitions of the term Afropolitan. Most definitions describe Afropolitans as Africans who (1) are multicultural in their expressions (fashion, language, dining), (2) are at home in a variety of international settings, (3) are academically or financially successful in diverse fields, (4) are a product of the migrants that left Africa from the 1960s to the 1980s or middle- to upper income Africans at home, (5) have spent a lot of time traveling between the West and Africa, and (6) have a unique relationship with Africa, in a way that allows them to both critique and celebrate Africa (Tuakli-Wosornu 2005; Makokha 2010; Tutton 2012).

The term has come under heavy criticism for its glorification of the lives of African elites, its celebration of Africanizing Western products, its embrace of consumer capitalism, and its classism, which is all disconnected from the lives of most Africans (Santana 2013; Tveit 2013). Indeed, many celebrations of Afropolitanism focus on materialism. The term does, however, bring up some important observations of a growing population of transnational Africans. Not only does the term Afropolitan describe many of Owusu's (2006) transnational Africans, it also describes Africans whose experiences include three or more countries besides their native country.

Temporarily setting aside the elitism in Afropolitanism, Tuakli-Wosornu's text roots Afropolitanism in migrant experiences and feelings of alienation from both home and host. The author focuses primarily on African migrants growing up in the West, growing up confronted with negative images of Africa and Africans. The social impact of the African migrant having to bear the familiar tropes of the poor, barely civilized African is partially responsible for Afropolitan identities (Tuakli-Wosornu 2005; Tutton 2012). Afropolitan identities allow migrants to create a counternarrative that challenges those familiar tropes, a counternarrative that presents an Africa that

"Make You No Forget": Representations of Migrant Experiences | 175

is trendy, cool, savvy, and international. This counternarrative of the trendy African should not be overlooked, given the significant role it serves as a response to and defense against the barely civilized African. Among these transnational African migrants there is also a sense of alienation from home, a difficulty in returning home as an insider when confronted with multiple cues that signal one's foreignness.

> Most of us grew up aware of "being from" a blighted place, of having last names from countries which are linked to lack, corruption. Few of us escaped those nasty "booty-scratcher" epithets, and fewer still that sense of shame when visiting paternal villages. Whether we were ashamed of ourselves for not knowing more about our parents' culture, or ashamed of that culture for not being more "advanced" can be unclear. (Tuakli-Wosornu 2005)

Scholarly support for Afropolitan identities may also position Afropolitanism as a psychosocial response to African tropes, either directly or as subtext. According to Miriam Pahl (2016), Mbembe and Eze present Afropolitanism as "an alternative to Afropessimism," or the view that Africa will continually be seen as problematic, destined to be plagued by poverty and corruption. Mbembe (2007) and Eze (2014) assert that Afropolitanism rejects this view of Africa and Africans as "victims." The Afropolitan African is now seen as having "a voice" and "agency" (Eze 2014; Pahl 2016). The Afropolitan proves this, in part, in their assimilation with global cultures, presenting a narrative of Africa that replaces the one constructed in Afropessimism. Tsitsi Jaji says that artists often use their narratives to challenge the monopolization of "the narration and documentation of history" (2014, 193).

Eze asserts that "being African has little to do with blood or skin colour; rather it has much more to do with moral topography, with how one positions oneself vis-à-vis the other people on that continent" (2014, 244). Advocates for defining an African identity as a nonracial hybrid cultural identity reject Pan-African identities, and claims of certain diaspora communities to an African identity. Pahl says that

Mbembe and Eze's reconstructions of African identities expressly reject what they call "nativism" and its attempts to maintain "cultural and racial purity and tradition" (2016, 76). Mbembe (2001, 2007) and Eze (2014, 2016) seem to promote hybrid identities that result in new, blended identities, versus the adoption of multiple identities. Chris Barker and Dariusz Galasiński (2001) discuss the concept of hybridity and identify two types of hybridity. The first results from "the mixing of difference and the production of the new" (159), resulting in a British-Ghanaian, or Mbembe and Eze's Afropolitan. The second type of hybridity results in a simultaneous identification with multiple cultures, resulting in a British and Ghanaian. Managing multiple identities was discussed in a review of scholarship on code-switching, cultural frame switching (CFS), and bicultural identity integration (BII) for an earlier publication on bicultural Black populations in America (Clark 2012b). The ability to code switch, or cultural frame switching, relates to the accessing "of multiple meaning systems and switching between different culturally appropriate behaviors depending on the context" (Jackson 2006, 67). Data suggests that the successful ability to manage multiple cultural identities results in an individual who is able to comfortably exist in multiple cultural environments, to possess "a positive perspective of each culture," and to "effectively communicate verbally and/or non-verbally" in each culture (Clark 2012b, 54). The Afropolitan's need for redefining "African" is connected to the dilemma of returning home, and to the sense of alienation abroad.

The dismissal of Pan-African identities, and the promotion of a postracialesque, multicultural utopia by scholars like Mbembe (2007) and Eze (2014, 2016), has largely caused a backlash against Afropolitanism. This backlash was first led by Binyavanga Wainaina's 2012 speech "I Am a Pan-Africanist, Not an Afropolitan," which provides an important critique of the term and its implication for a Pan-African identity (Santana 2013).

Critiques of Afropolitanism have also been raised around its disconnect from the masses of Africans, on the continent and abroad, who are less mobile. Emma Dabiri (2016) compares Afropolitanism to feminism, whose leaders have not acknowledged their own class and race privilege. In the case of Afropolitans it would be privilege based on class and mobility. There is also little acknowledgment of the underlying class implications, in which privilege and class are the subtexts used to make a case for a postracial utopia, in spite of significant evidence to the contrary. It is perhaps a *need* for a postracial utopia that makes some invested in stressing hybrid identities.

Despite Mbembe and Wainaina's criticisms, Pan-African and Afropolitan identities may not be mutually exclusive. Neither Mbembe nor Wainaina addresses the politicization of Afropolitans, as evidenced by their work and activism in community groups, grassroots movements, NGOs, . . . and through their art. The artists in this research express both Pan-African and Afropolitan identities.

The term Afropolitanism has, however, grown in popularity. The global popularity in the term's use has produced the Afropolitan Week of Fashion and Arts in Toronto, Afropolitan Sundays in Philadelphia, the AfropolitanDC Afro-Caribbean Mixer in Washington, DC, Afropolitan Vibes in Lagos, "Afropolitan" parties at Khao Suay in Paris, and the Afropolitan Dance Party in Oxford. Largely because of Afropolitanism's focus on consumerism and aesthetics, African literature and pop culture produced by "Afropolitans" have come under scrutiny. This includes criticisms of popular magazines like *Afropolitan* and *Arise* and entertainment programming like the YouTube series *An African City*.

Contemporary African literature has been especially hailed as an "Afropolitan renaissance." Teju Cole's (2007) *Every Day Is for the Thief*, Chimamanda Adichie's (2013) *Americanah,* and Taiye Selasi's *Ghana Must Go* have all been named as being among the texts leading this renaissance. Wainaina is especially critical of the "Afropolitan African novel," which he sees as being produced by and for "fellow Afropolitans" (Santana 2013). Many contemporary transnational African authors are categorized as Afropolitan due to their transnational lifestyles and the transnational themes of their literary works (Makokha 2010; Lee 2014; Dabiri 2016; Pahl 2016). Dabiri (2016) points out, however, that criticism of Afropolitanism has led some authors to distance themselves from the term, specifically Chimamanda Adichie, who used the term "African internationality" to describe trends of African mobility and transnationalism.

Books by authors labeled Afropolitan often explore African transnational experiences, while focusing mostly on representations of university-educated, multinational, financially secure African migrants. The books often present transnational experiences of multidimensional African characters who often have an inability to relate to less-mobile and lower-income African migrants and Africans at home, who are presented with much less depth and complexity.

In *Every Day Is for the Thief*, Teju Cole's construction of a Nigerian migrant's experience, the readers' introduction to the character begins with his return home. The main character's struggle with his return is played out in a series of experiences with poverty, corruption, and inefficiency. The main character is highly critical of Nigeria, speaking with the authority of a Nigerian who, with the benefit of education and wealth, can now see and articulate the flaws in his society. By comparison, while the musicians in this study come from similar socioeconomic backgrounds as Cole (as well as Adichie and Selasie), their music is more likely to address the complexities of return, of the contradictions found in the weak economic structures that exists alongside strong social structures. In the music there are strong criticisms of Africa but also attempts to construct an Africa that contradicts the single story. The musicians in this study, unlike many of the authors, also differ in that within their music they identify more with lower-income Africans and African Americans, and are often critical of American racism and its various manifestations.

Like the artists in this study, these African transnationals differ from the Africans who came to the United States in the 1960s and 1970s, as well as those that came in the 1980s and 1990s. On the migrants that came here in the 1980s, Takougang says that "unlike their counterparts in the 1960s and 70s who were anxious to return home after acquiring an American education in order to contribute in the task of nation building, an overwhelming majority of recent immigrants are more interested in establishing permanent residency in the United States" (2003, 1). This post-2000 group of migrants has learned and benefited from earlier migrations, as well as improvements in technology and communication that allowed them to maintain and expand transnational linkages. Some have moved back to Africa, some have stayed in the West, but many spend time traveling between the West, Africa, and other regions. Whether they have dual citizenship, permanent residency, US citizenship, or a visa, the question of home and return differs for them in some important ways.

In an interview with National Public Radio, Blitz the Ambassador credits Taiye Selasi and her 2005 article as the inspiration for his use of the term to describe himself and his 2014 album *Afropolitan Dreams:* "I was looking for something that described who I was in terms of being young, being creative and being global. But at the end of the day, I felt what the Afropolitan part of it really revolves around returning home" (Bazawule 2014). Blitz, a socially conscious artist, also claims a Pan-African identity, as in the title of the press release for his 2011 album *Native Sun:* "Diasporighteousness: Blitz the Ambassador Brings the Pan-African Noise with Native Sun." Blitz uses his music to address racial oppression of African Americans and Africans. In addition to his use of African American Vernacular English, his use of other African influences includes Swahili in the songs "Uhuru" and "Victory" to address political struggle, while the song "Wahala" channels Fela, and features artists from Brazil and the Democratic Republic of the Congo. Blitz claiming an Afropolitan and a Pan-African identity challenges both Mbembe's and Wainaina's assertions that the two identities are not compatible. In addition, his representations of migrant experiences of lower-income migrants as well as experiences of inner-city African Americans differ significantly from the representations presented by Afropolitan authors Adichie, Cole, and Selasi.

Other artists in this study see Afropolitanism as a movement or a direction that African (hip-hop) music is headed in, though they tend to express different views on what Afropolitanism means. In 2012, M.anifest spoke of the term Afropolitan in an interview discussing the future of African music. While not defining the term, he looked at it as expressing the global connectedness of African music (M.anifest 2012). In 2013, Krukid/Ruyonga called his music "Afropolitan rap," saying that it "infuses aspects of different African cultures to hip hop" (Semwezi 2013). Krukid/Ruyonga said that this was the direction African hip-hop was headed, and away from a simple imitation of American rap. In 2014, Wanlov and M3NSA performed at Afropolitan Vibes, a monthly music concert held in Lagos and spoke of the platform the concerts provide as being symbolic of a movement that is spreading across Africa and abroad (Afropolitan Vibes 2014).

While the term *Afropolitans* has been associated with elitism, it does speak to a changing African migrant experience and shifting African identities. For many transnationals home has been redefined. They can no longer return home and pick up where they left off. Home has changed, and so have they. So while allegiances continue to be to home countries, they have formed identities that are uniquely transnational but whose complexities are not adequately captured by *Afropolitanism*.

GRANT FARRED (2010) discusses the important linkages between culture and the diaspora, saying that culture articulates the experiences of the diaspora. Through the music of African hip-hop artists certain African migrant experiences are constructed. They are constructed through lyrics that inform the listener of African migrant experiences and the idea of return. Burns (2009) discusses how the music of Ghanaian artists in the diaspora changes over time, as it reflects contact with difference influences. He describes how artists often develop Pan-African identities in addition to national ones. Because of their involvement with hip-hop music and culture before migrating, the African hip-hop artists in this study started developing Pan-African identities earlier, and that those identities were reinforced once in the United States.

Perhaps because of these experiences and influences, these artists have also had to find their audience, who are often fellow transnationals. The return home often means negotiating a space within the local music scene for a voice that combines experiences from local and international contexts. In a 2014 interview with nydjlive.com (2014), Wanlov has stated that he has had problems connecting with Ghanaian audiences, that he and M3NSA were "treated as outcasts" (nydjlive.com 2014). In June 2016 a feud developed between M.anifest and fellow Ghanaian rapper Sarkodie. In addition to the dis tracks that sparked and fed the feud, much of the language coming from Sarkodie and his fan base focuses on M.anifest's time in the United

States and his right to claim his space in the Ghanaian hip-hop scene. Conversations around the style of English M.anifest uses, or the way he wears Ghanaian-print clothes, seek to depict M.anifest as a "returnee" who has become somewhat of an outsider. In conversations with Ghanaians in Ghana, several indicated that they did not fully understand or relate to much of the music of Blitz the Ambassador or M.anifest. All these artists are negotiating their place, influenced by both home and diaspora; their music differs in that the narratives they construct speak to transnational experiences of, especially, post-2000 African migrants.

The voices of African hip-hop artists among those post-2000 migrants have allowed for the construction of new narratives of African migrant experiences. US-based African hip-hop artists represent a coalescence of African and diaspora experiences and identities. Positioned at an intersection of both African and African American cultures, they are simultaneously alienated from both. It is thus through their music that a certain African immigrant experience is constructed, one connected to both diaspora and home. And it is through the artists themselves that we understand the impact of African migrant experiences on the idea of home and the importance of return.

African hip-hop weaves several narratives of African immigrant experiences and serves as commentary on broader discussions of migration, diaspora experiences, alienation, identity, and return. These US-based African hip-hop artists construct a reality of African immigrant experiences in America, contributing to existing literature on both African migration and the resonance of cultural representation. African hip-hop artists depict certain realities of African migrants in the United States, as well as the place of diaspora and home in African immigrant identities. This depiction informs its audience of African immigrant realities, while at the same time engaging fellow migrants, and would-be migrants, in conversations around those same realities.

> People of African descent are getting their voices heard . . . we're speaking for ourselves, so we can tell our stories.
>
> —Blitz the Ambassador (pers. comm., August 24, 2011)

6

"Brkn Lngwjz"

Language, Identity, and Cultural Appropriation

ACCORDING TO LEE Watkins (2012) and Williams and Stroud (2013, 2014), emcees use language to claim authenticity, "to reflect their roots, their social standing, and their multiplicity" (Watkins 2012, 66). An artist's language and appropriate use of cultural cues and symbols reinforce or contradict their claims of authenticity. This practice in hip-hop is also mentioned by Tanure Ojaide (2007) in his discussion of poetry—that a writer's own origins are important and reflected in their work. Ojaide (2007) sees the African writer as a voice for their people and as spokesmen/women for the poor and against government. Ojaide stresses that the African writer must represent Africa in a way that is honest. The importance of representation and authenticity in hip-hop mean that the African hip-hop emcee is also supposed to honestly represent their hood, their city, their country, and their continent; Blitz the Ambassador talks about having the entire "continent on my back."

Within hip-hop, representation is a core principle of the culture. Hip-hop culture stresses "keeping it real" and representing where you're from and who you are. Within hip-hop culture artists represent both specific locations and cultures, as well as a broader hip-hop culture, which is rooted in the urban Black experience. Hip-hop culture in Africa manifests in a hybrid of local African and global hip-hop cultures.

Hip-hop in Africa has produced communities in which youth often share cultural identities that, as Stuart Hall (1990) would say, are specific to the context within which their representations are created.

Hall's (1990) discussion on Black identities can be applied to participants of hip-hop culture in Africa. According to Hall, cultural identities are made up of two factors. First is the shared or collective self, in which common experiences and "shared cultural codes" can be seen in the ownership of a global Black identity (Hall 1990, 223). According to Catherine Appert, "for local rappers, their marginalized experiences of urban postcoloniality create a sense of contemporary connection with African American youth" (2016, 294). As such, many youth in urban Africa have cultivated shared identities through claims to a global hip-hop (Black) culture. The shared use of hip-hop slang and symbolism, as well as the shared experiences in urban environments, and sometimes confrontational relationships with the state, have developed shared cultural identities among hip-hop heads globally.

The second factor in the development of our cultural identities outlined by Hall (1990) is the differences that emerge from space and time. While African hip-hop heads may have ownership in a collective hip-hop (Black) identity, Hall argues that global migration (voluntary and involuntary), as well as diverging histories, have meant differences among cultural identities. Therefore, local realities and experiences have meant hip-hop identities are necessarily different across Africa.

In understanding the ways identities have been created and shaped by hip-hop culture in Africa it is helpful to examine the importance of language choice. The question of language choice has been discussed in research on African literature, and has resurfaced in hip-hop communities across Africa. In countries like Tanzania and South Africa the language artists choose to perform in has been the subject of debate over whether artists are being too Western by not performing in their local languages. This connection between language and class and culture is complex, with African hip-hop artists operating in more than one cultural context.

The coded language used by African hip-hop artists has implications for the development of Pan-African identities. The works of artists Samuel Bazawule (aka Blitz the Ambassador) and Kwame Tsikata (aka M.anifest) of Ghana, and Edwin Ruyonga (aka Krukid, now Ruyonga) of Uganda provide representations that help us understand how hip-hop is being used in the formation of not just transnational, but Pan-African identities. Each of the artists to varying degrees presents evidence of Pan-African identities through their use of African and African American coded language and cultural symbols.

Conversations on the connections between language and culture also necessitate discussions of cultural appropriations. There have been centuries of musical (and artistic) back-and-forth between Africa and the African diaspora (see chapter 1). The appropriation and localization of art, styles, symbols, and practices between Africa and the African diaspora will be examined, as will a discussion of misappropriations. The topic of misappropriations is a controversial one, primarily because the determination of whether an appropriation is a misappropriation is highly subjective. Within hip-hop culture there are frequent charges that African youth are simply trying to be American. It may therefore be helpful to engage these debates.

Language Choice

Various factors go into the crucial choice of which language an artist decides to perform in. A primary factor is selecting a language in which the artist is fluent. Additional considerations include the artist's desired audience and what social statements that artist aims to make. Many African artists mix languages, using a combination of Western and African languages in their music. Tanure Ojaide (2007) says that the nonnative English speaker has more linguistic tools with which to create poetry, allowing for greater creativity in content and structure. Similarly, many African hip-hop artists access and manipulate multiple languages in their hip-hop verses. Chuck D, founder of the American hip-hop group Public Enemy, has praised hip-hop in Africa on more than one occasion. He coined the term "super MC" to refer to MCs who rap in more than two languages. On June 2, 2016, Chuck D's tweet on African emcees went viral: "AFRICA is the future of all MCS in HIPHOP. . . . The continent been spitting RAP FIRE for the past 25YRS only USAers DON'T KNOW because they UN-TAUGHT." In writing lyrics African artists often access more than one cultural system, using multiple languages, symbols, and cultural cues to compose songs that claim ownership of multiple cultural systems. It is common in most countries for artists to rap in at least two languages. In Senegal several artists rap in Wolof and French; in Mali many rap in Bambara and French; in Tanzania many use Swahili and English; in Uganda it's Luganda and English.

There are also some hip-hop artists in Africa who rap in more than two languages. In Ghana both Edem and Eyirap rap in Ewe, Twi, and Pidgin English. Senegalese artist Sister Fa raps in Wolof, French, and Jola. In Kenya artists like Nazizi, Bamboo, and Abbas Kubaff rap in English, Swahili, and Sheng.[1] But accessing multiple cultural systems in the creation of lyrics often requires a certain level of cultural fluency. Many rap artists focus on the use of one primary language, occasionally borrowing words when needed from other languages. Artists who are fluent in more than one language but choose to rap in only one language often do so because they are more creatively comfortable in that language or they want to make a statement about their intended audience. For bilingual artists, the decision often comes down to whether to rap in a European or an African language.

According to Ngũgĩ wa Thiong'o (1986), historically the use, mastery, and promotion of adopted European languages in Africa encouraged alienation, as it caused Africans to view their world through the lens of another culture. Ngũgĩ says the creation of Pidgin English was a result of the "peasantry and working class" Africanizing European languages (1986, 23). It was a resistance to attempts by postcolonial governments to impose standard English as the lingua franca spoken by all. In looking at Alim's (2009) discussion of confrontations between African American Vernacular English (AAVE) varieties and the formal education system in the United States, we see similar confrontations between Pidgin English and formal education systems in anglophone Africa. Schools regularly discouraged, sometimes even punished, the use of nonstandard English or Pidgin English, or of local African languages. The decision for artists to rap in Pidgin English or in one of their local languages can often be reinforcing resistance to standard English-only policies. Indeed, Tope Omoniyi argues that "language choice can be a conscious act of political subversion and resistance" (2009, 124).

The choice of which language to rap in can go beyond a question of language fluency. Artists who are fluent in European languages yet choose to rap in African languages or dialects are making a conscious decision that is often influenced by the intended audience, marketability, authenticity, political views, and a desire to strengthen cultural connections. The result has sometimes meant the mainstreaming of African languages and dialects among the youth. Omoniyi (2009), for example, asserts that the use of Pidgin English and local languages in hip-hop helps to promote and elevate the status of those languages.

Hip-hop artists who use Pidgin English, like Ghanaian artists Wanlov the Kubolor and M3NSA, often do so as a way of identifying with the "peasantry and working class," and rejecting their inherited economic class status. This has helped to remove some of the stigma around the use of Pidgin English. In Nigeria, Omoniyi (2009) says that hip-hop artists often use several local languages, especially Pidgin English. The use of more than one language by hip-hop artists is likely a result of urban centers that are home to multiple ethnic groups living in close proximity. In Tanzania most artists rap in Swahili because Swahili, the official and national language of Tanzania, is spoken all over the country, and because a movement to promote Swahili in the late 1990s resulted in a push for Swahili-only hip-hop. This movement was backed by radio stations, especially Clouds FM. DJs at Clouds, which was created in 1998 by its current CEO, Joseph Kusaga, refused to play Tanzanian hip-hop that was performed in English. Unlike in the first days of hip-hop in Tanzania, today the vast majority of hip-hop artists there perform in Swahili, which has helped strengthen the popularity of the language among the youth.

In an interview South African hip-hop artist Kanyi said though she was fluent in English, she chose to rap in Xhosa. Kanyi said she was more comfortable in Xhosa and that English was more limiting in the topics she wants to explore. For her, rapping in Xhosa forced her to dig into and discover her language more. This decision establishes not only a South African identity but a Xhosa identity that reaches both urban and rural Xhosa. Kanyi's mastery of Xhosa is shown in her rapid flow and use of Xhosa metaphors in her lyrics. During the study several artists and hip-hop heads in South Africa commented that Kanyi's use of Xhosa was sometimes difficult to translate by South Africans raised in the urban areas, who in knowing several languages did not have the level of mastery over Xhosa.

There are bilingual African hip-hop artists who have decided to perform in English, often in an effort to connect with international audiences, even if it is not the language they are most fluent in. In separate interviews with Liberian artists 2C (based in the United States) and South Sudanese artists Emmanuel Jal (based in England) and Mxc Wol (based in Australia), all three indicated that they consciously chose to rap in English and AAVE in order to gain an international audience. The accent 2C uses swings between Liberia and the American south, and his lyrics are in English and AAVE, with little hint of the Pidgin English spoken in Liberia.

Emmanuel Jal is an interesting example of an artist whose use of English and AAVE is confronted by problems of language fluency and cultural proficiency. Jal's work on the album *Ceasefire* (2005) is performed in Dinka and Nuer, while his album *Warchild* (2008) is performed in English. While there is a noticeable decline in skill on the *Warchild* album, Emmanuel Jal felt it was important to rap in English on the album in order to get his message out to a broader audience. The choice of switching to English was an attempt to gain entry to an international audience. With songs like "Skirt Too Short" and "50 Cent," a dis track directed to American rapper 50 Cent, Jal's commentary on sexual explicitness and gangster rap reflect a lack of fluency in AAVE, as well as limited proficiency in African American cultural systems. In the chorus to "Skirt Too Short" Jal raps,

> Hey girl, your skirt's too short
> I can almost see your drawers
> Pay attention to this conversation
> I don't want you spoiling your reputation
> Hey girl, cover up your chest

I can almost see you breasts
Pay attention to this conversation
Leave a little to the imagination.

From a feminist perspective the song is problematic in its use of the familiar practice of slut shaming as a way to police women's bodies. Additionally, Jal's use of "standard" English instead of AAVE or East African English slang is an indicator of the artist's lack of fluency in varieties of English slang, including AAVE. The song becomes a lecture on morality instead of a conversation between men and women within hip-hop culture. Further evidence of Jal's challenges with language fluency appear in his song "50 Cent":

You've gone done enough damage selling crack cocaine
Now you've gotta kill a black man video game?
There ain't a Jewish or a White man, a Chinese or an Indian
Blowing up the brain of their own fellow men
We've lost a whole generation through this lifestyle
Now you want to put it in the game for a little child?
Bling, like guns, is fun
I'm sure your own son wouldn't be playing with one.

Often artists target other artists to gain attention or notoriety. But it is not clear what Emmanuel Jal's intentions are with the song "50 Cent." His message and use of English is awkward, even with his use of AAVE. There are two additional indicators of Jal's struggle with African American cultural proficiency. First, in American hip-hop culture there is an established tradition of dis records, but what is problematic in "50 Cent" is that within hip-hop culture one artist does not directly call out another artist for participating in illegal activities. Artists frequently speak out against drugs and confront glorifications of violence in hip-hop and Black culture. While the impacts of drugs in Black communities and the glorification of gangster lifestyles by artists in general are discussed, individual artists are not singled out by name. While drug dealing is often criticized, this is often done within discussions of the oppressive conditions of poverty, racism in drug laws, and the prison-industrial complex. Criticisms of drug violence are often articulated by artists who also articulate understandings of the role of institutional racism in perpetuating cycles of violence

Additionally, Jal asserts that video games do not depict people of Jewish, European, or Asian heritage killing other people, implying that it is only African Americans who are depicted killing other people. Not only is this not accurate, the subtext of the entire song is based on the familiar trope that depicts the African American man as the pathological criminal, personified by 50 Cent.

By comparison, Somali rapper K'naan released the song "What's Hardcore?" on his 2005 album *Dusty Foot Philosopher*. The song takes aim at gangster rap, specifically calling out 50 Cent. In the song K'naan uses his own experience in warlord-ruled Somalia to juxtapose life in Mogadishu with life in urban America. For two verses K'naan describes the violence and lawlessness of life in Mogadishu, rapping about guns going off at hospitals, refugees dying in boats, a lack of law enforcement, neighborhoods controlled by gangsters, and the popularity of the AK-47 assault rifle as the daily weapon of choice. In the chorus he simply asks, "So what's hardcore? Really, are you hardcore? Hmm." After two verses of describing life in Mogadishu he directly references gangster rap in America with the lines:

> I'm a spit these verses cause I feel annoyed
> And I'm not gonna quit till I fill the void
> If I rhyme about home and got descriptive
> I'd make 50 Cent look like Limp Bizkit
> It's true, and don't make me rhyme about you
> I'm from where the kids is addicted to glue
> Get ready, he got a good grip on the machete
> Make rappers say they do it for love like R. Kelly.

In the song K'naan uses AAVE in his juxtaposition of life in Mogadishu with life in the urban ghettos of America, claiming a space of authenticity within the culture. Taken in context with his entire album, K'naan repeatedly articulates an identification with African American culture, evidenced by the frequent and appropriate use of AAVE and symbols in his music. This contrasts with Emmanuel Jal, who takes aim at 50 Cent from a position outside the community, evidenced by his less frequent and less fluent use of AAVE and symbols in his music.

Both Emmanuel Jal and K'naan fled civil conflicts in their countries. Both fled first to Kenya, and then to the West. Jal went to England and K'naan went to Canada. Their experiences are a large part of their music and both write about surviving the conflicts, as well as the friends and family they lost due to the conflict. Through his book, documentary, and NGO, Emmanuel Jal has largely marketed himself to European audiences and human rights activist groups. He has not participated significantly in hip-hop communities in the United States or within Africa, outside of Sudan. K'naan on the other hand has worked with several US and African hip-hop artists and been visible on the hip-hop scene in the United States, Africa, and Europe.

Language, Identity, and Code-Switching

The process of identity formation is often composed of both internal and external influences, based on one's interactions with others and one's perceptions of self. The language one speaks and the use of that language are keys to understanding one's cultural identity. In his book *Decolonizing the Mind*, Ngũgĩ wa Thiong'o says language "is both a means of communication and a carrier of culture" (1986, 13). Carol Eastman (1985) used the idea of "group talk" to describe the appropriate use of language among people with shared cultural identities. According to Eastman, "Language use has a context-based domain structure comprising its setting, the language users, the purpose of language use, the actual intragroup use of language, and the rules for using language appropriately interpersonally" (7).

Within hip-hop the dominant language is English and certain slang terms or ways of speaking are well known and common in hip-hop cultures. Alim (2006) calls the variety of English and its regional variations spoken in hip-hop culture the Hip Hop Nation Language (HHNL). HHNL is similar to African American Vernacular English (AAVE), which, according to E. R. Thomas (2007), is also spoken mostly among working-class African American communities. Both

Alim and Thomas see HHNL and AAVE as related to, but different from, standard language structures in the African American community of what Alim calls Black Language (BL) and Thomas calls African American English. Both also recognize that HHNL and AAVE have regional variations. Outside the United States the use of HHNL/AAVE by hip-hop artists signals an identification with a global hip-hop community for which HHNL/AAVE is the linguistic foundation. Of Africans, Alim says they "practice hip hop as a critical site of identification with Black Americans and the development of hybrid identities" (2006, 11).

These African hip-hop artists demonstrate significant integration of their cultural identities and have the ability to easily move between African and African American linguistic communities. Their music often contains elements of integration of both local and African American culture, including language. Among African hip-hop artists in general we find varying levels of integration. Key to high levels of integration is their ability to switch between cultures, referred to as cultural frame switching (CFS) or code-switching (Y. Jackson 2006). CFS refers to the ability to "access multiple cultural meaning systems and switching between different culturally appropriate behaviors depending on the context" (Y. Jackson 2006). Crucial to this is the ability to effectively communicate verbally or nonverbally in both cultures (LaFromboise, Coleman, and Gerton 1993).

For African immigrants in America a foreign accent marks individuals as outsiders to their host culture. Likewise, an inability to speak their heritage language signals the same individuals as outsiders to other members of their immigrant community. This "outsider" status impacts individuals' interactions with others, as well as their identity.

Within hip-hop culture these identity fluctuations are reflected in the music African hip-hop artists produce. Within hip-hop, unlike in other genres of music, artists are obliged to write their own lyrics, making songs reflections of the thoughts, feelings, and perspectives of individual artists.

The research recognizes studies on code-switching and the work of scholars like Carol Myers-Scotton, which examine the alternating between two different languages. This study focuses not only on language but also on the use of symbols and cultural cues, as well as evidence of identification with multiple cultures.

This research shows us that the appropriate use of AAVE/HHNL and African American themes by US-based African hip-hop artists may be evidence of their Pan-African identities. The frequent code-switching, in this case using African and African American/hip-hop–coded language, indicates a level of fluency and competency with AAVE/HHNL. The use of code-switching to express both African and African American experiences indicates a level of identification with African and African American cultures.

The importance of the representation of self, space, and place in music, hip-hop in particular, is essential. The ways in which hip-hop artists "represent" through their music not only informs us of their experiences but also speaks to variations in cultural identities and cultural competencies among African hip-hop artists.

Using theories of cultural representation and language, we know that all representations emanate from a cultural system. While humans share many similar ways of processing certain cultural cues, our own cultural background (system) determines how we filter and process certain representations. When we understand a cultural system, we are better able to decipher the meanings being represented. In creating representations, the appropriate use of language and cultural cues is evidence of a level of cultural competency, even identification with the culture from which the representations emanate. For example, an analysis of the appropriate use of AAVE/HHNL to express African and diaspora experiences both speaks to African American cultural competency among some African migrants and reveals African migrant identities that are connected to both African and diaspora communities.

In *Decolonizing the Mind*, Ngũgĩ says that language "is both a means of communication and a carrier of culture." It encompasses the history, values, and experiences of a culture. Therefore, the understanding and creation of cultural representations requires an intimate understanding of the cultural system from which those representations emanate.

Each of the African migrant artists discussed in this book uses AAVE/HHNL and African American cultural symbols alongside African languages and cultural symbols. With frequent references to multiple African and diaspora experiences and symbols in their lyrics, many of these artists also challenge racial justice in America with the same conviction they use to challenge corrupt institutions at home. Among these artists there is an acknowledgment of a Pan-African identity that is both implicit and explicit in their lyrics.

For example, in Blitz the Ambassador's "Ghetto Plantation," he raps,

> Incarceration is the new plantation
> A new kind of slavery, a new foundation
> And it wouldn't even cost you much
> The project is the slave ship
> The corner is the auction block.

In this song Blitz, a Ghanaian, presents commentary on the relationship between slavery and the prison-industrial complex. Blitz is an artist whose music is infused with African drumming, jazz, and Afrobeat sounds. In his lyrics he expresses both African and African American identities in three ways. First, he assumes an African American identity, using AAVE/HHNL to present commentary on race in America. Through his lyrics he takes on an African American identity and uses African American cultural cues in his lyrics. In his song "Free at Last" he refers to himself as "Detroit Red[2] with a flow" and says that his music is "far from your average jigaboo, pickaninny rap shit." Second, Blitz assumes a Ghanaian identity and uses AAVE/HHNL to present commentary on Ghanaian and African immigrant experiences. In "Native Sun" he plays on the title of Richard Wright's classic novel, addressing the irony of struggling in the United States, while in Ghana people think that you are doing well because you are there. Third, Blitz assumes a Ghanaian identity and uses Ghanaian-coded language to discuss home. In the song "Akwaaba" (Welcome) Blitz switches completely to Twi and presents a distinct Ghanaian identity.

M.anifest also code-switches continuously in his lyrics. Unlike Blitz, who represents both African American and African themes, M.anifest uses AAVE/HHNL to represent mostly African themes.

M.anifest does address social issues in his music, but the topics do not dominate his music. His dual identities emerge in his mastery and appropriate use of AAVE/HHNL, as in his song "Represent":

> Who woulda knew that this cat from Africa
> Would come to America
> Verbally massacre these characters
> ...
> Ghanaian presence definin' the essence
> Ancestors blessed us beyond measure
> Deliver lyrical treasure like AZ[3] in the golden era
> Written, off the top, on beat, or acappella
> Every line, every rhyme relevant forever
> In the name of Mandela
> Masakela, Makeba
> Oral traditions in a flavor you can savor
> We never gave up
> True warriors, vainglorious
> It's obvious the gift is upon us.

"Represent" is a play on a common hip-hop word and refers to important verbal and nonverbal signals in which one shows pride in where they come from. M.anifest uses the term to represent not only Ghana but to affirm a representation of the entire continent.

Krukid/Ruyonga also uses mostly AAVE/HHNL throughout his music. He does this to such an extent that it's sometimes difficult to determine if he is talking about Uganda or the United States. Some of the stories he tells through his lyrics, whether they are spatially located in Uganda or not, appear to take place within African American contexts. There are two songs I want to highlight—"African" and "African American, American African"—in which Krukid expresses dual identities and addresses the relationship between Africans and African Americans, using AAVE/HHNL.

In "African American, American African," Krukid first adopts the identity of an African immigrant and considers the stereotypes of Africans as poor and uncivilized. In one line, "Et tu homie," he seems to question the furtherance of these stereotypes by African Americans, who are supposed to be his "homies."[4] In the next verse he switches to an African American identity and addresses the stereotypes of African Americans as violent criminals and drug addicts. In the chorus he raps, "African American, American African / See the same shit here, there and then back again / A race caring over who got the blackest skin." While the song speaks of stereotypes in general, the chorus seems to be speaking specifically to the presence of those stereotypes among African and African American communities.

In his song "African," Krukid/Ruyonga adopts a clear Pan-African identity. In the song he identifies with Africa as a whole, as well as with each nation, asserting a claim to an identification with all of Africa and the diaspora.

> I'm Ugandan I'm Kenyan I'm Tanzanian
> I'm Zambian, I'm Gambian, I'm Ghanaian
> I'm Algerian, Liberian, Nigerian
> American African, Afro American
> . . .
> I'm Angolan, I'm Mozambican
> I'm a raise my voice so you know I'm speaking
> It ain't by choice that I live and breathe it
> I bleed it, I'm still here even when I leave it
> . . .
> I'm Haitian, I'm Jamaican
> I carry my race like a conversation.

In Krukid/Ruyonga's song the artist makes a conscious and definitive identification with all African peoples, by calling out not only African countries by name but diaspora countries as well.

This presence of Pan-African identities among African migrant artists has implications for the tensions that have existed between African American communities and migrant communities from both the Caribbean and Africa. West Indian and African migrants, especially first-generation migrants, tended to distance themselves from African Americans because of a perceived loss in status (Waters 1999; Arthur 2000). Mary Waters's (1999) study of West Indian migrants and John Arthur's (2000) study of African migrants were seminal works on the migration experiences of both populations. Those studies found that many West Indian and African migrants believed the immigrant Black had a higher status that the US-born Black and would often emphasize their national identities as a way to distinguish themselves. According to Bonny Norton (1997), the connection between identity and distribution of resources and privilege influences how people identify.

Each of the artists in the study has returned home either permanently or temporarily, and all have taken ownership of African American and Ghanaian or Ugandan linguistic and cultural symbols. All are culturally situated at the nexus between both communities and construct African identities based on their African and diaspora experiences.

The regular and appropriate use of AAVE/HHNL and African American themes by US-based African hip-hop artists is evidence not only of their Pan-African identities but also of Pan-African identities among some African migrants. The importance of this code-switching among these artists is not simply because it is happening but because of why it is happening and because of the broader implications of its occurrence.

It is happening because of the more frequent movement of African peoples between African and the diaspora, either physically or virtually. This has come about because of increased travel and innovations in technology and social media. This study focuses on post-2000 African migrants to the United States because this is a population where scholars have found some of the highest rates of transnationalism, of Africans with experiences and cultural competencies in two or more cultures. The music these artists produce is speaking to specific audiences.

As for the implications, through references and language use that are familiar to post-2000 African migrants in the United States, as well as some diaspora populations, these artists are bringing together and reinforcing cultural networks and communities in Africa and the diaspora. This may be evidence of an easing of some of the tensions that have existed between African Americans and African migrants.

The Progression of Artists' Albums

Of writers who write of home, Ojaide says, "The writer tends to exploit memory and return to childhood days to garner images to clarify his or her visions" (2007, 24). For the artists in this study—Blitz the Ambassador, M.anifest, and Krukid/Ruyonga, for example—we see changes in their sound and lyrics as they moved closer to home, either permanently or semipermanently. All three artists began to include more music, language, and memories from home in their songs.

Krukid/Ruyonga's first album, *Raisin in the Sun* (2005) did not incorporate a lot from the languages or music of Uganda. The album has several mentions of his Ugandan experiences, but blended in with many of the sounds and styles produced by African American hip-hop artists. Krukid's lyrics primarily utilized AAVE/HHNL, and showed little trace of his Ugandan roots. His 2007 album, *Afr-I-Can*, on which he seems to reclaim his Ugandan roots, delves a bit more into his Ugandan and African identities. But it is his 2010 project, an EP collaboration with M.anifest entitled *Two Africans and a Jew*, that we see a stronger reclamation of home. Krukid/Ruyonga performs in Luganda for the first time on an album with the track "Breakdown." Krukid/Ruyonga permanently moved back to Uganda in 2011, changing his name from Krukid to Ruyonga upon his return. Ruyonga continues to perform mostly in English, but mixes English and Luganda on tracks like "Muhuliire?" and "Tutuuse."

M.anifest released *Manifestations* in 2007 and *Immigrant Chronicles: Coming to America* in 2011. On both albums M.anifest uses AAVE/HHNL throughout to produce tracks that address primarily African themes. A lot of his songs are traditional hip-hop tracks, which include both boasting and social commentary. His music looks at issues of poverty and racism, in both the African and African American communities. Like Blitz the Ambassador, evidence of M.anifest's identification with African American communities in his earlier music can be seen in his mastery and appropriate use AAVE as well as his articulation of African American cultural norms and nuances. M.anifest returned to Ghana after 2011, and his music signaled a shift back to Ghana. He continues to rap using AAVE/HHNL, as well as Pidgin English, and Twi. His songs "Someway Bi," "W'ani Aba," and "Makaa Maka" blend all three languages, and show M.anifest using both Ghanaian and African American symbols and cultural contexts.

As Blitz the Ambassador began to return to Ghana to perform, there was a noticeable move toward Ghana in his music. Blitz released *Soul Rebel* in 2005 (EP), *Double Consciousness* in 2009 (EP), and the album *Stereotype* in 2009. All three included a focus on an African American urban identity, continuously addressing urban ills, like violence, drugs, and the prison-industrial complex. On Blitz's 2011 album *Native Sun* we see more expressions of his Ghanaian identity, with tracks blending Twi lyrics, African beats, and lengthy discussions of African subjects. With songs like "Akwaaba," "Accra City Blues," and "Wahala," Blitz almost reclaims or reasserts a strong Ghanaian identity, alongside music and lyrics conveying an African American identity. He in fact refers to himself as a bridge between the two cultures. This trend continues with his 2014 album, *Afropolitan Dreams*.

(Mis)appropriations

In September 2015 a blog post written by Zipporah Gene, a British Nigerian, entitled "Black America, Please Stop Appropriating African Clothing and Tribal Marks" sparked a firestorm on Black social media.[5] Responses were immediate, and soon after posts went up taking on the debate. On news sites popular in Black social media, articles like "Black Americans Don't 'Appropriate' African Culture" by Jouelzy on TheRoot.com[6] and "Why It Isn't Possible for Black Americans to Appropriate African Culture" by Julia Cravan on HuffingtonPost.com[7] were published within weeks of the original blog post. The problematic nature of Gene's argument, along with her never having lived in the United States, left many suspecting the post was meant to spark debate and generate site traffic. While the post resonated with some, the reaction created an online discussion that produced two main arguments: (1) that African Americans, who are also Africans, cannot appropriate from a culture they are also a part of and (2) that Africans have also appropriated from African American culture. The premise of the first argument is that one cannot appropriate from one's own culture. Therefore, since African Americans are African, they cannot appropriate from their own culture. The second argument acknowledges the African origins of African American people and culture, but also the cultural differences between Africans and African Americans. This argument points to the historical-cultural give-and-take that has gone on between the two communities.

We will briefly explore the latter argument, which recognizes the cultural similarities and differences between African Americans and various African communities, as well as the regular cultural give-and-take that has historically occurred in the areas of music, fashion, and language. Though the term *appropriation* has negative connotations, appropriation in itself is not necessarily negative. Richard Rogers defines cultural appropriation as "the use of one culture's symbols, artifacts, genres, rituals, or technologies by members of another culture—regardless of intent, ethics, function, or outcome" (2006, 476). In distinguishing between appropriation in the form of cultural exchange versus appropriation in the form of cultural dominance or cultural exploitation, Rogers says that in cultural exchanges the appropriation is reciprocal and there is no dominance or imbalance of power. James Young's (2008) look at the appropriations that occur in the arts asserts that most artists engage in appropriations in various ways. This is especially true of hip-hop culture, which often appropriates, through sampling, music and styles from a variety of cultures.

African American and African communities have historically appropriated and localized each other's cultures. During the rise of Black pride and the Black Power movement in the United States in the 1960s, African Americans adopted and localized the West African dashiki, slightly changing the silhouette and using a variety of prints. The dashiki was worn by celebrities, activists, and models on the cover of popular African American magazines, becoming a popular way for African Americans to connect with African culture (Mead and Pederson 1995). In the 2000s the African American–style dashiki made a return, with young African Americans and Africans alike wearing it. Additionally, African Americans have appropriated and localized other aspects of African culture in their celebration of Kwanzaa, as well as the use of kente cloth as part of one's graduation regalia.

Africans have also appropriated diaspora culture and music and localized them. Before hip-hop, artists doing Afrobeat and Cape Jazz appropriated African American music and culture and localized their music with local sounds, instruments, and lyrics. In Nigeria, Fela Kuti, having been greatly influenced by the funk music and Black Power politics of Los Angeles in the late 1960s, would blend Nigerian and other West African instrumentals and sounds to pioneer Afrobeat. In South Africa, Cape Jazz emerged in Cape Town and blended African American and South African sounds and instruments. Many of the artists who were influential in the South African jazz scene left for the United States during apartheid, and some, like Abdullah Ibrahim, Hugh Masekela, and Miriam Makeba, were influenced by the Black Power movement in the United States, which would inform their music and their activism.

How then can culture be misappropriated? There are several examples tied to social power imbalances, when one culture's privilege allows it to incorrectly appropriate another culture in the creation or furtherance of harmful tropes and stereotypes. For example, when performing in blackface, White actors used their privilege to appropriate what they thought was African American culture, only to further negative tropes about the lazy, untrustworthy, and stupid African American.

When appropriations occur between marginalized groups, there are two categories of cultural appropriation that have at times been problematic. First is the appropriation done without a clear understanding of the originating culture. This often leads to distortions or incorrect interpretations of another culture. The second appropriation is done with the intent of becoming a member of the appropriated culture and adopting someone else's reality. In the arts, Young (2008) calls this latter instance subject appropriation, in which the lives and experiences of another culture are used as one's own. This may also be done without a clear understanding of the originating culture.

Assuming membership in another culture, or in multiple cultures, without an understanding of the appropriate cultural competency can be problematic, and in music it brings up questions of authenticity. According to Eastman, membership in a particular cultural group requires the appropriate use of "1. Vocabulary, 2. Topics, and 3. Attitudes in the appropriate speech act context" (1985, 5). Eastman says that vocabulary or language fluency is not enough for group membership. Newcomers wanting group membership require a knowledge and understanding of language patterns, social norms, and other speaking patterns. Christina Higgins (2009) points out that authenticity is often called into question by in-group members when out-group members fail to properly use the language and cultural cues of the in-group. This can happen even when fellow out-group members perceive the use of the in-group's language and cultural cues as authentic.

Misunderstandings and misappropriations of African American and hip-hop culture can be found in hip-hop and popular music produced by African artists, where African American and hip-hop-coded language and culture may be incorrectly appropriated via the use of familiar tropes about gangster culture, drug and alcohol use, and hypersexuality in African American and hip-hop culture. The representation of these tropes in hip-hop music and videos by some African artists reflects a lack of African American cultural competency, as well as an attempt to use the experiences and culture of African Americans as their own.

The use of the word *nigga* has been passionately debated within the African American community. The word has a long history in the United States and is tied to the racial oppression of African Americans and the brutalities and murders committed against African Americans. The word, for many, is a constant reminder of America's painful experience with racism. The word is nonetheless used often in AAVE and HHNL. Alim says that within hip-hop culture there has been a recognition that the "n-word" has "various positive in-group meanings, and pejorative out-group meanings, and thus [was] felt the need to reflect the culturally specific meanings with a new spelling" (2006, 77). Hence, within HHNL (and AAVE) the word *nigger* is spelled *nigga*. While the debate over the word *nigga* is important, for the purpose of this research what is important is the understanding of the word's history among the African artists who use it.

Among African artists who misunderstand or misappropriate African American culture, one often finds heavy use of the word *nigga*, alongside artists donning Timberland boots (in tropical weather), baggy jeans, and proclamations of "thug life." This replication of an African American stereotype originates from media representations of African American and hip-hop culture, and is mostly devoid of much real understanding of the history of the word *nigga*, the origins of Timberland boots in the working class, or the connection between the baggy jeans and the mass incarceration of African American men.

Repetition of familiar tropes can also be found in African American misunderstandings and misappropriations of African culture, where tropes around rural Africa, Mother Africa, or Africa in need of aid are common. The Mother Africa trope has often resulted in artists reinforcing the "country of Africa" image of a homogeneous Africa, where everyone speaks the same language, often Swahili. In Erykah Badu's 1997 song "Yeyo" the artist incorrectly says, "Yeyo means mother in Swahili." There are frequent representations of these tropes in music, films, and media produced by African Americans. If the "gangster African American" is an attempt for Africans to identify with, and replicate, African American culture, the homogeneous "Mother Africa" is an attempt for African Americans to identify with, and replicate, African culture. The problem may arise when a lack of cultural competency causes misappropriations, which lead in-group members to question the authenticity of out-group representations.

HIP-HOP ARTISTS IN Africa use language to "represent" their identities in ways that speak to variations in cultural identities and cultural competencies. The use of African American Vernacular English and the employment of code-switching by African hip-hop artists can be representations of transnational, Pan-African, identities. Alternately, while there have clearly been cultural appropriations among African and diaspora communities, there have also been misappropriations.

Understanding the connection language has to cultural identity and class leads us to an understanding of the role language choice plays in hip-hop, especially in Africa where artists are often fluent in more than one language. The continued impacts of colonial language policies,

English-only education policies, and the global dominance of the English language and American culture have resulted in a perception that English equals modern and developed, while African languages equal traditional and undeveloped. African artists have thus taken up the questions over language posed by African writers like Ngũgĩ wa Thiong'o and Chinua Achebe years before. Some artists have chosen to perform in European languages as a means to reach broader audiences. Others have chosen to perform in African languages in order to find an audience at home. In anglophone countries artists have chosen to perform in Pidgin English, which makes them accessible to international audiences but allows them to reach local audiences as well.

In looking at the relationship between language and identity, Burns (2009) discusses how African migrant artists often develop Pan-African identities in addition to national ones. Because of their involvement with hip-hop music and culture before migrating, the African hip-hop artists in this study started developing Pan-African identities before their arrival in the United States, and that those identities were reinforced once here.

Perhaps because of these experiences and influences, these artists have also had to find their audience, who are often fellow transnationals. In a 2014 interview Wanlov stated he has had problems connecting with Ghanaian audiences, that he and M3NSA were "treated as outcasts." In conversations with Ghanaians in Ghana, several indicated they did not fully understand or relate to Blitz the Ambassador's music. All these artists are negotiating their place, influenced by both home and diaspora; their music differs in that the narratives they construct speak to transnational experiences of, especially, post-2000 African migrants. These African hip-hop artists represent a coalescence of African and diaspora experiences and identities. It is thus through their music that a certain African immigrant experience is constructed, one that is connected to both diaspora and home. And it is through a look at the evolution of the artists themselves and through their music that we understand their relationships to the idea of home and the importance of return.

Appropriations have always been a part of the cultural give-and-take between Africa and the diaspora. African diaspora communities have both retained and appropriated aspects of African culture. Joseph Holloway's (2005) edited book *Africanisms in American Culture* contained several chapters detailing the African presence in diaspora culture and practices. There have also been deliberate appropriations of African culture, appropriations that are often localized to fit diaspora needs. Similarly, African communities have appropriated from the diaspora. We see this musically not just in African musical genres but also in the localization of diaspora genres like reggae in Africa. Additionally, African communities have appropriated other symbols and practices from the diaspora. The Black Consciousness Movement in South Africa was greatly impacted by the Black Power movement in the United States, but localized to be relevant to South African contexts.

The idea of misappropriations can be heavily debated. In examining that debate, I have attempted to expand on differences between appropriations and misappropriations. Discussing misappropriations allows us to clarify how these misappropriations can have real impacts on the perceptions of Africans held by African Americans, or the perceptions of African Americans held by Africans. Misappropriations that emanate from a lack of cultural competency can result in the reinforcement of negative tropes that can contribute to divisions and misunderstandings between Africans and African Americans. Misappropriations that are based on a desire to adopt wholesale another's culture can also lead to misunderstandings and charges of inauthenticity. In our increasingly globalized world, content produced anywhere in the world can go viral globally in less than twenty-four hours. Therefore, cultural appropriations are easily consumed by local and global audiences, which position themselves as barometers of authenticity and appropriateness of the appropriation.

Epilogue

IN 1996, I returned home to Tanzania to participate in a study abroad program at the University of Dar es Salaam. During that time, hip-hop had emerged as a dominant musical genre in Dar es Salaam. Every Sunday night was hip-hop night poolside at the Kilimanjaro Hotel in downtown Dar es Salaam. Every week youth from around the city would make their way to the hotel and listen to nothing but hip-hop into the late hours. Having grown up in the United States, a part of the hip-hop generation, I got involved in the hip-hop scene during my stay in Tanzania. I and my housemates, visiting students from America, attended performances, made friends with artists, and hosted house parties at our home in the Mwenge area, near the university. During that year in Tanzania we witnessed the initial heavy imitation phase that Dar es Salaam hip-hop went through as it began to find its own identity. Many artists were simply copying what was popular and had no investment in hip-hop culture. Artists for whom hip-hop was a passing fad quickly fell by the wayside over the years, while others helped build hip-hop culture in the city. Some of these more serious artists are still heavily involved in hip-hop culture in Tanzania. Going back and forth between Tanzania and the United States over the years, I witnessed the dominance of hip-hop (mid-1990s), the growth of bongo flava (late 1990s), and the resurgence of hip-hop culture through various collectives in Tanzania intent on keeping the culture alive (2000s).

In the meantime, in the 1990s hip-hop studies in the United States was growing into a respected field of research, thanks in large part to the work of scholars like Jeff Chang, Bakari Kitwana, Imani Perry, and Tricia Rose. Many of these scholars were hip-hop heads in their own right, hip-hop heads who had gone into academia. This put them in a position to help direct the academic gaze that academia was placing on hip-hop culture. In 2008, Adam Haupt, a South African hip-hop head and academic, published the first full-length book on hip-hop in Africa, *Stealing Empire: P2P, Intellectual Property and Hip Hop Subversion*. Like Rose, Perry, Chang, and Kitwana in the United States, Haupt helped usher in the serious study of hip-hop in Africa. Like Rose, Perry, Chang, and Kitwana, Haupt, a member of South Africa's hip-hop generation, had entered academia and would influence academic discourse around hip-hop in Africa. The hip-hop scholars mentioned have also often worked with artists on scholarly projects, giving those artists a voice on academic platforms that seek to debate the cultures these artists come from. This also serves to give those projects validity outside academia. This research praxis has been used by scholars in numerous disciplines and is a recognition of academic privilege that we as researchers have, as well as some of the historical distortion of non-Western cultures by scholars using Western lenses. During this research and in discussions with other academics in the field, conversations have often reflected on the criticism that as scholars we mostly take from, and do not benefit, the cultures we research. We fly in with our notebooks, collect data, do our analyses, and publish, while the communities with whom we come in contact may not benefit in any significant way. Additionally, those communities have little, if any, say in our published studies of their cultures.

This research stands on the shoulders of those hip-hop scholars who seek to influence and adjust the academic gaze placed upon hip-hop in Africa. This book has gone through several iterations and has seen other articles and books go from development to publication. This book was an ambitious attempt to survey many of the various representations within hip-hop culture across Africa and to make that research as accurate and as accessible as possible.

Academically, this research is where African studies and hip-hop studies meet, using cultural studies as a tool for dialogue. All three fields are highly interdisciplinary but also complementary. An examination of hip-hop in Africa must consider the relationship hip-hop culture in Africa has with both American and global hip-hop culture. Some scholars have used the term *glocal* to refer to hip-hop communities that exist in both local and global spaces (Alim and Pennycook 2007; Mose 2013, 2014). This book focuses specifically on hip-hop as its own distinct genre and culture in order to better understand how, like in other locations in Africa, hip-hop heads use hip-hop to represent their local realities. This approach to studying hip-hop culture in Africa, of linking it to global hip-hop culture, is not revolutionary and has been done by scholars like H. Samy Alim, Jeff Chang, Eric Charry, Adam Haupt, P. Khalil Saucier, and Quentin Williams.

This research has expanded on the work of these scholars, using cultural studies as a framework to examine cultural representations in Africa. In this way, the research also built on the work of Stewart Hall and his ideas around cultural representation. Hall's theory asserts that meaning is constructed for us via various cultural representations—TV, film, music, text, and so on. We are therefore able to understand hip-hop culture (a cultural representation) as a lens with which to understand local and global social, cultural, and political dynamics. Artists use hip-hop to construct new narratives around female sexuality that need to be understood; artists use hip-hop to construct contemporary African immigrant experiences; artists use hip-hop to engage the state around questions that may not be posed by traditional media. Scholars have examined the role various mediums of cultural representation play in shaping our understanding of the world (Cottle 2000; Jackson and Andrews 2004; Wright 2008; Barker 2012). In this research I chose to survey hip-hop as the medium of representation.

Understanding the important role of "representation" within hip-hop culture helped make this study a cultural-studies endeavor. The centuries of cultural dialogues that continue to occur between Africa and its various diasporas have also informed this research. Hip-hop is not the first musical genre to represent a blending of African and diasporic influences. It is not even the most recent musical genre to do so. Hip-hop has simply offered us one platform with which global Black cultures construct narratives that are in global dialogue, while informing us of local realities.

There is a serious need for additional research on hip-hop culture in Africa, especially in those countries that have had little coverage. It would be helpful, for example, to have more scholarship on hip-hop's narrative of politics and conflict in the Democratic Republic of the Congo, liberation movements in Western Sahara, and social resistance in Angola. There are many similarities in hip-hop culture across Africa, and this research attempts to draw attention to some of those parallels. There are also local realities that have influenced variations in the stories told and the communities represented in local hip-hop culture. An examination of each of those variations was beyond the scope of this project, but this research has shown the need for further explorations of local hip-hop communities.

By Way of an Afterword

Akosua Adomako Ampofo

WE ALL HAVE visions of the futures we want. For us Africans it is important that we are guaranteed space to live and thrive and be all that we can be in a world that seems increasingly hostile to us. Many feel buffeted on every side: our knowledge and products are denigrated, our customs belittled, and our very bodies cast off like filthy rags. As a people we are numbed to the pictures of a people dying from wars, and few ask why weapons are still promoted by European governments as a useful product to export to African nations. Droughts and famines come and go, bodies lie wasting, and it seems to matter little that we don't know how much the greenhouse gases produced in the global north have contributed to this devastation. Children as young as five years are trafficked to brothels and porn production centers around the globe because the sexual abuse of young black bodies is considered titillating. We need new prophets to proclaim a new world order for us and order us to occupy it. It is no exaggeration to say that Africa's future is writ large with the messages and sounds of hip-hop.

The timing of this pleasant assignment to write a "postword" for Msia Clark's *Hip-Hop in Africa: Prophets of the City and Dustyfoot Philosophers* meant that I read the manuscript over a few weeks between Accra, New York, Washington, DC, and Kumasi. I think that is a fitting metaphor for the way the music has traveled and its influences and influencers. Clark does away with the need to settle who did what first in her mapping of the forward and backward linkages and influences of the music between Africa and the diaspora, the connections among global and local hip-hop cultures. No need to prove the authenticity of African hip-hop, not by language nor content, for "as long as an artist is representing his or her reality and experiences as an African, through hip-hop, it can be seen as African hip-hop."

This is a very important text. To say that I learned a lot about the artists and their music, so many I had never even heard of before, and the intricacies of hip-hop music and culture would be an understatement; I came away having totally enhanced my own pop-culture credibility. I have heard Msia Clark speak to her work, and she brings to the story of today's hip-hop storytellers the passion of the historian who must give voice to a phenomenon, a movement, a future that we must recognize and appreciate. From Algeria to Zimbabwe we feel the angst of the artist. We hear the pain and anger of the revolutionary. We learn of Ghanaian preferences for the innuendos of proverbs, and the Senegalese penchant for direct confrontation (and that there are between three and five thousand hip-hop artists in Dakar alone!). We learn of genesis, becoming popular and becoming political. We learn of censorship in southern Africa and depoliticization in Tanzania. We learn about the power of emcees in the hip-hop scene. And we learn about the vagaries of the industry, including having their music banned, arrests, and imprisonment. We learn of succumbing and co-optations. We are reminded of the Prophet's humanity, vanity, and susceptibility to corruption of the flesh. And we applaud the courage and creativity, all the above notwithstanding.

The story of women in hip-hop allows us to appreciate the complicated world of gender and social protests. From the Black Panther movement in the United States, to Egypt's Tahrir Square protests, through the revolutionary stripping of African mothers, to the recent protests around police brutalities in the United States and Europe, the silencing of black women's voices, and the policing and abuse of their bodies, has been a subject both on and off the social and political stages. Clark brings the female emcee to the center of the narrative by illustrating how the hip-hop tradition of braggadocio is employed by female artists "to force a space for themselves in hip-hop communities,

By Way of an Afterword | 211

and to be able to challenge prevailing ideas of femininity." Sexuality, violence, agency, the "African" woman—all these are themes they employ. At a time when feminism is no longer cool, at least not the kind from the earlier feminist "waves," female emcees bring the old message in new, poignant ways that resonate, even if they don't have the continental and international reach of their male counterparts. Yes, sometimes their in-your-face reverse sexualizing makes some of us cringe. But this should serve as a renewed call to us all to continue working to change the unequal terrain. A recent call to young girls by Ghana's minister for Gender, Children and Social Protection reminds us how women are often implicated in our own oppression: "If you wear a short dress it's fashionable but know that it can attract somebody who would want to rape or defile you. You must be responsible for the choices you make."[1] The solution is not a war to place the "true" feminists on the throne but a war to dismantle the capitalist patriarchal order that simultaneously promotes the objectification of women while condemning them for not conforming to conservative femininity—a very confusing world for young women to live in.

In my own country, Ghana, the pop-culture world, and hiplife musicians in particular (as we refer to our brand of hip-hop), have been an important feature of many recent sociopolitical happenings. In the lead-up to our December 2016 general elections, which eventually saw a handing over of the government from the National Democratic Congress to the New Patriotic Party (NPP), hiplife music and its messengers played significant roles. In September 2016 the award-winning group Praaye (Broom) joined a long and growing list of celebrities to endorse the NPP's flagbearer, Nana Addo Dankwa Akufo-Addo, who won the 2017 elections. Since the country returned to so-called democratic rule in 1992, with its attendant winner-take-all character, Ghana's election periods have conveyed a do-or-die atmosphere. Warnings about how the country will be fragmented if the political parties don't behave in a civil manner crowd the airwaves and civil-society activism. We are reminded about Rwanda, Kenya, Sierra Leone and Liberia, with some arguing that Ghanaians are a "peaceful people" and others cautioning what happened there can happen to us. In 2008, hiplife artist Obour released the socially conscious album and project *One Ghana Peace Project/Obour for President*, ahead of the general elections and went on to embark on a nationwide peace campaign. Interestingly, Obour was later selected as one of twelve "emerging leaders" by the African Leadership Initiative, to pursue training with the reputable Aspen Global Leadership Network. And why is all this important? Because, as Misa Clark makes evident throughout her book, Africa's overlooked demographic dividend—her youth—are not sitting back and waiting for their future to be written for them. And one of the most powerful ways they are calling out their elders, including politicians and religious leaders and other duty bearers, is through today's *akyeame*, or griots. *Akyeame*, plural of *Ɔkyeame*, is the Akan title for the adviser and spokesperson of the king.[2] *Mɛ san aba*, literally, "I will return" or, "I will be back," is the title of a hiplife song by the duo Akyeame. Since akyeame are usually seasoned elders, by calling themselves Akyeame the duo speaks to the notion that young people can also be wise advisers regarding Africa's future. They do this by considering her past and by reclaiming her stories and reviving a cultural project that expresses our identities and needs. Today many African youth have developed what Dennis Howard (2012), writing about Jamaicans, refers to as a "schizophrenic" relationship with their countries. Indeed, Howard writes about the "rantin" against the state reflected in dancehall music that is deeply embedded in hip-hop and hiplife music, much as in the civil rights anthems. Akyeame are just one example of hiplife artists calling the state to order. *Mɛ san aba*, with its hiplife style, which uses traditional overtures, and mixtures of Ghanaian languages and English, speaks to this eclectic mix that forms the identities of many of today's youth, something Clark addresses powerfully. They straddle urban and rural, elite Afropolitanism and the everyday ghetto, mother and colonial tongues, so-called modern and so-called traditional. "*Mɛ san aba*" can also be read as the kind of threat—"just you wait, I'll be back to deal with you"—that informs much of civil society's language as it engages with the state's failure to deliver on the promises it made to its citizens.

As Clark describes so eloquently in her first chapter, "'Boomerang': Hip-Hop and Pan-African Dialogues," the continent's hip-hop messengers all link back to the community of black cultures in content, style, vocabulary, and rhyming, thereby creating an opportunity for today's youth to understand the legacies of their communities. It is important for today's messengers to see themselves not as pioneers but as a continuation of a larger and longer struggle for the emancipation of black lives. Sometimes they miss this; it has come home to me most forcefully in some of the rhetoric of the #BlackLivesMatter and #RhodesMustFall activists that is sometimes dehistoricized and decontextualized from the earlier Pan-African and civil rights movements. And yet we are not left with a romanticized picture. Problematized are lyrics, the controversial place of braggadocio with all its consumer-capitalist and exploitative overtones, and the mainstreaming of protest.

An afterword should cement our hope. And *Hip-Hop in Africa* offers hope because our griots and akyeame have moved off the hallowed forest paths of sometimes fossilized "tradition" onto the social, political, and economic highways. They move with speed. They are not respectfully silent. They are the *abrafo*, the royal army, claiming their Africa. The continental and diasporic connections that Clark maps, both in music and in larger projects such as documentaries, are evidence of the blurring of lines among this generation of black people. If we take America's M-1 and DJ Awadi's "The Roots" (2010), or Ghanaian Blitz the Ambassador and Chuck D's "The Oracle" (2011), we see conversations about the lives of black people across borders. While the African Union may be slow in dismantling artificial borders, while we may still need visas just to transit from one African country to another, continental hip-hop collaborations such as Professor Jay (Tanzania) and Kwaw Kese (Ghana)'s "Who Be You" (2010), and M.anifest (Ghana) and Krukid (Uganda)'s African Rebel Movement that birthed the album *Two Africans and a Jew* have already found ways to transcend the borders and bring together young Africans from all over the world, not just Africa.

Two Ghanaian gems bring my comments to a close. One of Ghana's best music videos for 2016, Flowking Stone's "Rapping Drums," represents the best of hip-hop and hiplife, incorporating diverse dance moves from across Ghana, including Damba, Adowa, Kete, and Agbadja. At Wiyaala's debut performance to outdoor her self-titled album in 2014, she invited her parents onto the stage. Flowking Stone represents the reuniting of people from diverse backgrounds and Wiyaala, the reuniting of the generations. Here's to our future, filled with dustyfoot, transformational philosophers and soldiers!

Appendix 1

Artist Interviews

This list includes the name of each artist, their country of origin, and the date and location of the interview.

Abramz (of Breakdance Project Uganda) | Uganda | December 29, 2013 | Kampala.

Amkoullel l'enfant Peulh | Mali | multiple interviews, 2011–16 | Los Angeles, Hartford, Washington, DC.

Panji Anoff (of Pidgen Music) | Ghana | July 23, 2011 | Accra.

Baay Bia | Senegal | January 21, 2012 via telephone.

Babaluku (of Bavubuka Foundation) | Uganda | multiple interviews, 2007–13 | via telephone and Kampala.

Black Athena | South Africa | July 14, 2016 | Cape Town.

Black Bird | Zimbabwe | September 27, 2012 | via Skype.

Blitz the Ambassador | Ghana | August 24, 2011 | Brooklyn, NY.

Burni Aman (of Godessa) | South Africa | March 1, 2014 | Cape Town.

Chazz le Hippie | South Africa | July 5, 2016 | via telephone.

Cindy Rulz | Tanzania | January 26, 2014 | Dar es Salaam.

Coin Moko, Ehks B, and Rage Prophetional, (of Rebel Sonz) | Tanzania | August 16, 2009 | Dar es Salaam.

D-Black | Ghana | September 1, 2010 | Accra.

Da Brains | Senegal | August 6, 2009 | Dakar.

Devour Ke Lenyora | South Africa | July 2, 2016 | Johannesburg.

DJ Colors | Democratic Republic of the Congo | December 24, 2013 | Kampala.

Balozi Dola (aka Balozi) | Tanzania | July 10, 2011 | Chicago.

Doom E. Right | Zimbabwe | August 26, 2011 | via telephone.

Dope Saint Jude | South Africa | July 14, 2017 | Cape Town.

Edem | Ghana | multiple interviews, 2011–17 | via telephone and Accra.

Emmanuel Jal | South Sudan | February 24, 2009 | Washington, DC.

Fafi Threepercent | Zimbabwe | June 4, 2011 | Tucson, AZ.

Fid Q | Tanzania | multiple interviews, 2010–12 | Dar es Salaam.

Duke Gervalius | Tanzania | July 27, 2014 | Dar es Salaam.

Hashim | Tanzania | September 18, 2010 | Dar es Salaam.

JCB | Tanzania | August 8, 2010 | Dar es Salaam.

J-Town | Ghana | September 3, 2010 | Accra.

Just Lyphe (aka Dumi) | Zimbabwe | March 24, 2011 | Los Angeles.

Kama (of Kalamashaka) | Kenya| October 16, 2011 | Palo Alto, CA.

Kanyi | South Africa | July 13, 2016 | Cape Town.

KBC (of Kwanza Unit) | Tanzania | multiple interviews, 2010–17 | via telephone.

Keyti | Senegal | August 2, 2009| Dakar | October 18, 2016 | Washington, DC.

Krukid/Ruyonga | Uganda | December 25, 2013 | Kampala.

M.anifest | Ghana | September 6, 2011 | Minneapolis.

Mangwea | Tanzania | August 3, 2010 | Dar es Salaam.

Mastah Boobah | Ivory Coast | June 15, 2011 | Washington, DC.

Mkuki Bgoya (of Kina Klothing) | Tanzania | August 10, 2010 | Dar es Salaam.

M3NSA | Ghana | February 17, 2013 | Los Angeles.

Mxc Wol | South Sudan | January 25, 2012 | via telephone.

Nazlee | South Africa | July 14, 2016 | Cape Town.

Ncha Kali | Tanzania | August 20, 2010 | Dar es Salaam.

Nikki Mbishi | Tanzania | multiple interviews, 2013–14 | Dar es Salaam.

One the Incredible | Tanzania | multiple interviews, 2013–14 | Dar es Salaam.

Quame Junior | Ghana | September 1, 2010 | Accra.

Reggie Rockstone | Ghana | September 15, 2010 | Accra.

Saba Saba | Uganda | January 15, 2010; December 25, 2011 | Los Angeles.

Saigon | Tanzania | August 23, 2011 | Dar es Salaam.

Salu T | Tanzania | May 24, 2014 | Dar es Salaam.

Sarkodie | Ghana | September 6, 2010 | Tema.

Shaheen Ariefdien (of Prophets of da City) | South Africa | September 5, 2011 | Toronto.

Shameema (of Godessa) | South Africa | July 17, 2016 | Cape Town.

Sister Fa | Senegal | January 18, 2012 | via telephone.

Slim Emcee (UG) the poet | Uganda | December 24, 2013 | Kampala.

Songa | Tanzania | multiple interviews, 2013–14 | Dar es Salaam.

Stosh | Tanzania | multiple interviews, 2013–14 | Dar es Salaam.

Sugu | Tanzania | August 23, 2011 | Dar es Salaam.

Guin Thieuss | Senegal | May 29, 2011 | Los Angeles.

Tifa | Tanzania | multiple interviews, 2013–14 | Dar es Salaam.

Trigmatic | Ghana | September 3, 2010 | Accra.

2C | Liberia | June 7, 2011 | Atlanta.

Wachata Crew | Tanzania | multiple interviews, 2013–16 | online and Dar es Salaam.

Wakazi | Tanzania | July 10, 2011 | Chicago.

Wanaitwa Uhuru | Tanzania | multiple interviews, 2013–14 | Dar es Salaam.

Michael Wanguhu | Kenya | February 18, 2011 | Los Angeles.

Wanlov the Kubolor | Ghana | September 1, 2010 | Accra.

Waterflow | Senegal | August 14, 2011 | Washington, DC.

Witnesz | Tanzania | multiple interviews, 2010–14 | Dar es Salaam.

Xuman | Senegal | August 7, 2009 | Dakar | October 18, 2016 | Washington, DC.

Yaa Pono | Ghana | July 25, 2011 | Accra.

Yugen Blakrok | South Africa | July 1, 2016 | Johannesburg.

Zavara aka Rhymson | Tanzania | multiple interviews, 2013–17 | via phone and Dar es Salaam.

Appendix 2

Companion Website

The companion site for this book can be found at:

https://hiphopafrican.com/hip-hop-in-africa

The companion site features resources, by chapter, and provides audiovisual material, links to material discussed in the book, and links to artists' websites.

Notes

Chapter 1: "Boomerang"

The title of the chapter refers to the song and album titled *Boomerang*, released by the Senegalese hip-hop duo Daara J in 2004. The album title signified hip-hop's return to Africa.

1. RAP é attitude / . . . / rimas potentes por cima de beats fats / esperámos muito tempo agora é a nossa vez / . . . / esse é o nosso amor / e nós levamos a peito / queremos ouvidos / queremos vosso respeito / criticamos o país pro bem da nação / as nossas calças largas é questão de identificação/não usamos fardas mas lutamos pelo país / guerrilheiros fora da mata / soldados civis / guerrilheiros fora da mata / soldados civis.

2. The Black Arts movement came out of the black nationalist movement in America. Its confrontation of racism, its embrace of black ascetics, and its rage are said to have heavily influenced hip-hop (Gladney 1995; Hoch 2006; Ongiri 2009)

3. *Hip-hop head* is a common term for an active member of hip-hop culture. Urbandictionary.com provides a comprehensive definition: "someone that embodies the Hip Hop culture usually consisting of an avid interest or participation in Hip Hop Music, MCing, Djing, Breakdancing and Graffiti Art. A Hip Hop Head is usually more into underground/independant [sic] Hip Hop rather than the more commercial/mainstream rap heard on the radio. A Hip Hop Head also has a great knowledge in the history of Hip Hop stemming from the roots in the South Bronx up until the modern day."

Chapter 2: "Understand Where I'm Coming From"

The title of the chapter refers to the song "Understand Where I'm Coming From," released by South African hip-hop pioneers Prophets of da City in 1993 on their album *Age of Truth*.

1. Frances Cress Welsing was an African American psychiatrist whose writings on white supremacy in America were influential in African-centered thought and activism in America.
2. The country code for Kenya is 254.
3. Translation provided by Fid Q.

Chapter 3: "Lettre à Mr le Président"

The title of the chapter refers to the song "Lettre à Mr le Président," released by Cameroonian hip-hop artist Valsero in 2009. The song was a protest against President Biya, and it got Valsero in trouble with authorities.

1. Titles, translation, and lyrics provided by Fid Q. Swahili version:

> KIDUMU CHAMA CHA MASELA Ukoloni mambo leo umetupa uhuru wa bendera / tuone kufuru za wenye hela / TANZANIA ni demu wa mtungo wanamuiita CHA WOOTE / HANGOVER . . . anaikimbia kwa kupiga mtungi saa zote . . . Mkubwa anazuga atasolve matatizo ya nchi yake / na gari bovu . . . halisukumwi kwa kukaa ndani yake / MAENDELEO ni ile ndoto . . . hakuna UHURU wa kweli (Africa) msidanganywe na illusion / na daily tunafeli sababu ya POLITICAL institutions / CIVILIZATION imeadvance sasa wanatuua economically / hakuna utumwa mbaya kama ule wa kujiona uko free.

2. The term *queer* refers to people who identify as lesbian, gay, bisexual, transgender, or other gender as well as to other sexual identities that are not heteronormative.
3. "They [the citizens] sell okra."
4. "A better life for every Tanzanian."
5. A serial killer who killed more than a dozen people in South Africa in 2004.
6. Boer are descendants of the original Dutch settlers in the region; "moer" (rhymes with "poor") means "attack violently."
7. Slang term for police.
8. Translation by Msia Kibona Clark (2012a). Original:

> Modwene se eda fom, gyae nipa rebre / Obi te Canada, nee obei koraa, osre/Burgers yi bebree na entaa nka nokore / Anka mobehunu se amanone mpo ye foo kyere / Wote Ghana pam adee nya wo sika / Nea wobɛdi, woanya koraa wowo beebi da / Woaboa sika ano de akogye visa / Wope se wotu kwan ko America ko bre kwa / Afutuo nsakyere nipa na koso hwe / . . . Amanehunu kwa, wei eye hwan na fault / Obre a wote

Ghana anka woabie sukuu ama Tigo afa wo manager / Na wote obi man so pra kwan ho / Ewo se woso ho, efiri se wonni beebi da.

9. Suburban neighborhoods where poor migrants often live.

10. Translation by Christopher Stroud (2015). Original:

> At home, um-Somalia is black / Xenophobia is wack / iNigeria yhi plek yama-Afrika Respect! / [Chorus] Liphalel'igazi / Yhile xenophobia... Ulahlekelw'umfazi / Yhile xenophobia... Sikhathel'emzantsi / Yhile xenophobia... Ma-Afrik'ay'phele le xenophobia ... / eMalaw'eZambia/eGhan'eTopia... eZimbabw'eGambia / All over Afrika.

11. Translation provided by azlyrics.com/lyrics/knaan/soobax. Original:

> Dadki waa dinten nagalaa soobax / Dibki waa butten nagalaa soobax / Deegii waa butten nagalaa soobax / Duulki waa guubten nagalaa soobax / Nagalaa soobax / Nagalaa soobax.

12. Sean Bell was an African American man who was shot and killed by police in New York City in 2006.

13. Trayvon Martin was an African American teenage boy who was shot and killed by a neighborhood watch patroller in 2012. Martin's death greatly contributed to the start of the #BlackLivesMatter movement.

14. The Basters are a group with biracial backgrounds similar to South African Coloureds. They are a mix of white Boers and black Khoisan residents of South Africa, who migrated to Namibia, where they maintained a separate identity (Lang 1998).

15. Fallists, in the context of the social movements in South Africa, are activists advocating for the fall of school fees, statues and buildings honoring people who represent apartheid (Cecil Rhodes), and politicians who have they feel have betrayed the antiapartheid struggle. It is also a largely women-led movement that also often espouses African feminist and queer politics.

16. A reference to the 1976 Soweto uprisings.

17. The Gupta family has been seen by many South Africans as colluding with Jacob uma in several corruption scandals.

Chapter 4: "Femme de Combat"

The title of the chapter refers to the song "Femme de Combat" (Fighting woman), a 2009 release by BlackTiger, Burni Aman, René

Mosele, and Thaïs on the album *Rogue State of Mind*, pt. 2. The song features Swiss and South African female emcees speaking on women confronting various social oppressions.

1. "They call us cold."
2. "A UFO burst on the scene."
3. "Ugh, but this train is not turning around."
4. *Emi* means "I'm."
5. *Eyin* means "if."
6. Translation by Clark 2014. Original:

Jua kuja battle nami, wazi ukajipange joh / . . . we kwangu utakaa/ Mi toka moyoni we darasani / . . . Style zako fake copy and pasting mi ndo queen of flowz.

7. Translation by Mose 2013 and the author. Original:

First Lady kwa beat / kama hii iki-pump kwa ma-streets za Nai- / robbery town tuki-represent washe / na wadhii / wanaojiunga name / juu hii sound ya Ukoo Flani na mi / N-A, Z-I, zi / toka Mau Mau wapate uhuru sa tuko free / ku-rock ma-crowds so wanacheza nasi / hawawezi kataa instead wana-agree / that we the illest / kwa hii crowd ya wasanii / that's why tunachaguliwa na mateenie / wa Zimmer, South B na Eastleigh.

8. Translation by africaresource.com 2010. Original:

Bien sappé le matin tu parts à la course du temps / Tu ne prends pas tout ton temps à marcher comme au printemps / Tu ne donnes pas tellement d'importance à celui qui pretend / Que la vie en milieu rural est difficile / Car toi rak ndaw tu ne vis que des choses faciles / Pour faire tes courses tu as là ta très jolie bagnole / Tu t'y promènes aisément comme un tout petit rossignol / Pendant que moi tot le matin je parts pour les rizieres / Bébé porté au dos je parcours des kilometers / Deguisée en haillons comme si je n'avais rien à mettre / Pour vivre heureuse c'est le travail que je dois admettre / J y dépense toute mon énergie sans aucun remord / Et pour prouver ma bravoure je me mets tout simplement à chantonner.

9. Saartjie "Sarah" Baartman was a Khoi woman born in Southern Africa in the late 1700s. She was taken to Europe and paraded around Europe nude as a spectacle because of her large breasts and buttocks. She would later be driven to prostitution, before she eventually died in her midtwenties.

10. "This one is gay." (This and the following three translations provided by the artist.)
11. "Get with it, I'm the shit."

12. "A streetwise hustler, a boss who is able to adjust to any situation and make it better."

13. "You feel me my dog!"

14. Heteronormativity is the idea that heterosexuality is normal.

Chapter 5: "Make You No Forget"

"Make You No Forget" is a 2014 song by Ghanaian rapper Blitz the Ambassador and Nigerian Musician Seun Kuti. In the song's chorus Kuti sings, "Make you no forget where you from."

1. "Hold post" is a slang term for maintaining a presence in a location.

2. Khat is a plant that grows in the horn of Africa and produces a feeling of euphoria in those who chew its leaves.

3. This is a reference to Rakim's 1987 song "Paid in Full."

4. California emcees Dr. Dre and Snoop Dogg.

5. Popular slang term used frequently in the western United States by Latino (often Mexican) males to refer to other Latino males.

6. Slang for the American south.

7. Slang for Atlanta, Georgia.

8. Airport code for Miami International Airport and, by extension, the city itself.

9. "Ali boomaye" (Ali, kill him) was chanted by Congolese during the 1974 heavyweight fight between Muhammad Ali and George Foreman in the Democratic Republic of the Congo (then Zaire).

10. For example, James Burns (2009) examines the articulation of migrant experiences by Ghanaian performers in the diaspora. He presents Koo Nimo's song "Abrokyire Abrabo" (Overseas life), by an artist who, like the four artists in this study, describes the anticipation of migration followed by the difficult realities faced by many African immigrants in the West.

11. B visas are nonimmigrant visas given to foreign citizens traveling to the United States for short periods.

12. Not maintaining full-time status in school can jeopardize the legal status of international students.

13. Kelewele is a popular Ghanaian dish made from fried plantains. Fufu is a popular West African dish made with cassava flour.

Chapter 6: "Brkn Lngwjz"

"Brkn Lngwjz" (Broken Languages) is a 2010 release by the Ghanaian duo Fokn Bois, made up of Wanlov the Kubolor and M3NSA. The song, a celebration of the culture that the two artists come from, is done entirely in Pidgin English.

    1. Sheng is a mix of Swahili, English, and other Kenyan languages.

    2. Detroit Red was Malcolm X's nickname before he converted to Islam.

    3. AZ is a New York rap artist who was popular in the late 1990s and early 2000s.

    4. The term *homie* has roots in AAVE/HHNL and is used to refer to someone who is from your home, specifically your neighborhood—someone who has your back and is like family.

    5. The term *Black social media* refers to the network of social media content creators and consumers who create and consume content that is relevant to, or directly speaks to, black people and culture. Popular content creators on black social media often have tens of thousands of followers (consumers) each, who will often spread news stories, memes, and commentary produced by those content creators, ensuring that popular posts easily reach over a million people.

    6. TheRoot: https://www.theroot.com/black-americans-don-t-appropriate-african-culture-1790861102.

    7. HuffPost: https://www.huffingtonpost.com/entry/is-it-cultural-appropriation-when-africans-wear-jordans_us_56099b3be4b0768126fea24d.

By Way of an Afterword

    1. The comment was made during her speech at Krobo Girls Presbyterian Senior High School's annual Speech and Prize-Giving Day, 2017. https://citifmonline.com/2017/03/26/social-media-fumes-as-otiko-tells-girls-no-to-attract-rapists-with-short-skirts/.

    2. *Ɔkyeame* has often been inappropriately translated into English as "linguist."

References

Abdellatif, B. H. 2010. "African Skilled Labour Migration: Dimensions and Impact." In *International Migration within, to and from Africa in a Globalised World,* edited by Aderanti Adepoju, 97–118. Accra: Sub-Saharan Publishers.

Abdulai, David. 1992. "Rawlings 'Wins' Ghana's Presidential Elections: Establishing a New Constitutional Order." *Africa Today* 39 (4): 66–71.

Acheampong, E. O. 2015. "The U.S. Visitor Visa (B-Visa); What Does It Really Entail?" *Ghanaweb.com,* September 12. http://www.ghanaweb.com/GhanaHomePage/features/The-U-S-Visitor-Visa-B-Visa-What-Does-It-Really-Entail-381172.

Adepoju, A. 2010. "Rethinking the Dynamics of Migration within, from and to Africa." In *International Migration within, to and from Africa in a Globalised World,* 9–45. Accra: Sub-Saharan Publishers.

Adichie, C. N. 2009. *The Danger of a Single Story* (video file). https://www.ted.com/talks/chimamanda_adichie_the_danger_of_a_single_story.

Africaresource.com. 2010. "Sister Fa." http://www.africaresource.com/lifestyle/profiles/699-sister-fa.

African Urbanism. 2014. "In Dakar, a Graffiti Festival Connects Artists, Cultures and Ideas." *AfricanUrbanism.com,* April 24. http://africanurbanism.net/2014/04/24/dakar-festigraff-2014/.

Afropolitan Vibes. 2014. *Fokn Bois, Bantu.* Afropolitan Vibes, June 18. https://www.youtube.com/watch?v=WIVM2vf9AAk.

Al Jazeera. 2011. "Angolan Youths Arrested for Staging Rally." Al Jazeera English, September 4. http://www.aljazeera.com/news/africa/2011/09/20119441813571546.html.

Ali, A. A. G. 2002. "Structural Adjustment Programs and Poverty in Sub-Saharan Africa: 1985–1995." In *African Voices on Structural Adjustment: A Companion to Our Continent, Our Future,* edited by T. Mkandawire and C. C. Soludo, 189–228. Trenton, NJ: Africa World Press.

Alim, H. S. 2003. "On Some Serious Next Millennium Rap Ishhh: Pharoahe Monch, Hip Hop Poetics, and the Internal Rhymes of Internal Affairs." *Journal of English Linguistics* 31 (1): 60–84.

———. 2006. *Roc the Mic Right: The Language of Hip Hop Culture*. Routledge.

———. 2009. "Creating 'an Empire within an Empire': Critical Hip Hop Language Pedagogies and the Role of Sociolinguists." In *Global Linguistic Flows: Hip Hop Cultures, Youth Identities, and the Politics of Language*, edited by Alim, A. Ibrahim, and A. Pennycook, 213–30. New York: Routledge.

Alim, H. S., and A. Pennycook. 2007. "Glocal Linguistic Flows: Hip-Hop Culture(s), Identities, and the Politics of Language Education." *Journal of Language, Identity and Education* 6 (2): 89–100.

Altman, D. 2004. "Sexuality and Globalization." *Sexuality Research and Social Policy* 1 (1): 63–68.

Anderson, M. 2015. "African Immigrant Population in U.S. Steadily Climbs." *Pew Research Center*. http://www.pewresearch.org/fact-tank/2015/11/02/african-immigrant-population-in-u-s-steadily-climbs/.

Appert, C. M. 2016. "On Hybridity in African Popular Music: The Case of Senegalese Hip Hop." *Ethnomusicology* 60 (2): 279–99.

Apraku, K. K. 1991. *African Emigres in the United States: A Missing Link in Africa's Social and Economic Development*. New York: Praeger.

Arango, J. 2000. "Explaining Migration: A Critical View." *International Social Science Journal* 52 (165): 283–96.

Ariefdien, S., and M. Burgess. 2011. "Putting Two Heads Together: A Cross-generational Conversation about Hip-Hop in South Africa." In *Native Tongues: An African Hip-Hop Reader*, edited by P. K. Saucier, 219–52. Trenton, NJ: Africa World Press.

Ariefdien, S., and R. Chapman. 2014. "Hip Hop, Youth Activism, and the Dilemma of Coloured Identity in South Africa." In *Hip Hop and Social Change in Africa: Ni Wakati*, edited by M. K. Clark and M. W. Koster, 94–111. Lanham: Lexington Press.

Arnfred, S., ed. 2004. *Re-thinking Sexualities in Africa*. Uppsala: Nordiska Afrikainstitutet.

Arthur, J. A. 2000. *Invisible Sojourners: African Immigrant Diaspora in the United States*. Westport, CT: Praeger.

Attwood, F. 2006. "Sexed Up: Theorizing the Sexualization of Culture." *Sexualities* 9 (1): 77–94.

Awokoya. J. T. 2012. "Reconciling Multiple Black Identities: The Case of 1.5 and 2.0 Nigerian Immigrants." In *Africans in Global Migration: Searching for Promised Lands*, edited by J. A. Arthur, J. Takougang, and T. Y. Owusu, 97–116. Lanham, MD: Lexington Books.

B-Global Indigenous Hip Hop Gathering. n.d. https://www.facebook.com/BGlobalIndigenousHipHop/info.

Bâ, S. W. 1973. *The Concept of Negritude in the Poetry of Léopold Sédar Senghor.* Princeton: Princeton University Press.

Bagnall, R. S., R. Casagrande-Kim, A. Ersoy, and C. Tanriver, eds. 2016. *Graffiti from the Basilica in the Agora of Smyrna.* New York: NYU Press.

Bailey, D. 2006. "Stemming the Immigration Wave." *BBC News*, September 10. http://news.bbc.co.uk/2/hi/europe/5331896.stm.

Bakhtin, M. M. 1986. *Speech Genres and Other Late Essays.* Translated by Vern W. McGee. Austin: University of Texas Press.

Baloyi, B., and G. Isaacs. 2015. "South Africa's 'Fees Must Fall' Protests Are about More Than Tuition Costs." *CNN.com*, October 28. http://www.cnn.com/2015/10/27/africa/fees-must-fall-student-protest-south-africa-explainer/.

Barker, C. 2012. *Cultural Studies: Theory and Practice.* 4th ed. London: Sage.

Barker, C., and D. Galasiński. 2001. *Cultural Studies and Discourse Analysis: A Dialogue on Language and Identity.* London: Sage.

Barlow, S., and B. Eyre. 2005. "African Hip Hop in Tanzania—Highlights of a Conversation with Alex Perullo." *Afropop.org*. http://www.afropop.org/multi/interview/ID/67/AFRICAN+HIP+HOP+IN+TANZANIA+-+Highlights+of+a+Conversation+with+Alex+Perullo.

Bavubuka Foundation. n.d. Bavubuka Foundation. http://www.bavubuka.org.

Bazawule, S. [Blitz the Ambassador]. 2014. "Ghanaian Rapper Hopes to Take His 'Afropolitan Dreams' Back Home." NPR, July 31. http://www.npr.org/2014/07/31/336829806/ghanaian-rapper-hopes-to-take-his-afropolitan-dreams-back-home.

BBC World Service. 2000. "African Unions Want Libya Violence Inquiry." *BBC News*, October 25. http://news.bbc.co.uk/2/hi/middle_east/990917.stm.

———. 2013. "Lampedusa Boat Disaster: Death Toll Rises to 232." *BBC News*, October 7. http://www.bbc.co.uk/news/world-europe-24436779.

Beah, I. 2007. *A Long Way Gone: Memoirs of a Boy Soldier.* New York: Farrar, Straus and Giroux.

Beekman, D. 2010. "From the Bronx, Birthplace of Hip-Hop Music, Comes Ghana's 'Hiplife.'" *New York Daily News,* June 29. http://www.nydailynews.com/new-york/bronx/bronx-birthplace-hip-hop-music-ghana-hiplife-article-1.178974.

Berktay, A. 2014. "Beyond Y'en A Marre: Pikine's Hip Hop Youth Say 'Enough Is Enough' and Pave the Way for Continuous Social Change." In *Hip Hop and Social Change in Africa: Ni Wakati,* edited by M. K. Clark and M. M. Koster, 112–43. Lanham, MD: Lexington Books.

Boffard, R. 2011. "Hip-Hop: Who Represents South Africa?" *Guardian,* February 17. http://www.guardian.co.uk/music/2011/feb/17/south-african-hip-hop-the-future.

Bond, P., and G. Dor. 2003. "Uneven Health Outcomes and Political Resistance under Residual Neoliberalism in Africa." Life after Capitalism: Health. *ZNet at the World Social Forum,* January 25. Porto Alegre, Brazil. http://www.zcommunications.org/uneven-health-outcomes-and-political-resistance-under-residual-neoliberalism-in-africa-by-patrick-bond-1.

Boorstin, J. 2013. "Facebook vs. Twitter: Here's How They're Different." *CNBC,* October 4. http://www.cnbc.com/id/101087718.

Boyer-Rossol, K. 2014. "From the Great Island to the African Continent through the Western World: Itineraries of a 'Return to the Origins' through Hip Hop Music in Madagascar 2000–2011." In *Hip Hop and Social Change in Africa: Ni Wakati,* edited by M. K. Clark and M. M. Koster, 178–97. Lanham, MD: Lexington Books.

Bradley, A. 2009. *Book of Rhymes: The Poetics of Hip Hop.* New York: Basic Civitas Books.

Branch, D. 2011. *Kenya: Between Hope and Despair, 1963–2011.* New Haven: Yale University Press.

Brown, S. 2001. "Authoritarian Leaders and Multiparty Elections in Africa: How Foreign Donors Help to Keep Kenya's Daniel arap Moi in Power." *Third World Quarterly* 22 (5): 725–39.

Brydon, L., and K. Legge. 1996. *Adjusting Society: The World Bank, the IMF and Ghana.* London: Tauris Academic Studies.

Burns, J. 2009. "'The West Is Cold': Experiences of Ghanaian Performers in England and the United States." In *The New African Diaspora,* edited by I. Okpewho and N. Nzegwu, 127–45. Bloomington: Indiana University Press.

Campbell, E. 2010. "Irregular Migration within and to the Republic of South Africa and from the African Continent to the European Union: Tapping Latent Energy of the Youth." In *International Migration within, to and from Africa in a Globalised World*, edited by A. Adepoju, 169–207. Accra: Sub-Saharan Publishers.

Casco, J. A. 2012. "From Music to Politics: Hip Hop in Africa as a Political Option for the Youth: The Case of Tanzania." In *Youth and the City: Expressive Cultures, Public Space Appropriation, and Alternative Political Participation*, 1–18. Madrid: 8º Congreso Ibérico de Estudios Africanos.

Chaddha, A., and W. J. Wilson. 2010. "Why We're Teaching 'The Wire' at Harvard." *Washington Post*, September 12, p. 9.

Chale. 2011. "Didier Awadi's Presidents d'Afrique Pays Tribute to Pan-African Leaders" (blog), February 19. http://www.museke.com/node/7430.

Chang, J., and DJ Kool Herc. 2005. *Can't Stop, Won't Stop: A History of the Hip-Hop Generation*. New York: Picador.

Charry, E. 2012. "A Capsule History of African Rap." In *Hip Hop Africa: New Music in a Globalizing World*, edited by E. Charry, 1–25. Bloomington: Indiana University Press.

Cho, G. 2010. "Hiplife, Cultural Agency and the Youth Counter-public in the Ghanaian Public Sphere." *Journal of Asian and African Studies* 45 (4):406–23.

Christen, R. S. 2003. "Hip Hop Learning: Graffiti as an Educator of Urban Teenagers." *Journal of Educational Foundations* 17 (4): 57.

Clark, M. K. 2009a. "Emmanuel Jal Sheds Light on Struggles in Southern Sudan." *allAfrica.com*, April 3. http://allafrica.com/stories/200904030753.html.

———. 2009b. "Questions of Identity among African Immigrants in America." In *The New African Diaspora*, edited by I. Okpewho and N. Nzegwu, 255–70. Bloomington: Indiana University Press.

———. 2011. "Bongo Flava and Hip Hop." *allAfrica.com*, April 25. http://allafrica.com/stories/201104251053.html.

———. 2012a. "Hip Hop as Social Commentary in Accra and Dar es Salaam." *African Studies Quarterly* 13 (3): 23–46. http://sites.clas.ufl.edu/africa-asq/files/Clark-V13Is3.pdf.

———. 2012b. "Identity Formation and Integration among Bicultural Immigrant Blacks." In *Africans in Global Migration: Searching for Promised Lands*, edited by J. A. Arthur, J. Takougang, and T. Owusu, 45–66. Lexington Press.

———. 2013. "The Struggle for Hip Hop Authenticity and against Commercialization in Tanzania." *Journal of Pan African Studies* 6 (3): 5–21.

———. 2014. "Gendered Representations among Tanzanian Female Emcees." In *Hip Hop and Social Change in Africa: Ni Wakati*, edited by M. K. Clark and M. M. Koster, 144–69. Lanham, MD: Lexington Books.

Clay, A. 2003. "Keepin' It Real: Black Youth, Hip-Hop Culture, and Black Identity." *American Behavioral Scientist* 46 (10): 1346–58.

Cobb, W. J. 2007. *To the Break of Dawn: A Freestyle on the Hip-Hop Aesthetic.* New York: NYU Press.

Cole, J. 2013. "Let Nas Down." Recorded by J. Cole on *Born Sinner*. Dreamville/ByStorm/Roc Nation/Columbia/Sony.

Cole, J., and B. Guy-Sheftall. 2003. *Gender Talk: The Struggle for Women's Equality in African American Communities.* New York: One World/Ballantine.

Collins, E. J. 1987. "Jazz Feedback to Africa." *American Music* 5 (2): 176–93.

———. 2012. "Contemporary Ghanaian Popular Music since the 1980s." In *Hip Hop Africa: New Music in a Globalizing World*, edited by E. Charry, 211–33. Bloomington: Indiana University Press.

Cottle, S., ed. 2000. *Ethnic Minorities and the Media: Changing Cultural Boundaries.* Philadelphia: Open University Press.

Cowie, D. F. 2009. "K'naan: The Beautiful Struggle." *Exclaim!*, January 25. http://exclaim.ca/music/article/knaan-_beautiful_struggle.

Crowder, N. 2015. "The Breaks: Uganda's Break Dance Culture Pops and Locks into Perfect Milnor Form." *Washington Post*, February 4. https://www.washingtonpost.com/news/in-sight/wp/2015/02/04/the-breaks-ugandas-break-dance-culture-pops-and-locks-into-perfect-form/.

Dabiri, E. 2016. "Why I Am (Still) Not an Afropolitan." *Journal of African Cultural Studies* 28 (1): 1–5.

Dennis, C. 2012. *Afro-Colombian Hip-Hop: Globalization, Transcultural Music, and Ethnic Identities.* Lanham, MD: Lexington Books.

Devonish, H. 1986. *Language and Liberation: Creole Language Politics in the Caribbean.* London: Karia Press.

Dina, J. 2001. "The Hazomanga among the Masikoro of Southwest Madagascar: Identity and History." *Ethnohistory* 48 (1–2): 13–30.

Diouf, S. n.d. "The New African Diaspora." Schomburg Center for Research in Black Culture. http://www.inmotionaame.org/texts/?migration=13&topic=99&type=text.

Dosi, M. A. M., L. Rushubirwa, and G. A. Myers. 2007. "Tanzanians in the Land of Oz: Diaspora and Transnationality in Wichita, Kansas." *Social and Cultural Geography* 8 (5): 657–71.

Durham, A., B. C. Cooper, and S. M. Morris. "The Stage Hip-Hop Feminism Built: A New Directions Essay." *Signs* 38 (3): 721–37.

Dyson, M. E. 2004. *The Michael Eric Dyson Reader*. New York: Basic Civitas Books.

Eastman, C. M. 1985. "Establishing Social Identity through Language Use." *Journal of Language and Social Psychology* 4 (1): 1–20.

ECA (Economic Commission for Africa). 1989. *African Alternative Framework to Structural Adjustment Programmes for Socio-economic Recovery and Transformation (AAF-SAP): A Popular Version*. Addis Ababa: ECA.

Elliot, M. 2001. "Watcha Gon' Do?" Recorded by M. Elliot and T. Mosely. On *Miss E . . . So Addictive* (CD). Goldmind/Elektra.

Engels, B. 2015. "Political Transition in Burkina Faso: The Fall of Blaise Compaoré." *Governance in Africa* 2 (1): 1–6.

Englert, B. 2003. "Bongo Flava (Still) Hidden: 'Underground' Rap from Morogoro, Tanzania." *Stichproben (Wiener Zeitschrift für kritische Afrikastudien)* 5 (3): 73–93. http://www.univie.ac.at/ecco/stichproben/nr5_english.htm.

Essence. 2009. "K'Naan: 'Rap Music Helped Me Learn English.'" *Essence.com*, December 16. http://www.essence.com/2009/05/14/knaan-rap-music-helped-me-learn-english.

Eze, C. 2014. "Rethinking African Culture and Identity: The Afropolitan Model." *Journal of African Cultural Studies* 26 (2): 234–47.

———. 2016. "'We, Afropolitans.'" *Journal of African Cultural Studies* 28 (1): 114–19.

Fallon, A. 2015. "From Headlines to Hip-Hop: The Ugandan TV Show Rapping the News." *Guardian*, June 10. http://www.theguardian.com/world/2015/jun/10/uganda-hip-hop-tv-presenter-rapping-the-news-newzbeat.

Fanon, F. 2004. *The Wretched of the Earth*. New York: Grove Press.

Farred, G. 2010. "Out of Context: Thinking Cultural Studies Diasporically." In *The African Diaspora and the Disciplines*, edited by T. Olaniyan and J. H. Sweet, 256–78. Bloomington: Indiana University Press.

Fenn, J. 2012. "Style, Message, and Meaning in Malawian Youth Rap and Ragga Performances." In *Hip Hop Africa: New Music in a Globalizing World*, edited by E. Charry, 109–28. Bloomington: Indiana University Press.

Fernandes, S. 2012. "The Mixtape of the Revolution." *New York Times*, January 29. http://www.nytimes.com/2012/01/30/opinion/the-mixtape-of-the-revolution.html?_r=0.

Fessy, T. 2011. "Senegal Rapper Thiat Rocks President Wade." *BBC News*, August 4. http://www.bbc.co.uk/news/world-africa-14403302.

Flock, E. 2014. "A Female Rapper Busts onto Senegal's Male-Dominated Hip Hop Scene." *Global Post*, June 22. http://www.globalpost.com/dispatch/news/regions/africa/senegal/140616/toussa-senerap-GOTAL-rapper-west-african-hip-hop.

Flynn, M., and C. J. Cannon. 2009. "The Privatization of Immigration Detention: Towards a Global View." Global Detention Project. http://citeseerx.ist.psu.edu/viewdoc/download?doi=10.1.1.366.4051&rep=rep1&type=pd.

Foner, N., ed. 2001. *Islands in the City: West Indian Migration to New York*. Berkeley: University of California Press.

Forman, M. 2002. *The 'Hood Comes First: Race, Space, and Place in Rap and Hip-Hop*. Middletown, CT: Wesleyan University Press.

Fredericks, R. 2014. "'The Old Man Is Dead': Hip Hop and the Arts of Citizenship of Senegalese Youth." *Antipode* 46 (1): 130–48.

Gallagher, J. 2015. *Images of Africa: Creation, Negotiation and Subversion*. Manchester University Press.

Garang, M. 2009. "Kenyan Female Artistes Breaking the Glass Ceiling." *Saturday Nation*, November 26. http://www.nation.co.ke/lifestyle/lifestyle/-/1214/812746/-/8nn091/-/index.html.

Garcia, M., and J. Fares. 2008. "Why Is It Important for Africa to Invest in Its Youth?" In *Youth in Africa's Labor Market*, edited by Garcia and Fares, 3–14. Washington, DC: World Bank.

Geiger, S. N. 1998. *TANU Women: Gender and Culture in the Making of Tanganyikan Nationalism, 1955–1965*. Portsmouth, NH: Heinemann.

Gene, Z. 2015. "Black America, Please Stop Appropriating African Clothing and Tribal Marks." *Those People* (blog), September 3. https://thsppl.com/black-america-please-stop-appropriating-african-clothing-and-tribal-marks-3210e65843a7#.8ofxwlmpo.

George, N. 2005. *Hip Hop America*. New York: Penguin.

Gladney, M. J. 1995. "The Black Arts Movement and Hip-Hop." *African American Review* 29 (2): 291–301.

Goethe Institute. n.d. "The Spoken Word Project: Stories Travelling through Africa." *Goethe Institute*. http://www.goethe.de/ins/za/prj/spw/plc/all/enindex.htm.

Gonzalez, D. 2007. "When American Dream Leads to Servitude." *New York Times*, April 24, p. 1B.

Gordon-Chipembere, N., ed. 2011. *Representation and Black Womanhood: The Legacy of Sarah Baartman*. New York: Palgrave Macmillan.

Guardian. 2008. "Is Hip-Hop Haunted by Ghostwriters?" *Guardian*, August 5. http://www.theguardian.com/music/musicblog/2008/aug/05/ishiphophauntedbyghostwriters.

Gueye, M. 2011. "Modern Media and Culture in Senegal: Speaking Truth to Power." *African Studies Review* 54 (3): 27–43.

———. 2013. "Urban Guerrilla Poetry: The Movement Y'en a Marre and the Socio-political Influences of Hip Hop in Senegal." *Journal of Pan African Studies* 6 (3): 22–42.

Guiraudon, V. 2002. "Immigration Policy in France." Brookings Institution, US-France Analysis, January 1. http://www.brookings.edu/articles/immigration-policy-in-france/.

Gunkel, H. 2010. *The Cultural Politics of Female Sexuality in South Africa*. New York: Routledge.

Haaken, J., J. Wallin-Ruschman, and S. Patange. 2012. "Global Hip-Hop Identities: Black Youth, Psychoanalytic Action Research, and the *Moving to the Beat* Project." *Journal of Community and Applied Social Psychology* 22 (1): 63–74.

Haas, H. de. 2006. "Trans-Saharan Migration to North Africa and the EU: Historical Roots and Current Trends." *Migration Policy Institute*. http://www.migrationinformation.org/feature/display.cfm?id=484.

Hall, S. 1990. "Cultural Identity and Diaspora." In *Identity: Community, Culture, Difference*, edited by J. Rutherford, 222–37. London: Lawrence and Wishart.

———. 2013. "The Work of Representation." In *Representation: Cultural Representations and Signifying Practices*, edited by Hall, 13–69. London: Sage.

Halpern, S., and B. McKibben. 2014. "How a Tightknit Community of Ghanaians Has Spiced Up the Bronx." *Smithsonian Magazine*, June. http://www.smithsonianmag.com/arts-culture/how-tightknit-community-ghanaians-spiced-up-bronx-180951434.

Harris-Perry, M. V. 2011. *Sister Citizen: Shame, Stereotypes, and Black Women in America*. New Haven: Yale University Press.

Harter, P. 2004. "Slavery: Mauritania's Best Kept Secret." *BBC News*, December 13. http://news.bbc.co.uk/2/hi/africa/4091579.stm.

Haupt, A. 2001. "Black Thing: Hip-Hop Nationalism, 'Race' and Gender in Prophets of da City and Brasse Vannie Kaap." In *Coloured by History, Shaped by Place: New Perspectives on Coloured Identities in Cape Town*, edited by Zimitri Erasmus, 173–80. Cape Town: Kwela Books.

———. 2003. "Hip-Hop, Gender and Agency in the Age of Empire." *Agenda* 17 (57): 21–29.

———. 2008. *Stealing Empire: P2P, Intellectual Property and Hip Hop Subversion*. Cape Town: Human Sciences Research Council (HSRC.

Hawley, C. 2000. "Libyan Unrest over Immigration." *BBC News*, September 29. http://news.bbc.co.uk/2/hi/africa/949208.stm.

Hebdige, D. 2004. "Rap and Hip-Hop: The New York Connection." In *That's the Joint!: The Hip Hop Studies Reader*, edited by M. Forman and M. A. Neal, 223–32. New York: Routledge.

Herson, B. 2011. "A Historical Analysis of Hip-Hop's Influence in Dakar from 1984–2000." *American Behavioral Scientist* 55 (1): 24–35.

Herson, B., M. McIlvaine, and C. Moore (directors). 2009. *African Underground: Democracy in Dakar* (film). United States, Nomadic Wax/Sol Productions Foundation.

Hess, M. 2009. "'It's Only Right to Represent Where I'm From': Local and Regional Hip Hop Scenes in the United States." In *Hip Hop in America: A Regional Guide*, edited by Hess, vii–xxx. Santa Barbara: Greenwood.

Higgins, C. 2009. "From da Bomb to Bomba: Global Hip Hop Nation Language in Tanzania." In *Global Linguistic Flows: Hip Hop Cultures, Youth Identities, and the Politics of Language*, edited by Alim, A. Ibrahim, and A. Pennycook, 95–112. New York: Routledge.

Hill Collins, P. 2002. *Black Feminist Thought: Knowledge, Consciousness, and the Politics of Empowerment*. 2nd ed. New York: Routledge.

Hip Hop Foundation of Zambia. n.d. Facebook post. https://www.facebook.com/group.php?gid=120106723323.

Hoch, D. 2006. "Toward a Hip-Hop Aesthetic: A Manifesto for the Hip-Hop Arts Movement." In *Total Chaos: The Art and Aesthetics of Hip-Hop*, edited by J. Chang, 349–63. New York: Basic Civitas Books.

Holloway, J. E. 2005. *Africanisms in American Culture*. Bloomington: Indiana University Press.

Howard, D. 2012. *Rantin from Inside the Dancehall*. Kingston, Jahmento Publishing.

Human Rights Watch. 2011. "Angola: End Violence against Peaceful Protests." Human Rights Watch, December 7. http://www.hrw.org/news/2011/12/07/angola-end-violence-against-peaceful-protests.

Hurt, B. (director). 2006. *Hip-Hop: Beyond Beats and Rhymes* (film).
Ingram, B. 2010. "Music." In *Cultural Studies: A Practical Introduction*, edited by M. Ryan, Ingram, and H. Musiol, 105–21. Malden, MA: Wiley-Blackwell.
IOM (International Organization for Migration). 2008. "Irregular Migration from West Africa to the Maghreb and the European Union: An Overview of Recent Trends." IOM Migration Research Series. http://www.iom.int/jahia/webdav/site/myjahiasite/shared/shared/mainsite/published_docs/serial_publications/MRS-32_EN.pdf.
Jackson, S. J., and D. L. Andrews, eds. 2004. *Sport, Culture and Advertising: Identities, Commodities and the Politics of Representation*. New York: Routledge.
Jackson, Y. 2006. *Encyclopedia of Multicultural Psychology*. Thousand Oaks, CA: Sage.
Jaji, T. E. 2014. *Afropolitanism as Critical Consciousness: Modernism, Music, and Pan-African Solidarity*. New York: Oxford University Press.
Jason, S. 2015. "Women in South African Hip-Hop: 6 Leading Female Rappers." *OkayAfrica.com*, April 15. http://www.okayafrica.com/news/south-african-hip-hop-female-rappers/6/.
Jones, M. 2013. "Township Textualities." *Race, Power and Indigenous Knowledge Systems* 20 (1): 26–51.
Jones, N. 2002. "Warrior Song." Recorded by N. Jones and A. Cook. On *God's Son* (CD). Ill Will/Columbia.
Juma4. 2009. "The Hip Hop Generation and Elections in Gabon." *Africanhiphop.com*, August 31. http://www.africanhiphop.com/featurestories/the-hip-hop-generation-and-elections-in-gabon/.
———. 2011. "Hip Hop from Eastern Congo: Salaam Kivu All Stars." *Africanhiphop.com*, June 30. http://www.africanhiphop.com/africanhiphopnews/hip-hop-from-eastern-congo-salaam-kivu-all-stars/.
Jumare, I. M. 1997. "The Displacement of the Nigerian Academic Community." *Journal of Asian and African Studies* 32 (1–2): 110–19.
Kafuabotsi, P. 2015. "U.S. Embassy Fleeces Visa Applicants—and Treats Ghanaians Like Slaves." *Chronicle*, October 19. http://allafrica.com/stories/201510193029.html.
Kahf, U. 2011. "Arabic Hip-Hop: Claims of Authenticity and Identity of a New Genre." In *That's the Joint! The Hip-Hop Studies Reader*, edited by M. Forman and M. A. Neal, 116–33. New York: Routledge.
Kalmijn, M. 1996. "The Socioeconomic Assimilation of Caribbean American Blacks." *Social Forces* 74:911–30.

Kambarami, M. 2006. "Femininity, Sexuality and Culture: Patriarchy and Female Subordination in Zimbabwe." South Africa: ARSRC.

Kellerer, K. 2013. "'Chant Down the System 'till Babylon Falls': The Political Dimensions of Underground Hip Hop and Urban Grooves in Zimbabwe." *Journal of Pan African Studies* 8 (3): 43–64.

Kenyan Poet. 2009. *Emcee Africa 2—Search for Africa's Premier Freestyle MC/Rapper on 23rd May at WAPI* (blog), May 6. http://kp.motogari.co.ke/2009/05/06/emcee-africa-2-search-for-africas-premier-freestyle-mcrapper-on-23rd-may-at-wapi/.

Kenyon, P. 2009. "Migrants Risk Lives for Europe." *BBC News*, September 14. http://news.bbc.co.uk/2/hi/africa/8251376.stm.

Keyes, C. L. 1996. "At the Crossroads: Rap Music and Its African Nexus." *Ethnomusicology* 40 (2): 223–48.

———. 2002. *Rap Music and Street Consciousness*. Urbana: University of Illinois Press.

———. 2008. "The Roots and Stylistic Foundations of the Rap Music Tradition." In *The Hip Hop Reader*, edited by T. Strode and T. Wood, 3–16. New York: Pearson-Longman.

Kidula, J. N. 2012. "The Local and Global in Kenyan Rap and Hip Hop Culture." In *Hip Hop Africa: New Music in a Globalizing World*, edited by E. Charry, 171–86. Bloomington: Indiana University Press.

Kilkey, M., and L. Merla. 2014. "Situating Transnational Families' Care-Giving Arrangements: The Role of Institutional Contexts." *Global Networks* 14 (2): 210–29.

Kimble, J. 2014. "How Nas Turned America's Largest Housing Project into a Historic Landmark." *Complex*, April 18. http://www.complex.com/pop-culture/2014/04/how-nas-turned-the-queensbridge-houses-into-a-landmark.

Kistler, M. E., and M. J. Lee. 2009. "Does Exposure to Sexual Hip-Hop Music Videos Influence the Sexual Attitudes of College Students?" *Mass Communication and Society* 13 (1): 67–86.

Kitwana, B. 2002. *The Hip Hop Generation: Young Blacks and the Crisis in African American Culture*. New York: Basic Civitas Books.

K'Naan. 2011. "A Son Returns to the Agony of Somalia." *New York Times*, September 24. http://www.nytimes.com/2011/09/25/opinion/sunday/returning-to-somalia-after-20-years.html?_r=3&ref=opinion.

———. 2012. "Censoring Myself for Success." *New York Times*, December 8. http://www.nytimes.com/2012/12/09/opinion/sunday/knaan-on-censoring-himself-for-success.html?_r=0.

Konadu-Agyemang, K. 2000a. "The Best of Times and the Worst of Times: Structural Adjustment Programs and Uneven Development in Africa: The Case of Ghana." *Professional Geographer* 52 (3): 469–83.

———. 2000b. *The Political Economy of Housing and Urban Development in Africa: Ghana's Experience from Colonial Times to 1998.* Santa Barbara, CA: Praeger.

Kostka, R. 1974. "Aspects of Graffiti." *Visible Language* 8 (4): 369–75.

Kramarae, C., and D. Spender. 2004. *Routledge International Encyclopedia of Women: Global Women's Issues and Knowledge.* New York: Routledge.

Krukid. 2005. "African American, American African." On *Raisin in the Sun* (CD). Champaign, IL: Cash Hill Records.

———. 2007. "City Life." On *Rawkus 50 Presents Afr-I-Can* (CD). Champaign, IL: Rawkus 50.

Künzler, D. 2007. "The 'Lost Generation': African Hip Hop Movements and the Protest of the Young (Male) Urban." In *Civil Society: Local and Regional Responses to Global Challenges*, edited by M. Herkenrath, 89–128. Zurich: Deutsche Nationalbibliothek.

———. 2011a. "Rapping against the Lack of Change: Rap Music in Mali and Burkina Faso." In *Native Tongues: An African Hip-Hop Reader*, edited by P. K. Saucier, 23–50. Trenton, NJ: Africa World Press.

———. 2011b. "South African Rap Music, Counter Discourses, Identity, and Commodification beyond the Prophets of Da City." *Journal of Southern African Studies* 37 (1): 27–43.

Kwenaite, S., and A. Van Heerden. 2011. "Dress and Violence: Women Should Avoid Dressing Like 'Sluts' to Avoid Being Raped." *South African Journal of Art History* 26 (1): 141–55.

Kyere, A. 2012. "A Comparative Study of the Lives and Works of Selected Ghanaian Female Musicians from 1980–2010." Doctoral dissertation, University of Ghana.

LaFromboise, T., H. Coleman, and J. Gerton. 1993. "Psychological Impact of Biculturalism: Evidence and Theory." *Psychological Bulletin* 114 (3): 395–412.

LaMayne, G. 2016. "South African Rapper Gigi LaMayne on the Struggle of Her Generation." Interview by N. Makhonjwa, *OkayAfrica.com*, April 27. http://www.okayafrica.com/news/gigi-lamayne-fees-must-fall/.

Lang, H. 1998. "The Population Development of the Rehoboth Basters." *Anthropos* 93 (4–6): 381–91. http://www.jstor.org/stable/40464838.

Langa, M. 2010. "Lyricism and Other Skizims." Master's thesis, University of the Witwatersrand.

Lee, F. R. 2014. "New Wave of African Writers with an Internationalist Bent." *New York Times,* June 30, p. A1.

Lemelle, S. J. 2006. "'Ni wapi Tunakwenda': Hip Hop Culture and the Children of Arusha." In *The Vinyl Ain't Final: Hip Hop and the Globalization of Black Popular Culture,* edited by D. Basu and Lemelle, 230–54. London: Pluto Press.

Lena, J. C. 2004. "Meaning and Membership: Samples in Rap Music, 1979–1995." *Poetics* 32 (3–4): 297–310.

———. 2006. "Social Context and Musical Content of Rap Music, 1979–1995." *Social Forces* 85 (1): 479–95.

Lennon, J. 2014. "Assembling a Revolution: Graffiti, Cairo and the Arab Spring." *Cultural Studies Review* 20 (1): 237–375.

Lewis. D. 2011. "Representing African Sexualities." In *African Sexualities: A Reader,* edited by S. Tamale, 199–216. Oxford: Pambazuka Press.

Lewis, D., and A. Ross. "Connected and Angry, African Youth Groups Push for Democracy." Reuters, May 1. https://www.reuters.com/article/us-africa-democracy-insight/connected-and-angry-african-youth-groups-push-for-democracy-idUSKBN0NM3UT20150501.

Lewis, S. K. 2006. *Race, Culture, and Identity: Francophone West African and Caribbean Literature and Theory from Négritude to Créolité.* Lanham, MD: Lexington Books.

Ley, D. 2013. "Does Transnationalism Trump Immigrant Integration? Evidence from Canada's Links with East Asia." *Journal of Ethnic and Migration Studies* 39 (6): 921–38.

Ley, D., and R. Cybriwsky. (1974. "Urban Graffiti as Territorial Markers." *Annals of the Association of American Geographers* 64 (4): 491–505.

Li, T., M. Ogihara, and Q. Li. 2003. "A Comparative Study on Content-Based Music Genre Classification." In *Proceedings of the 26th Annual International ACM SIGIR Conference on Research and Development in Information Retrieval,* 282–89. ACM, July.

Liu, L. S. 2011. "New Zealand Case Study of PRC Transnational Migration: Returnees and Trans-Tasman Migrants." *Transmigration and the New Chinese: Theories and Practices from the New Zealand Case,* 57–101. Pokfulam: University of Hong Kong.

Livesay, C. 2010. "Music You're Not Supposed to Hear." NPR.org, June 30. http://m.npr.org/news/front/128216493?page=0.

Liviga, A. J. 2011. "Economic and Political Liberalization in Tanzania and Its Unintended Outcomes." *Eastern Africa Social Science Research Review* 27 (1): 1–31.

Lo, S. 2014. "Building Our Nation: Senegalese Hip Hop Artists as Agents of Social and Political Change." In *Hip Hop and Social Change in Africa: Ni Wakati*, edited by M. K. Clark and M. M. Koster, 27–48. Lanham, MD: Lexington Books.

Loots, L. 2003. "Being a 'Bitch': Some Questions on the Gendered Globalisation and Consumption of American Hip-Hop Urban Culture in Post-apartheid South Africa." *Agenda Feminist Media* 57:65–73. http://www.jstor.org/stable/4066391?origin=JSTOR-pdf.

Ludl, C. 2008. "'To Skip a Step': New Representation(s) of Migration, Success and Politics in Senegalese Rap and Theatre." *Stichproben: Wiener Zeitschrift für kritische Afrikastudien* 14 (8): 97–122.

Lugalla, J. L. P. 1997. "Economic Reforms and Health Conditions of the Urban Poor in Tanzania." *African Studies Quarterly* 1 (2): 19–37.

Magubane, V., and E. Offer. 2007. *Counting Headz: South Afrika's Sistaz in Hip Hop* (film). Chop Shop Multimedia.

Makokha, J. K. S. 2010. "In the Spirit of Afropolitanism." Introduction to *Negotiating Afropolitanism: Essays on Borders and Spaces in Contemporary African Literature and Folklore*, edited by J. Wawrzinek and Makokha, 13–24. Amsterdam: Rodopi.

Makoni, B. 2011. "Multilingual Miniskirt Discourses in Motion: The Discursive Construction of the Female Body in Public Space." *International Journal of Applied Linguistics*, 21 (3): 340–59.

Malone, C., and G. Martinez. 2010. "The Organic Globalizer: The Political Development of Hip-Hop and the Prospects for Global Transformation." *New Political Science* 32 (4): 531–45.

M.anifest. 2012. "M.anifest: 'The Spotlight Is Shining Brightly on African Music.'" Interview by C. Jones. *Guardian/Observer*, August 15. http://www.theguardian.com/music/2012/aug/26/manifest-african-express-ghanaian-rapper.

Manji, F. 2012. "African Awakenings: The Courage to Invent the Future." In *African Awakening: The Emerging Revolutions*, edited by Manji and S. Ekine, 1–18. Cape Town: Pambazuka Press.

Manning, P. 2009. *The African Diaspora: A History through Culture*. New York: Columbia University Press.

Marschall, S. 2008. "Transforming Symbolic Identity: Wall Art and the South African City." *African Arts* 41 (2): 12–23.

Marsh, C., and S. Petty. 2013. "Globalization, Identity, and Youth Resistance: Kenya's Hip Hop Parliament." *MUSICultures* 38:132–43.

Mawuko-Yevugah, L. C. 2010. "Governing through Developmentality: The Politics of International Aid Reform and the (Re)production of Power, Neoliberalism and Neocolonial Interventions in Ghana." ProQuest Dissertations and Theses (NR55972).

Mayer, R., R. Neumayer, and A. Rauber. 2008. "Rhyme and Style Features for Musical Genre Classification by Song Lyrics." *ISMIR 2008—Session 3a—Content-Based Retrieval, Categorization and Similarity,* September, 337–42.

Mazaza, S. M. 2015. "Dope Saint Jude: Hip-Hop, Feminism, Race Politics and Cape Town Queer Culture." *Okay Africa,* March 27. http://www.okayafrica.com/video/dope-saint-jude-hip-hop-feminism-race-politics-cape-town-queer-culture/.

Mbaye, J. 2011. "Hip-Hop Political Production in West Africa: AURA and Its Extraordinary Stories of Poto-Poto Children." In *Native Tongues: An African Hip-Hop Reader,* edited by P. K. Saucier, 51–68. Trenton, NJ: Africa World Press.

Mbembe, A. 2001. "Ways of Seeing: Beyond the New Nativism." *African Studies Review* 44 (2): 1–14.

———. 2007. "Afropolitanism." In *Africa Remix: Contemporary Art of a Continent,* edited by N. Simon and L. Durán, 26–30. Johannesburg: Johannesburg Art Gallery.

McLeod, K. 1999. "Authenticity within Hip-Hop and Other Cultures Threatened with Assimilation." *Journal of Communication* 49 (4): 134–50.

Mead, P. C., and E. L. Pederson. 1995. "West African Apparel Textiles Depicted in Selected Magazines from 1960 to 1979: Application of Cultural Authentication." *Family and Consumer Sciences Research Journal* 23 (4): 430–52.

Mengara, D. M., ed. 2001. *Images of Africa: Stereotypes and Realities.* Trenton, NJ: Africa World Press.

Migiro, K. 2011. "Kenya Stalls on Justice for Poll Killings: HRW." *Reuters Africa,* December 9. http://af.reuters.com/article/topNews/idAFJOE7B807X20111209.

Mikell, G. 1997. *African Feminism: The Politics of Survival in Sub-Saharan Africa.* Philadelphia: University of Pennsylvania Press.

Milnor, K. 2009. "Literary Literacy in Roman Pompeii: The Case of Virgil's *Aeneid.*" In *Ancient Literacies: The Culture of Reading in Greece and Rome,* edited by W. A. Johnson and H. N. Parker, 288–319. Oxford: Oxford University Press.

Mittell, J. 2010. "*The Wire* in the Context of American Television." *Media Commons: A Digital Scholarly Network,* 9.

Moore, A. R. 2013. *The American Dream through the Eyes of Black African Immigrants in Texas*. Lanham, MD: University Press of America.

Morgan, J. 2000. *When Chickenheads Come Home to Roost: A Hip-Hop Feminist Breaks It Down*. New York: Simon and Schuster.

Morgan, M. 2005. "Hip-Hop Women Shredding the Veil: Race and Class in Popular Feminist Identity." *South Atlantic Quarterly* 104 (3): 425–44.

Mose, C. 2011. "Jua Cali Justice: Navigating the 'Mainstream Underground' Dichotomy in Kenyan Hip-Hop Culture." In *Native Tongues: An African Hip-Hop Reader*, edited by P. K. Saucier, 69–104. Trenton, NJ: Africa World Press.

———. 2013. "'Swag' and 'Cred': Representing Hip-Hop in the African City." *Journal of Pan African Studies* 6 (3): 106–32.

———. 2014. "Hip Hop Halisi: Continuities of Heroism on the African Political Landscape." In *Hip Hop and Social Change in Africa: Ni Wakati*, edited by M. K. Clark and M. M. Koster, 3–26. Lanham, MD: Lexington Books.

Moyer, E. 2005. "Street-Corner Justice in the Name of Jah: Imperatives for Peace among Dar es Salaam Street Youth." *Africa Today* 51 (3): 31–58.

Mullard, S. 2007. "Madagascar Rap Star Name Six Appointed First-Ever Junior Goodwill Ambassador." *UNICEF*. http://www.unicef.org/infobycountry/madagascar_40057.html.

Murunga, G. R., and S. W. Nasong'o. 2007. *Kenya: The Struggle for Democracy*. Cape Town: Zed Books.

Mwangi, E. 2004. "Masculinity and Nationalism in East African Hip-Hop Music." *Tydskrif vir letterkunde* 41 (2): 5–20.

Mwangi, E., and W. Mbure. 2010. "Passion in a Mathree: Metropolitan Love in Nazizi Hirji's 'Kenyan Girl/Kenyan Boy.'" *Women and Language* 32 (2): 25–31.

Mwaũra, M. W. 2007. "Artistic Discourse and Gender Politics in the Gĩkũyũ Popular Song." In *Songs and Politics in Eastern Africa*, edited by K. Njogu and H. Maupeu, 49–73. Dar es Salaam: Mkuki na Nyota.

Nation. 2014. "Being Gay Is Not a Crime, Says Sasha P." *Nation*, January 29. http://thenationonlineng.net/being-gay-is-not-a-crime-says-shasha-p/.

Neff, A. C. 2010. "Meet Toussa, Senegal's New Woman Rapper." *Ethnolyrical*, September 13. http://www.ethnolyrical.org/?p=677.

———. 2015. "Roots, Routes and Rhizomes: Sounding Women's Hip Hop on the Margins of Dakar, Senegal." *Journal of Popular Music Studies* 27 (4): 448–77.

Ngũgĩ wa Thiong'o. 1986. *Decolonising the Mind*. London: James Currey.
Nnaemeka, O., ed. 2005. *Female Circumcision and the Politics of Knowledge: African Women in Imperialist Discourses*. Westport, CT: Greenwood Publishing Group.
Norton, B. 1997. "Language, Identity, and the Ownership of English." *TESOL Quarterly* 31 (3): 409–29.
Notununu, A. 2009. "South African Hip Hop History." *South African Hip Hop*. Retrieved from http://www.sahhp.co.za/history.html.
Ntarangwi, M. 2009. *East African Hip Hop: Youth Culture and Globalization*. Champaign: University of Illinois Press.
———. 2010. "African Hip Hop and Politics of Change in an Era of Rapid Globalization." *History Compass* 8 (12): 1316–27.
NTV Kenya. 2014. "Nazizi on Music, Career and Life." AM LIVE AUG 29, 2014. https://www.youtube.com/watch?v=EOgKHDCAIMI.
Nwadiora, E. 1995. "Alienation and Stress among Black Immigrants: An Exploratory Study." *Western Journal of Black Studies* 19 (1): 58–71.
Nyairo, J., and J. Ogude. 2005. "Popular Music, Popular Politics: Unbwogable and the Idioms of Freedom in Kenyan Popular Music." *African Affairs* 104 (415): 225–49.
Nydjlive.com. 2014. "The Music Industry Treats Us as Outcasts—Wanlov the Kubolor." Ghanaweb.com, July 23. http://www.ghanaweb.com/GhanaHomePage/NewsArchive/artikel.php?ID=318161.
Nzegwu, A. 2009. "Redefining 'Africa' in the Diaspora with New Media Technologies: The Making of AfricaResource.com." In *The New African Diaspora*, edited by I. Okpewho and Nzegwu, 358–83. Bloomington: Indiana University Press.
Obiakor, F. E., and M. O. Afoláyan. 2007. "African Immigrant Families in the United States: Surviving the Sociocultural Tide." *Family Journal* 15 (3): 265–70.
Odamtten, H. N. K. 2011. "Hip-Hop Speaks, Hip-Life Answers: Global African Music." In *Native Tongues: An African Hip-Hop Reader*, edited by P. K. Saucier, 147–78. Trenton, NJ: Africa World Press.
Ojaide, T. 2007. *Ordering the African Imagination: Essays on Culture and Literature*. Lagos: Malthouse Press.
Okoa Mtaa Foundation. n.d.. http://www.okoamtaa.com/.
Okome, M. O. 2002. "The Antinomies of Globalization: Causes of Contemporary African Immigration to the United States of America." *Ìrìnkèrindò: A Journal of African Migration* 1. http://www.africamigration.com/.
———. 2012. "African Immigrant Relationships with Home Countries." In *Africans in Global Migration: Searching for Promised Lands*,

Oloruntoba-Oju, T. 2006. "'Dèdè n dẹ ku ikú n dẹ Dèdè̩': Fe/male Sexuality and Dominance in Nigerian Video Films (Nollywood)." *Stichproben: Wiener Zeitschrift für kritische Afrikastudien* 11:5–26.

Ombati, M. 2013. "Graffiti: A Powerful Innovative Weapon Broadening the Horizons of Social Transformation in Kenya." Paper presented at the Conference on Children and Youth Affected by Armed Conflict in Kampala, Uganda.

Omoniyi, T. 2009. "'So I Chose to Do Am Naija style': Hip Hop, Language, and Postcolonial Identities." In *Global Linguistic Flows: Hip Hop Cultures, Youth Identities, and the Politics of Language*, edited by H. S. Alim, A. Ibrahim, and A. Pennycook, 113–37. New York: Routledge.

Ongiri, A. A. 2009. *Spectacular Blackness: The Cultural Politics of the Black Power Movement and the Search for a Black Aesthetic*. Charlottesville: University of Virginia Press.

Opoku, D. K. 2008. "Political Dilemmas of Indigenous Capitalist Development in Africa: Ghana under the Provisional National Defence Council." *Africa Today*, 55 (2), 25–51

Opoku-Dapaah, E. 1992. "Ghana 1981–1991: A Decade of Forced Repression and Migration." *Refuge* 11 (3): 8–13.

———. 2006. "African Immigrants in Canada: Trends, Socio-demographic and Spatial Aspects." In *The New African Diaspora in North America: Trends, Community Building, and Adaptation*, edited by K. Konadu-Agyemang, B. K. Takyi, and J. A. Arthur, 69–93. Lanham, MD: Lexington Books.

Oripeloye, H. 2012. "Exile and Narration of Self/Communal in Syl Cheney-Coker's *Concerto for an Exile*." *Neohelicon* 39 (2): 423–38.

Otoo-Oyortey, N. 2007. "Expressing Sexual Fantasy through Songs and Proverbs." *Sexuality in Africa Magazine* 4 (3): 7–8.

Oware, M. 2009. "A 'Man's Woman'? Contradictory Messages in the Songs of Female Rappers, 1992–2000". *Journal of Black Studies* 39 (5): 786–802.

Owusu, T. 2006. "Transnationalism among African Immigrants in North America: The Case of Ghanaians in Canada." In *The New African Diaspora in North America: Trends, Community Building, and Adaptation*, edited by K. Konadu-Agyemang, B. K. Takyi, and J. A. Arthur, 273–86. Lanham, MD: Lexington Books.

Pahl, M. 2016. "Afropolitanism as Critical Consciousness: Chimamanda Ngozi Adichie's and Teju Cole's Internet Presence." *Journal of African Cultural Studies* 28 (1): 73–87.

Parris, A. 2008. "Reaching towards Hip-Hop's Homeland." In *The Hip Hop Reader,* edited by T. Strode and T. Wood, 208–17. New York: Pearson-Longman.

Pearce, J. 2015. "Contesting the Past in Angolan Politics." *Journal of Southern African Studies* 41 (1): 103–19.

Penna-Diaw, L. 2013. "Songs by Wolof Women." In *Women's Songs from West Africa,* edited by T. A. Hale and A. G. Sidikou, 124–35. Bloomington: Indiana University Press.

Pennycook, A. 2007. "Language, Localization, and the Real: Hip-Hop and the Global Spread of Authenticity." *Journal of Language, Identity, and Education* 6 (2): 101–15.

———. 2010. *Language as a Local Practice.* New York: Routledge.

Pennycook, A., and T. Mitchell. 2009. "Hip Hop as Dusty Foot Philosophy: Engaging Locality." In *Global Linguistic Flows: Hip Hop Cultures, Youth Identities, and the Politics of Language,* edited by H. S. Alim, A. Ibrahim and Pennycook, 25–42. New York: Routledge.

Perry, I. 2004. *Prophets of the Hood: Politics and Poetics in Hip Hop.* Durham, NC: Duke University Press.

———. 2008. "The Venus Hip Hop and Pink Ghetto: Negotiating Spaces for Women." In *The Hip Hop Reader,* edited by T. Strode and T. Wood, 134–46. New York: Pearson-Longman.

Perullo, A. 2005. "Hooligans and Heroes: Youth Identity and Hip-Hop in Dar es Salaam, Tanzania." *Africa Today* 51 (4): 75–101.

———. 2012. "Imitation and Innovation in the Music, Dance, and Camps of Tanzanian Youth." In *Hip Hop Africa: New Music in a Globalizing World,* edited by E. Charry, 187–210. Bloomington: Indiana University Press.

Perullo, A., and A. P. Fenn. 2003. "Language Ideologies, Choices, and Practices in Eastern African Hip Hop." In *Global Pop, Local Language,* edited by H. M. Burger and M. T. Carroll, 19–52. Jackson: University Press of Mississippi.

Peterson, S. H., G. M. Wingood, R. J. DiClemente, K. Harrington, and S. Davies. 2007. "Images of Sexual Stereotypes in Rap Videos and the Health of African American Female Adolescents." *Journal of Women's Health* 16 (8): 1157–64.

Phillips, L., K. Reddick-Morgan, and D. P. Stephens. 2005. "Oppositional Consciousness within an Oppositional Realm: The Case of Feminism and Womanism in Rap and Hip Hop, 1976–2004." *Journal of African American History* 90 (3): 253–77.

Pottie-Sherman, Y. 2013. "Vancouver's Chinatown Night Market: Gentrification and the Perception of Chinatown as a Form of Revitalization." *Built Environment* 39 (2): 172–89.

Pough, G. D. 2004. *Check It while I Wreck It: Black Womanhood, Hip-Hop Culture, and the Public Sphere*. Boston: Northeastern University Press.

Prince, E. 2011. "Rwanda: Gender Equality through Hip Hop." *allAfrica.com*, 16 May. http://allafrica.com/stories/201105160294.html.

Rabine, L. W. 2014. "The Graffiti Art Movement in Dakar." *African Studies Quarterly* 14 (3): 89–112. http://www.africa.ufl.edu/asq/v14/v14i3a6.pdf.

Richardson, E. 2007. "'She Was Workin Like Foreal': Critical Literacy and Discourse Practices of African American Females in the Age of Hip Hop." *Discourse and Society* 18 (6): 789–809.

Reuster-Jahn, U. 2008. "Bongo Flava and the Electoral Campaign 2005." *Stichproben: Wiener Zeitschrift für kritische Afrikastudien* 14 (8): 41–69.

Rogers, R. A. 2006. "From Cultural Exchange to Transculturation: A Review and Reconceptualization of Cultural Appropriation." *Communication Theory* 16 (4): 475–503.

Rong, X. L., and F. Brown. 2001. "The Effects of Immigrant Generation and Ethnicity on Educational Attainment among Young African and Caribbean Blacks in the United States." *Harvard Educational Review* 71 (3): 536–66.

———. 2002. "Socialization, Culture, and Identities of Black Immigrant Children: What Educators Need to Know and Do." *Education and Urban Society* 34 (2): 247–73.

Rose, T. 2008. *The Hip Hop Wars: What We Talk About When We Talk About Hip Hop—and Why It Matters*. Jackson, MS: Basic Civitas Books.

Saber, R. 2014. *Untouched: Egypt's Revolution in Graffiti*. Delizon Press.

Said-Moorhouse, L. 2013. "Colorful, Creative, Inspiring: The World of African Street Art." *CNN.com*. http://www.cnn.com/2013/09/27/world/africa/creative-inspiring-african-street-art/.

Sajnani, D. 2013. "Troubling the Trope of 'Rapper as Modern Griot.'" *Journal of Pan African Studies* 6 (3): 156–80.

Santana, S. B. 2013. "Exorcizing Afropolitanism: Binyavanga Wainaina Explains Why 'I Am a Pan-Africanist, Not an Afropolitan' at ASAUK 2012." *Africa in Words* (blog), February 8, http://africainwords.com/2013/02/08/exorcizing-afropolitanism

-binyavanga-wainaina-explains-why-i-am-a-pan-africanist-not-an-afropolitan-at-asauk-2012/.
Saucier, P. K., ed. 2011. *Native Tongues: An African Hip-Hop Reader*. Trenton, NJ: Africa World Press.
———. 2015. *Necessarily Black: Cape Verdean Youth, Hip-Hop Culture, and a Critique of Identity*. East Lansing: Michigan State University Press.
Scaringella, N., G. Zoia, and D. Mlynek. 2006. "Automatic Genre Classification of Music Content: A Survey." *IEEE Signal Processing Magazine* 23 (2): 133–41.
Scholtes, P. S. 2006. "Payback Is a Motherland: How African Hip Hop 'Gives Back' to Two Continents." *Minneapolis City Pages*, July 12. http://www.citypages.com/2006-07-12/music/payback-is-a-motherland/full/.
Schraeder, P. J., and B. Endless. 1998. "The Media and Africa: The Portrayal of Africa in the 'New York Times' (1955–1995)." *Issue: A Journal of Opinion* 26 (2): 29–35
Sekyiamah, N. D. 2012. "I Thought the US Was the Land of Gold. Now I See It as Rude and Disrespectful." *Guardian*, November 17. https://www.theguardian.com/commentisfree/2013/nov/17/ghana-america-exchange-expats-immigration-war.
Semwezi, S. 2013. "Ruyonga's Raw Talent Sparks Rap Renaissance in Uganda." *Observer*, June 21. http://observer.ug/index.php?option=com_content&view=article&id=25967:ruyongas-raw-talent-sparks-rap-renaissance-in-uganda.
Sene, C. (director). 2012. *100% Galsen* (film). Senegal, AfricanHipHop.com.
Séverino, J-M., and O. Ray. 2012. *Africa's Moment*. Translated by D. Fernbach. Cambridge: Polity.
Shain, R. M. 2002. "Roots in Reverse: Cubanismo in Twentieth-Century Senegalese Music." *International Journal of African Historical Studies* 35 (1): 83–101.
Shaw-Taylor, Y. 2007. "The Intersection of Assimilation, Race, Presentation of Self, and Transnationalism in America." In *The Other African Americans: Contemporary African and Caribbean Immigrants in the United States*, edited by Shaw-Taylor and S. A. Tuch, 1–48. Lanham, MD: Rowman and Littlefield.
Shipley, J. W. (producer). 2007. *Living the Hiplife* (motion picture). United States: Third World Newsreel.
———. 2009. "Aesthetic of the Entrepreneur: Afro-cosmopolitan Rap and Moral Circulation in Accra, Ghana." *Anthropological Quarterly* 82 (3): 631–68.

———. 2012. "The Birth of Ghanaian Hiplife: Urban Style, Black Thought, Proverbial Speech." In *Hip Hop Africa: New Music in a Globalizing World,* edited by E. Charry, 29–56. Bloomington: Indiana University Press.

———. 2013. *Living the Hiplife: Celebrity and Entrepreneurship in Ghanaian Popular Music.* Durham, NC: Duke University Press.

Shivji, I. 2010. "Pan-Africanism and the Challenge of East African Community integration." *Pambazuka News,* 503 (November 3. http://pambazuka.org/en/category/features/68395.

Shonekan, S. 2011. "Sharing Hip-Hop Cultures: The Case of Nigerians and African Americans." *American Behavioral Scientist* 55 (1): 9–23.

———. 2012. "Nigerian Hip Hop: Exploring a Black World Hybrid." In *Hip Hop Africa: New Music in a Globalizing World,* edited by E. Charry, 147–70. Bloomington: Indiana University Press.

Shryock, R. 2015. "Senegal's First Female Graffiti Artist Is Leaving a Fearless Mark." *Takepart.com,* June 17. https://www.takepart.com/article/2015/06/17/first-female-graffiti-artist-senegal.

Smith, A. D. 2014. "'Africa's Che Guevara': Thomas Sankara's Legacy." *BBC-News,* April 30. http://www.bbc.com/news/world-africa-27219307.

Smith, D. 1999. "Fear Not of Man." Recorded by D. Smith. On *Black on Both Sides* (CD). Rawkus/Columbia.

Smitherman, G. 1997. "'The Chain Remain the Same': Communicative Practices in the Hip Hop Nation." *Journal of Black Studies* 28 (1): 3–25.

Sommers, M. 2003. "Youth, War, and Urban Africa: Challenges, Misunderstandings, and Opportunities." In *Youth Explosion in Developing World Cities: Approaches to Reducing Poverty and Conflict in an Urban Age,* edited by B. A. Ruble, J. S. Tulchin, D. H. Varat, and L. M. Hanley. http://www.wilsoncenter.org/topics/pubs/ACF1AEF.pdf#page=30.

Sopitshi, A. 2012. "'Won't Nobody Even Try to Reach Her Mind . . .'" *Feminist Africa: Researching Sexuality with Young Women: Southern Africa* 17:129–32.

SoundwayRecords. 2012. *Batida—Cuka.* Video file. https://www.youtube.com/watch?v=SLaj5rEzDvA.

Soyinka, W. 2001. "Voices from the Frontier: The Nobel Laureate Wole Soyinka, Who Once Fled Nigeria, Considers the Plight of Writers in Exile." *Guardian,* July 13. http://www.theguardian.com/books/2002/jul/13/poetry.wolesoyinka.

Spocter, M. A. 2004. "This Is My Space: Graffiti in Claremont, Cape Town." *Urban Forum* 15 (3): 292–304.

Stebleton, M. J. 2012. "The Meaning of Work for Black African Immigrant Adult College Students." *Journal of Career Development* 39 (1): 50–75.

Stephens, D. P., and A. L. Few. 2007. "The Effects of Images of African American Women in Hip Hop on Early Adolescents' Attitudes toward Physical Attractiveness and Interpersonal Relationships." *Sex Roles* 56 (3–4): 251–64.

Stroud, C. 2015. "Orraait—Own Your Linguistic Citizenship." *Mail and Guardian*, May 22. http://mg.co.za/article/2015-05-21-orraait-own-your-linguistic-citizenship.

Subzzee. 2010a. "Motswako: Hip Hop Styles Request" (Msg 2572140). Message posted to http://www.discogs.com/help/forums/topic/206538#2572140.

———. 2010b. "Spaza: Hip Hop Styles Request" (Msg 2572135). Message posted to http://www.discogs.com/help/forums/topic/206538#2572135.

Suriano, M. 2007. "'Mimi ni msanii, kioo cha jamii': Urban Youth Culture in Tanzania as Seen through Bongo Fleva and Hip Hop." *Swahili Forum* 14:207–23.

Swank, A. 2012. "Why the Angolan Government Framed and Beat Rapper Ikonoklasta." *OkayAfrica.com*, July 19. http://www.okayafrica.com/stories/ikonoklasta-angola-framed-drug-smuggling/.

Sy, T. 2006. "Mother's Battle against Senegal Migration." *BBC News*, November 6. http://news.bbc.co.uk/2/hi/africa/6109736.stm.

Takougang, J. 2003. "Contemporary African Immigrants to the United States." *Ìrìnkèrindò: A Journal of African Migration* 2:1–15.

Tang, P. 2007. *Masters of the Sabar: Wolof Griot Percussionists of Senegal.* Philadelphia: Temple University Press

———. 2012. "The Rapper as Modern Griot: Reclaiming Ancient Traditions." In *Hip Hop Africa: New Music in a Globalizing World*, edited by E. Charry, 79–90. Bloomington: Indiana University Press.

Taylor, A. 2017. "Over 1,000 Migrants and Refugees Have Died Crossing the Mediterranean So Far This Year." *Washington Post*, April 25. https://www.washingtonpost.com/news/worldviews/wp/2017/04/25/over-1000-migrants-and-refugees-have-died-crossing-the-mediterranean-so-far-this-year/?utm_term=.1e11ec6c0d83

Taylor, D. 2013. "South Africa's Graffiti Outlaw Now a Top Artist." *VOA News*, September 16. http://www.voanews.com/content/south-africas-graffiti-artist-sandile-radebe/1750800.html.

Tchakam, S. 2011. "Valsero, a Hip-Hop Artist against Censorship." *GuinGuinBali.com*, May 17. http://www.guinguinbali.com/index.php?lang=en&mod=news&task=view_news&cat=4&id=1966.

Thomas, E. R. 2007. "Phonological and Phonetic Characteristics of African American Vernacular English." *Language and Linguistics Compass* 1 (5): 450–75.

Thompson, K. D. 2011. "Zanzibari Women's Discursive and Sexual Agency: Violating Gendered Speech Prohibitions through Talk about Supernatural Sex." *Discourse and Society* 22 (1): 3–20.

Thorpe, D. 1999. "Chuck D by David Thorpe." *Bomb Magazine*, July 2. https://bombmagazine.org/articles/chuck-d/

Traoré, F. A. 2007. "Women's Taarab Lyrics in Contemporary Zanzibar." *Swahili Forum* 14:181–95.

Trotter, T. 2008. "I Will Not Apologize." Recorded by T. Trotter, T. Green, K. Jenkins, and G. Porn. On *Rising Down*. Def Jam.

Tuakli-Wosornu, T. 2005. "Bye-Bye Babar." *LIP*, March 3. http://thelip.robertsharp.co.uk/?p=76.

Tutton, M. 2012. "Young, Urban and Culturally Savvy, Meet the Afropolitans." *CNN.com*, February 17. http://edition.cnn.com/2012/02/17/world/africa/who-are-afropolitans.

Tveit, M. 2013. "The Afropolitan Must Go." *Think Africa Press*, November 5. http://thinkafricapress.com/culture/afropolitan-must-go.

Ukadike, N. F. 1994. "Reclaiming Images of Women in Films from Africa and the Black Diaspora." *Frontiers: A Journal of Women Studies* 15 (1): 102–22. http://doi.org/10.2307/3346615.

UnderGround Angle. 2009. "UnderGround Style: Spaza Rap, More Than Just a Cipher outside the Corner Store" (blog), April 14. http://theundergroundangle.blogspot.com/2009/04/if-youve-ever-heard-driemanskap-joint.html.

UZN (Universal Zulu Nation). n.d. "The Five Elements of Hip Hop." Universal Zulu Nation. http://new.zulunation.com/elements/.

Urbandictionary.com. n.d. *Urban Dictionary*, s.v. *Hip hop head*. http://www.urbandictionary.com/define.php?term=Hip%20Hop%20Head.

USCIS. "Immigrants Admitted by Region and Country of Birth: Fiscal Years 1989–2004" (table 3). *United States Citizenship and Immigrations Services*. http://uscis.gov/graphics/shared/statistics/yearbook/YrBk04Im.htm.

Veal, M. E. 2007. *Dub: Songscapes and Shattered Songs in Jamaican Reggae*. Middletown, CT: Wesleyan University Press.

Veney, C. R. 2009. "The Effects of Immigration and Refugee Policies on Africans in the United States: From the Civil Rights Movement to the War on Terrorism." In *The New African Diaspora*, edited by

I. Okpewho and N. Nzegwu, 196–214. Bloomington: Indiana University Press.

Vincent, L. 2008. "Women's Rights Get a Dressing Down: Mini Skirt Attacks in South Africa." *International Journal of the Humanities* 6 (6): 11–18.

Waddacor, C. 2014. *Graffiti South Africa*. Atglen, PA: Schiffer Publishing.

Wahlrab, A. 2014. "Speaking Truth to Power: Hip Hop and the African Awakening." In *Hip Hop and Social Change in Africa: Ni Wakati*, edited by M. K. Clark and M. M. Koster, 49–64. Lanham, MD: Lexington Books.

Walser, R. 1995. "Rhythm, Rhyme, and Rhetoric in the Music of Public Enemy." *Ethnomusicology* 39 (2): 193–217.

Wanguhu, M., and R. Kenya. 2007. *Ni Wakati*. DVD. Chatsworth, CA: Emerge Media Group.

Warner, R. 2011. "Colouring the Cape Problem Space: A Hip-Hop Identity of Passions." In *Native Tongues: An African Hip-Hop Reader*, edited by P. K. Saucier, 105–44. Trenton, NJ: Africa World Press.

Waters, M. C. 1999. *Black Identities: West Indian Immigrant Dreams and American Realities*. Cambridge, MA: Harvard University Press.

Watkins, L. 2012. "A Genre Coming of Age: Transformation, Difference, and Authenticity in the Rap Music and Hip Hop Cultures of South Africa." In *Hip Hop Africa: New Music in a Globalizing World*, edited by E. Charry, 57–75. Bloomington: Indiana University Press.

Watkins, S. C. 2005. *Hip Hop Matters: Politics, Pop Culture, and the Struggle for the Soul of a Movement*. Boston: Beacon Press.

Watson, I. 2001. "Slavery Lives on in Mauritania: Tradition Thrives Thanks to a Confluence of Cultures." NPR, *All Things Considered*, August 28. http://www.npr.org/programs/specials/racism/010828.mauritania.html.

Weil, P., and J. Crowley. 1994. "Integration in Theory and Practice: A Comparison of France and Britain." *West European Politics* 17 (2): 110–26.

Weiss, B. 2009. *Street Dreams and Hip Hop Barbershops: Global Fantasy in Urban Tanzania*. Bloomington: Indiana University Press.

Werwath, T. 2006. "The Culture and Politics of Graffiti Art." *Art Crimes*, 19.

White, B. W. 2002. "Congolese Rumba and Other Cosmopolitanisms." *Cahiers d'études africaines* 4:663–86.

Williams, Q., and C. Stroud. 2013. "Multilingualism Remixed: Sampling, Braggadocio and the Stylisation of Local Voice." *Stellenbosch Papers in Linguistics* 42:15–36.

———. 2014. "Battling the Race: Stylizing Language and Coproducing Whiteness and Colouredness in a Freestyle Rap Performance." *Journal of Linguistic Anthropology* 24 (3): 277–93.

Wilson, J. H. 2003. "African Immigrants in Metropolitan Washington: A Demographic Overview." Proceedings of the 2003 African Immigrants and Refugees Foundation Conference.

Winter, J. 2006. "Senegal Migrant Song Hits the Net." *BBC News*, July 10. http://news.bbc.co.uk/2/hi/africa/5155592.stm.

Wipper, A. 1972. "African Women, Fashion, and Scapegoating." *Canadian Journal of African Studies/Revue canadienne des études africaines* 6 (2): 329–49.

World: The Global Hit. 2007. "South African Hip Hop." *PRI's The World Podcast.* http://www.pri.org/theworld/?q=node/11662.

Wright, T. 2008. *Visual Impact: Culture and the Meaning of Images.* New York: Berg.

York, G. 2015. "Hip-Hop Music Speaking for Africa's Disenfranchised Youth." *Globe and Mail*, December 23. http://www.theglobeandmail.com/arts/music/hip-hop-music-speaking-for-africas-disenfranchised-youth/article27922096/.

Young, J. O. 2008. *Cultural Appropriation and the Arts.* Malden, MA: Blackwell.

Index

#Angola15, 112
#BlackLivesMatter, 214, 225
#FeesMustFall, 41, 102, 112, 115
#RhodesMustFall, 41, 112, 115, 214
100% Galsen, 29
2 Proud. *See* Sugu
2C, 151, 152, 188
50 Cent, 188–90

Abbas Kubaff, 78, 186
Abena Rockstar, 125, 138
Abiola, Saratu, 140
Abramz, 55
Accra, 16, 90, 105, 141, 163
Adamiz, 52
Adichie, Chimamanda Ngozi, 37, 178–80
African American/s, xv, xvi, xvii, 5–9, 12, 14, 38, 59, 66, 68, 74, 101, 134, 135, 147, 149, 151, 156, 157, 158, 170, 173, 179–205, 224, 225
African American Vernacular English (AAVE), 186, 188–95, 197, 198, 202, 228. *See also* Hip Hop Nation Language (HHNL)
Africanhiphop.com, 52
African Hip Hop Radio, 52
African Rebel Movement, 10, 214
African Underground: Democracy in Dakar, 51, 108
Afrika Bambaataa, 6
Afrobeat, 9, 11, 24, 194, 201
Afrolution, 151
Afropolitan(ism), xiv, 150, 174–81, 199
Afropolitan Vibes, 178, 180

Afropolitan Week of Fashion and Arts, 178
Ajegunle, 16
AK-47, 30, 100, 156, 190
Akon, 65
albinism, 96
Albino Fulani, 96
Algeria, 41, 71, 93, 196, 211
alienation, xiv, 150, 159, 166–70, 175, 176, 177, 182, 186
AliThatDude, 103
Al Jazeera, 90
al-Shabaab, 155
Alternative Kerriculum for Mentoring Youth (ALKEMY), 84
Amaa Rae, 138
Aman, Burni, 128, 129, 142, 225
Amkoullel l'enfant Peul, 15, 87
Annansi Clothing, 65
Anoff, Panji, 27
Anta, 125
Anta Ba, 142
antepenultimate syllable (triple) rhyme, 20, 21
Anti-Homosexuality Bill [Uganda], 64, 105
apartheid, xii, xiii, xv, 30, 42–44, 101–3, 113, 116, 128, 137, 174, 201, 225
A-Plus, 87
appropriation, xv, xvii, 14, 81, 87, 183, 185, 199–205
Arab Spring, 42, 56, 110, 111
Ariefdien, Shaheen, 28, 29, 44, 54
Arusha, 46, 54
assimilation, 72, 74, 82, 152, 170, 176
Atlanta, 227

257

authenticity (hip hop), xii, xv, xvi, 12–19, 29, 121, 183, 187, 190, 202, 203, 205, 211

Baartman, Saartjie "Sarah," 134, 226
Baay Bia, 96
Babaluku, 49, 85
Balai Citoyen, 41, 110
Baloberos Crew, 111
Bamboo, 78, 186
banlieues, 94
Bantu Pound Gangsters, 16
Baster, 103, 225
Bataka Squad, 49, 85
Bataka Underground, 85
battle, 19, 123, 125
BBC, 2, 93
b-boy, 14, 15, 54
Beah, Ismael, 30
Beirão, Luaty, xiii, 88, 111, 112
Ben Ali, Zine El Abidine, 41
Benin, 20, 41, 130, 172
Ben Sharpa, 88, 89
b-girl, 14
B-Global Indigenous Hip Hop Gathering, 49, 85
bicultural identity integration (BII), 177
Big Mike, 52
Bi Kidude, 20
Biko, Steve, 69, 104
Biya, Paul, 111, 224
Black Arts movement, 25, 223
Black Athena, 113
Black Bird, 62
Black Consciousness, 22, 104, 205
Black Hawk Down, 154
Black Jeez, 52
Black Noise, 30, 84, 103, 113
Black Panther Party, 46, 66
Black Power movement, 8, 9, 200, 201, 205
Black Tiger, 128
Black Vulcanite, 103
Black women, 128, 134, 135, 136, 146, 147, 211
Blahzay Blahzay, 16
Blaise, 98, 125, 130, 132

Bling Is Dead, 65, 98
Blinky Bill, 87
Blitz the Ambassador, 9, 20, 21, 50, 68, 87, 148, 151, 160–63, 169, 172, 173, 180, 182, 183, 185, 194, 198, 199, 204, 214, 227
Boko Haram, 132
Bongo, Ali, 76
bongo flava, 13, 20, 24, 26–28, 46, 79, 206
Bongo Republic, 65
Book Café, The, 59
Boomerang, 5, 223
Botswana, 28
Bouncing Cats, 55
braggadocio, xiii, 118, 119–25, 139, 145, 146, 211, 214
Brasse Vannie Kaap (BVK), 84
break beats, 19
Breakdance Project Uganda, 55
breakdance(r), 13, 47, 49, 53–55, 84
Brooklyn, 173
Burkina Faso, 41, 51, 53, 75, 87, 93, 94, 96, 107, 110

Cabral, Amílcar, 66
Cairo, 58
call-and-response, 5, 6
Cameroon, 41, 60, 72, 111, 224
Camp Mulla, 10
Canada, 37, 91, 99, 154, 174, 191, 224
Cape Flats, 56
Cape Jazz, 201
Cape Town, 16, 56, 103, 104, 113, 121, 126, 143, 201
Cape Verde, 66, 104, 153
Carbono, 111
Caribbean, 6, 7, 8, 25, 66, 178, 196
Cassper Nyovest, 102
Césaire, Aimé, 68
chain rhyme, 21–23
Chama cha Demokrasia na Maendeleo (Chadema), 80
Chama Cha Mapinduzi (CCM), 78, 82, 83
Channel O, 52, 81
Chazz Le Hippie, 28
Cheney-Coker, Syl, 166

Chicago, 157
child soldier, 30, 100
Chiwawa, 78
Chosan, 65, 98, 101, 153
Chuck D, xvi, 9, 35, 185, 214
Cibil Nyte, 52
Civil Rights movement, 214
Cleo Ice Queen, 139
Clouds FM, 62, 187
CNN, 2, 35, 56
code-switching, xvi, 177, 191–93, 197, 203
Cole, Teju, 178, 179
Coloured (South Africa), 103, 104, 128, 129, 225
Columbus, 155
combat literature, xiii, 71, 73, 107, 110, 116
Common, 60
Compaoré, Blaise, 41, 110
Comrade Fatso, 88
Côte d'Ivoire, 41, 60
Coumbis Sorra, 121, 131
Counting Headz: South Afrika's Sistaz in Hip Hop (film), 64
Coz ov Moni (film), 65
Crazy Legs, 55
C-Real, 52
Crosby, 113
Cuba, 8
cultural appropriation, xv, 185, 200, 201, 203, 205
cultural competency, 193, 201, 202, 203, 205
cultural frame switching (CFS), 177, 192
cultural representation, 1–3, 35–39, 73, 133, 159, 182, 193, 208
cultural studies, xvii, 1, 2, 3, 35, 73, 133, 207, 208
cypher (hip-hop freestyle), 6, 19, 46, 47, 62, 124–26

Daara J [Family], 5, 93, 94, 223
Da Brains, 115
Daddy Spencer, 113
Dakar, 16, 32, 43, 51, 54, 58, 108, 125, 211
Dama do Bling, 138
Dandora, 16, 85

Dar es Salaam, 16, 31, 46, 47, 48, 57, 59, 60, 61, 79, 97, 105, 135, 206
Das Primeiro, xii, 34
dashiki, 200
D'Banj, 115
Dead Prez, 9, 60, 64, 65
Dein, 125, 142
Democratic Republic of the Congo, 41, 96, 98, 116
De-Plow-Matz, 31, 45
Devour Ke Lenyora, 10, 126, 142
Diamond Platnumz, 20
Diaspora, African, xiv, xv, 3, 4, 7, 8, 11, 49, 64, 68, 69, 151, 155–59, 166, 168, 176, 181, 182, 185, 193, 194, 196, 197, 201, 203, 204, 205, 208, 211, 227
Didier (DJ) Awadi, 9, 10, 23, 67, 68, 93, 214
Diouf, Abdou, 107
DJ, 5, 14, 15, 32, 49, 53–55, 62, 84, 126, 187, 223
DJ Kool Herc, 7
DJ Naida, 10, 126
DJ Ready D, 62
DJ Red Alert, 7
DJ Texas, 46
Djibouti, 41
Djily Bagdad, 109
domestic violence, 96, 131, 132, 146
Dominant 1, 10
Doom (Dumi) E. Right, 29, 151
Dope Saint Jude, 104, 143, 144
dos Santos, José Eduardo, 111, 112
Dr. Dre, 227
Driemanskap, 21, 28, 95
Dustyfoot Philosopher, 1, 73

East Africa, 30, 46, 52, 55, 76, 87, 100, 135, 136, 155, 189
Eastern Cape, 23
Eavesdrop, 142
Eazzy, 138, 139
Edem, 15, 26, 101, 102, 186
E.D.N.A., 142
Egypt(ian), 40, 41, 55, 58, 72, 75, 116, 211
EJ von Lyrik, 142
El Général, 41
el-Sisi, Abdel Fattah, 58

Index | 259

Emcee Africa competition: Emcee Africa II, 52
Emile YX?, 84, 113
Eminem, 20
Erykah Badu, 203
Ewe, 121
Explosivo Mental, 111
Eyirap, 121, 125, 186

Facebook, 50–51
Falko1, 56
Fanon, Frantz, xiii, 11, 33, 71–73, 75, 81, 82, 109
fashion, 35, 37, 60, 65, 70, 154, 175, 178, 200, 212
Faso Kombat, 87
female genital cutting (FGC), 96, 98, 105, 131, 132, 133, 146
feminism/t, 118, 119, 120, 126, 127, 137, 141, 144, 145, 146, 177, 189, 212, 225
Feminist Africa, 137
FemiOne Shikow, 131
Festival International de Graffiti en Afrique, International African Graffiti Festival, Festigraff, 58
Fete Jen, 60
Fid Q, 20, 50, 59, 62, 64, 66, 69, 82, 83, 224
FidStyle Fridays, 64
fifth element of hip-hop, xi, xii, xiii, 32
Fikrah Teule, 87
Filimbi, 41, 111
Flavour, 140
Fodeba, Keita, 75
Fokn Bois, 65, 105, 172, 227
France, 66, 93, 94
francophone, 4, 30, 32, 86
freestyle, 19, 46, 52, 124, 125
French, xv, xvi, 23, 94, 158, 186

Gabon, 41, 76
Gabon Hip Hop Festival, 76
Galxboy, 65
Gambia, The, 6
gender, xiii, 2, 4, 107, 110, 117, 118, 119, 126, 127, 133, 135–38, 143, 145, 146, 147, 211, 224; identity, xiii, 4, 119, 137, 142

Général Valsero, 111
Gervalius, Duke, 46, 48
Ghana(ian), 8, 24, 25, 26, 27, 28, 31, 33, 42, 43, 66, 68, 87, 90, 91, 92, 93, 95, 101, 105, 119, 121, 125, 136, 138, 139, 140, 141, 142, 148, 151, 160, 163, 165, 166, 168, 169, 171, 172, 174, 177, 178, 181, 182, 185, 186, 187, 194, 195, 196, 197, 198, 199, 204, 211, 212, 213, 214, 224, 225, 227
Ghana-must-go, 169
Ghetto Radio, 60
Gidi Gidi Maji Maji, 77
Gigi LaMayne, 10, 34, 113, 126, 127, 132
Godessa, 67, 128, 129, 146
Goethe Institute, 60
Good Hope FM, 62, 84
GOTAL, 59, 125
graffiti, xiv, 2, 11, 14, 15, 32, 35, 36, 37, 49, 53, 54, 55–59, 70, 84, 158, 223
Grandmaster Flash, 7
griot, 5, 6, 15, 213, 214
group talk, 191
Guinea, 53, 75
Guinea Bissau, 111
Guru, 30

Hardstone, 31
Headwarmaz, 62
heteronormativity, 143, 144, 227
highlife, 8, 11, 24, 25
Hiphocalypse, 52
Hip Hop Colony (film), 64
Hip Hop Foundation of Zambia, 53
Hip Hop Kilinge (Cypher), 46, 47
Hip Hop Nation Language (HHNL), xvi, 191–95, 197, 198, 202, 228. *See also* African American Vernacular English (AAVE)
Hip Hop Pantsula (HHP), 9, 10, 28
Hip Hop Parliament, 78
Hip Hop Revolution (film), 64
hip-hop studies, xi, 14, 133, 206
Hip-Hop Summit, 85
Hip Hop Thursdays, 62
Hip Hop World (magazine), 62
hiplife, 13, 24–28, 31, 140, 141, 212, 213, 214

260 | Index

Holstar, The, 10
homosexuality, xiii, 65, 86, 105–6
Hustlajay Maumau, 87
hypermasculine, 106, 144
hypersexual(ity), 119, 133, 134, 142, 202

Ikonoklasta, xiii, 111
imitation, 14, 31, 72, 82, 180, 206
Immigration and Nationality Act of 1965, 150
immigration law, 149, 151, 159, 165
internal rhyme, 21, 24
International Criminal Court, 187
International Monetary Fund (IMF), 39, 87
Islam/Muslim, 43, 131, 133, 143, 228
Izzo Bizness, 45

Jackson, Michael, 9
Jal, Emmanuel, 65, 99, 100, 101, 188–91
Jammeh, Yahya, 110
Jay-Z, 65, 76
J. Cole, 9
Johannesburg, 16, 22, 23, 56, 60
Jolof 4 Life, 65, 66, 108
Jose Chameleone, 85
Journal Rappé, 62
J-Town, 52
Jua Cali, 10
Juliana Kanyomozi, 85
Just Lyphe, 151

Kabila, Joseph, 111
Kalamashaka, 31, 34, 35, 67, 68, 84, 85
Kalibrados, 17
Kama, 35, 84, 85
Kampala, 49, 60, 85, 105, 135, 152, 161, 172, 173
Kanye West, 6
Kanyi, iv, 132, 142, 187, 188
kasi (ghetto), 16, 17
KasiTime, 16
Kayvo Kforce, 78
KBC, 29, 60, 61. *See also* Singo, Kibacha
Kenya, 9, 10, 13, 15, 17, 31, 33, 34, 41, 52, 54, 56, 57, 60, 64, 65, 67, 67, 75, 76, 77–78, 84, 87, 99, 100, 119, 121, 123, 124, 127, 131, 136, 138, 141, 154, 158, 186, 191, 196, 212, 224, 228
Kenya, Russell, 64
Kenya African National Union (KANU), 77
Kenyatta, Uhuru, 77, 78
Keur Gui, 45, 108, 109, 110
Keyti, 43, 62
Khaligraph Jones, 10
Khayelitsha, 16
Khusta, 113
Kibaki, Mwai, 75, 77
Kidjo, Angélique, 20, 172
Kikwete, Jakaya, 45, 79, 80, 83
Kilifeu, 45, 108, 109
Kimba Mutanda, 148
Kina Klothing, 65, 66
K'naan, 1, 9, 11, 21, 33, 37, 50, 51, 65, 73, 99–101, 152–58, 167, 190, 191
KORA Awards, 52
Kritsi Ye'Spaza, 28
Krukid, 10, 98, 152, 160, 161, 169, 171, 172, 173, 180, 185, 195, 196, 198, 214. *See also* Ruyonga
Kuti, Fela, 8, 9, 65, 157, 201, 227
kwaito, 13, 24, 26, 27, 28
Kwanza Unit, xii, 29, 30, 31, 34, 60, 61, 201
Kwaw Kese, 10, 214

Lady Zee, 125
Lagos, 16, 178, 181
language, xii, xv, xvi, xvii, 2, 3, 6, 11, 15, 23, 25–28, 31, 33, 34, 44, 45, 66, 85, 118, 121, 125, 145, 158, 171, 185, 186, 199, 202, 203, 204, 211, 213, 228; choice, xvi, 183, 185–91, 203; coded/code-switching, xv, 38, 39, 56, 184, 185, 191–97, 202; multiple language use, xvi, 28, 175, 185–88, 199, 203
LGBTQI, xiii
Liberia, 30, 33, 151, 152, 188, 196, 212
Libya, 45, 92, 93, 109
Lila, 125
Lil' Kim, 141
Limp Bizkit, 190
Linkris the Genius, 113
Little Accra, 151

Lness, 127
Lord's Resistance Army, 55
Los Angeles, 9, 32, 25, 151, 157, 201
Luanda, 60
Lufunyo, 62
Luganda, 85, 158, 173, 186, 198
Lumumba, Patrice, 68
Lutte pour le Changement (LUCHA), 111
Lyricist Lounge, 60

M-1, 9, 64, 90, 214
M3NSA, 65, 172, 180, 181, 187, 204, 227
Madagascar, 17, 60
Magubane, Vusi, 64
Magufuli, John, 83
Makoa, 17
Malade, Fou, 108
Malawi, 10, 15, 16, 21, 41, 95, 148, 149
Mali(an), 15, 21, 53, 60, 87, 94, 186
Malle Marxist, 46
Manaz, 99
Mandela, Nelson, 65, 68, 195
Mangwair, Albert, 79, 80
M.anifest, 9, 10, 21, 33, 50, 68, 151, 152, 150, 161, 168–74, 180, 181, 182, 185, 194, 195, 198, 199, 214
MarazA, 52
Marley, Damian, 155
Martin, Trayvon, 101, 225
Matador, 108
matatu, 56, 85, 158
Mau Mau, 35, 68, 82, 124, 226
Mauritania, 41, 43, 92
mbalax, 11, 29, 32
Mbembe, Achille, 174, 175, 176, 177, 178, 180
Mbeya, 80
MCK, 88, 111, 112
MC Solaar, 30
M.I., 10
migrants, xiv, 3, 7, 17, 30, 90–95, 116, 148–53, 158–71, 174, 175, 176, 179, 180, 182, 192, 193, 196, 197, 204, 225, 227
migration, xiv, 2, 3, 4, 12, 30, 85, 86, 90, 93, 104, 107, 116, 149, 150, 151, 159, 160, 171, 179, 182, 184, 197, 227
miniskirt, 138

Minista of Agrikulcha, 153
Minneapolis, 12, 151, 169
Miss Celanious, 104
Missy Elliot, 9
Missy RBK, 28
Mitchells Plain, 56
mixtape, 51, 52, 152
Mizchif, 9
Mkapa, Benjamin, 75, 82
Mo'Cheddah, 122, 125, 138
ModeNine, 9, 52
Mogadishu, 11, 99, 153, 156, 190
monorhymes, 21
monosyllable rhyme, 20, 21
Moona, 130, 131
Morocco, 41, 87, 92, 93, 138
Mos Def, 9, 60
Mosele, René, 128, 226
Mother Africa, 127, 203
mother/hood, 127, 128, 129, 130, 144, 172, 203, 211
motswako (rap), 25, 26, 28
Mozambique, 56, 119, 138
Mponjika, Zavara, 31. See also Zavara
Mr. II. See Sugu
MTV Africa Music Awards, 52
MTV Base Africa, 52, 81
Muna, 125
Museveni, Yoweri, 75, 76
Mwangi, Stella, 138, 139. See also STL
Mxc Wol, 188
Mzbel, 141
Mz Porsche, 138

Naeto C, 10, 52
Nairobi, 16, 46, 49, 56, 60, 85, 123, 135, 139, 158
Namibia, 10, 41, 103, 119, 121, 126, 138, 225
Nas, 6, 9, 55
Nash MC, 46
National Alliance, The (TNA), 78
National Rainbow Coalition (NARC), 77
Navio, 10
Nazizi, 9, 10, 52, 123, 124, 141, 186
Nazlee, 59, 113, 114, 143, 144
Ncha Kali, 62

262 | *Index*

N'Dour, Youssou, 54
Negritude, 167
Nelly Majestic, 99
neocolonialism, 44, 74
neoliberalism, 40, 42, 83
New York (city), 7, 12, 14, 15, 30, 55, 58, 60, 124, 151, 153, 157, 158, 173, 210, 225, 228
New York Times, 41, 134, 158
NewzBeatUganda, 62
Nigeria(n), 8, 9, 10, 11, 12, 13, 20, 52, 62, 76, 90, 93, 95, 98, 105, 115, 119, 122, 125, 130, 138, 140, 152, 157, 163, 166, 179, 187, 196, 199, 201, 225, 227
nigga, 14, 157, 202, 203
Niggas with Matatizo, 16
Nikki Mbishi, 24, 46
Nilsa, 142
Nima, 16
Ni Wakati, 34, 64, 68
N'Kashh, 96
Nkrumah, Kwame, 66, 68, 82
Nomadic Wax, 51
North Africa, 56, 92, 93, 94, 110
Nthabi, 59, 160, 142
NWA, 30
Nyerere, Julius, 66, 67, 68

Obour, 212, 213
Obrafour, 13
Odinga, Raila, 77
Okoa Mtaa, 46, 53, 54
O'Neal, Pete and Charlotte, 46
One the Incredible, 46
open-mic, 46, 59, 60
Orange Democratic Movement (ODM), 78
Ouagadougou, 41, 110
Oum, 87
out-group, 202, 203
out-migration, xiv
out of contextness, 166
Outspoken, 88, 89
Oxmo Puccino, 87

Pambazuka, 40, 41
Pan-African(ism), xii, xiv, xv, xvi, 5, 7, 8, 64, 66, 95, 104, 110, 150, 170, 176, 177, 178, 180, 181, 184, 185, 193, 194, 196, 197, 203, 204, 213, 214
Parti Démocratique Sénégalais (Senegalese Democratic Party, PDS), 107
Parti Socialiste du Sénégal (Socialist Party of Senegal, PS), 107
Pawa254, 46
Pharoahe Monch, 19
Pidgin English/Pidgin, 21, 25, 31, 33, 125, 168, 169, 170, 172, 173, 186, 187, 188, 199, 204, 228
Pikine, 16
pimp rap, 25
Platform, The (magazine), 62
Poetry Addiction, 59
Point Blank, 52
pop culture, 211, 212
Positive Black Soul (PBS), 30, 32, 34
postapartheid, 103, 116, 137, 174
postcolonial, 33, 166, 167, 184, 186
postracial, 177, 178
poverty reduction strategy papers (PRSPs), 39
POW, 64
Praaye, 212
Présidents d'Afrique, 10, 68
Princess Mwamba, 139
prison-industrial complex, 189, 194, 199
Professor Jay, 10, 45, 52, 80, 81, 82, 214
Professor X, 6
Prophets of da City, xii, xiii, 1, 28, 30, 34, 44, 54, 62, 84, 103, 223
protest literature, xiii, 71, 75, 81, 82
ProVerb, 9, 10
P-Square, 13, 115, 140
P the MC, 46
Public Enemy, 30, 44, 185

Q'ba, 16, 126
Queen Latifah, 125
Queen Mother (trope), 136
queer, xiii, 86, 106, 126, 143, 144, 224, 225

race, xv, 8, 86, 89, 101–4, 150, 177, 194, 196
Rage Prophetional, 52

Rakim, 157, 227
Ready D Show, The, 62, 84
Rebel Music, 51
Redman, 35
refugee, 40, 93, 99, 108, 190
reggae, 13, 20, 24, 25, 26, 31, 85, 205
Reggie Rockstone, 26, 27, 31, 90, 163
reverse migration, 171
rhyme pattern, 18–22
rhyme scheme, 18, 21
Rhymson. See Zavara
Riz One (Ridhiwan), 45, 80
Roma, 87, 88
Roots, The, 9, 214
rumba, 8
Ru the Rapper, 10, 126
Ruyonga, 10, 98, 152, 160, 161, 169, 171, 172, 173, 180, 185, 195, 196, 198, 214. *See also* Krukid
Rwanda, 10, 119, 212

Saba Saba, 85, 158
same-sex relationships, 144
same-sex rights, 105
Sankara, Thomas, 41, 66, 68, 82, 93, 110
Sarkodie, 10, 20, 21, 25, 26, 90, 91, 181
Sasa Klaas, 10, 126, 131
Sasha, 105, 125, 138, 139
Say'hu, 151
Scar, 132
Sefyu, 94
Selasi, Taiye, 175, 178, 180. *See also* Tuakli-Wosornu, Taiye
Senegal [ese], xix, 5, 6, 8, 10, 11, 12, 15, 23, 29, 30, 32, 33, 34, 40, 41, 42, 43, 44, 45, 46, 51, 53, 54, 56, 58, 59, 62, 65, 66, 67, 72, 75, 76, 87, 92, 93, 94, 96, 99, 107–10, 116, 119, 121,125, 126, 129, 130, 131, 133, 142, 143, 151, 186, 211, 223
Senghor, Léopold, 166, 167
Sen Kumpë, 45
Sensai T8, 52
sexual identity, xiii, 106, 137, 138, 142, 145
sexuality, 65, 119, 120, 133–47, 208, 227; female, xiv, 134, 135, 137, 138, 140, 144, 146, 147, 208; gender, xiii, 119, 133, 135, 145; homosexuality, xiii, 64, 65, 86, 105, 106; hypersexuality, 133, 202
Shameema, 142
Sheng, xvi, 186, 228
Shot B, 56
Sidibe, Dieynaba, 59
Sierra Leone(an), 14, 17, 30, 65, 98, 101, 212
Sima da Black Philosopher, 88
Singo, Kibacha, 29, 60, 61. *See also* KBC
Sister Fa, 96, 98, 99, 129, 131, 186
Skwatta Kamp, 10
Skye Wanda, 130
Slim Emcee (UG) the poet, 106
Smockey, 10, 41, 51, 87, 94, 96, 110
Snazz the Dictator, 52
social media, 37, 40, 50, 51, 60, 65, 107, 145, 159, 168, 197, 199, 228
Somalia/Somali, 1, 6, 11, 21, 33, 37, 87, 92, 95, 98, 99, 100, 153–58, 166, 190, 225
Songa, 46, 47, 96
South Africa(n), 8, 9, 10, 11, 13, 15, 16, 21, 22, 24, 25, 26, 27, 28, 29, 30, 33, 34, 40, 41, 42, 43, 44, 52, 53, 54, 56, 59, 60, 62, 64, 65, 66, 67, 68, 75, 76, 84, 86, 88, 89, 95, 101, 102, 103, 104, 112, 115, 116, 119, 122, 126, 128, 129, 130, 132, 137, 138, 142, 143, 144, 174, 184, 187, 188, 201, 205, 207, 223, 225, 226
South Bronx, 3, 223
South Sudan(ese), 188, 98–100, 188
Soweto, 16, 82, 102, 113, 122, 225
spaza (rap), 25, 26, 28
spoken-word artist, 114
spoken-word culture/event, 59, 60
spoken-word pieces, 148–49
Spoken Word Project, 60
Star Wars, 23
STL, 138, 139. *See also* Stella Mwangi
structural adjustment program, 39, 90
Sudan, 41, 100, 191
Sugu, 31, 45, 80
Swahili/Kiswahili, 44, 45, 81, 186, 187, 203, 228

Sway, 101
Swaziland, 41, 138
Sylvester, 55

taarab music/singer, 136
Tahrir Square, 211
Talking Drums, 26, 31
Tamaduni Muzik, 46
Tanzania(n), xii, xix, 6, 10, 13, 15, 16, 17, 20, 24, 26, 27, 28, 29, 31, 33, 34, 42, 44, 45, 46, 52, 53, 54, 57, 59, 60, 62, 64, 65, 66, 67, 69, 75, 76, 77, 78–81, 82, 83, 87, 88, 96, 119, 122, 136, 138, 143, 184, 186, 187, 196, 206, 211, 214, 224
Tassou, 6, 33,
Tata Pound, 87
Teeto, 52
Temeke, 16, 31
Thaïs, 128, 142, 226
The National Alliance (TNA), 78
Thiat, 41, 108, 109, 110
Thieuss, Guin, 62, 63
Thionck Essyl, 98, 131
Thiong'o, Ngũgĩ wa, 186, 191, 193, 204
Tifa Flowz, 122
Togo, 53, 76
Toure, Kwame, 8
transgender, 144, 224
translinguality, xvii
transnational, xiv, 137, 149, 150, 173–76, 178, 179, 181, 182, 185, 197, 203, 204
Trinity International Hip-Hop Festival, 109
Tuakli-Wosornu, Taiye, 175, 178, 180. *See also* Selasi, Taiye
Tunisia, 40, 41, 72, 75, 93, 116
Twista, 157
Twitter, 50, 51

Uganda, 152, 158, 160, 161, 171
Ujamaa Hip Hop, 46
Ukoo Flani Mau Mau, 68, 77, 85, 124
Umi, 64
United African Alliance Community Center, 46
United States, xiv, xvi, 1, 3, 4, 7, 8, 9, 12, 17, 25, 26, 29, 37, 40, 42, 49, 51, 55, 57, 59, 65, 66, 74, 82, 86, 88, 90, 94, 103, 104, 115, 116, 119, 124, 130, 132, 135, 137, 149–56, 158, 160–63, 166, 171, 172, 174, 179, 181, 182, 186, 188, 191, 192, 194, 195, 197, 199, 200, 201, 202, 204–7, 211, 227
United States of Africa: Beyond Hip Hop, 9, 10, 84
Universal Zulu Nation, 14
urbanization, 40, 42

VA Capsi Revolution, 93
Vector tha Viper, 10
Venus, 125
violence against women, 86, 96, 98, 119, 127, 130–33, 146

Wachata Crew, 57
Wade, Abdoulaye, 41, 45, 75, 107–9
Wagalla massacre, 87
Wainaina, Binyavanga, 177, 178, 180
Wakazi, 158
Wale, 9, 11, 152, 158
Wanaitwa Uhuru, 46, 48, 87, 88
Wanguhu, Michael, 64, 85
Wanlov the Kubolor, 33, 50, 65, 90, 101, 105, 160, 162–65, 168–73, 180, 181, 187, 204, 227
Wardhiigley, 156
Washington, DC, 151
Waterflow, 43, 54, 158
Welsing, Frances Cress, 35, 224
West Africa, 5, 6, 8, 11, 30, 31, 43, 49, 86, 87, 90, 92, 93, 133, 135, 167, 180, 200, 201, 227
Williams, Pharrell, 9
Wire, The, 38
Witnesz, 96, 97
Wiyaala, 214, 215
Wolof, 125, 186
wordplay, 3, 39, 45, 118, 120, 125
World Bank, 39, 87
World Cup, 51, 158
Wretched of the Earth, The, 71
Wyclef Jean, 81

X, Malcolm, 66, 68, 228
xenophobia, 95, 225

Xhosa, 21, 23, 28, 132, 142, 187, 188
Xuman, 43, 62, 109

Yaa Pono, 25
Yaoundé, 60, 111
Yayra, 125
Yeleen, 87, 94
Y'en a Marre (Enough Is Enough), 41, 108–10
YFM, 62
Young D, 52
Yugen Blakrok, 16, 22, 23, 68

Zaiid, 46
Zambia, 10, 15, 53, 95, 119, 139, 196, 225
Zavara, 31. *See also* Mponjika, Zavara
zef (rap), 25, 28
Zimbabwe, 9, 10, 15, 29, 41, 51, 52, 53, 59, 62, 76, 88, 89, 95, 119, 126, 138, 151, 152, 211
Zubz, 95
Zuluboy, 84, 88, 89
Zuma, Jacob, 75, 116